Migration and Islamic Ethics

Studies in Islamic Ethics

VOLUME 2

The titles published in this series are listed at *brill.com/sie*

Migration and Islamic Ethics

Issues of Residence, Naturalisation and Citizenship

Edited by

Ray Jureidini
Said Fares Hassan

BRILL

LEIDEN | BOSTON

Library of Congress Cataloging-in-Publication Data
Names: Jureidini, Ray, editor. | Hassan, Said Fares, editor.
Title: Migration and Islamic ethics : issues of residence, naturalisation and citizenship / edited by Ray Jureidini, Said Fares Hassan.
Description: Leiden ; Boston : Brill, 2020. | Series: Studies in Islamic ethics, 2589-3947 ; vol. 2 | Includes bibliographic references and index. | Summary: "Migration and Islamic Ethics, Issues of Residence, Naturalisation and Citizenship addresses how Islamic ethical and legal traditions can contribute to current global debates on migration and displacement; how Islamic ethics of mu'ākhā, diyāfa, ijāra, amān, jiwār, sutra, kafala, among others, may provide common ethical grounds for a new paradigm of social and political virtues applicable to all humanity, not only Muslims. The present volume more broadly defines the Islamic tradition to cover not only theology but also to encompass ethics, customs and social norms, as well as modern political, humanitarian and rights discourses. The first section addresses theorizations and conceptualizations using contemporary Islamic examples, mainly in the treatment of asylum-seekers and refugees; the second, contains empirical analyses of contemporary case studies; the third provides historical accounts of Muslim migratory experiences"-- Provided by publisher.
Identifiers: LCCN 2019039745 (print) | LCCN 2019039746 (ebook) | ISBN 9789004406407 (hardback) | ISBN 9789004417342 (ebook)
Subjects: LCSH: Asylum, Right of--Religious aspects--Islam. | Emigration and immigration--Religious aspects--Islam. | Iraq War, 2003-2011--Refugees. | Syria--History--Civil War, 2011---Refugees. | Islamic ethics. Classification: LCC BP190.5.A85 M54 2020 (print) | LCC BP190.5.A85 (ebook) | DDC 297.2/7--dc23
LC record available at https://lccn.loc.gov/2019039745
LC ebook record available at https://lccn.loc.gov/2019039746

Typeface for the Latin, Greek, and Cyrillic scripts: "Brill". See and download: brill.com/brill-typeface.

ISSN 2589-3947
ISBN 978-90-04-40640-7 (hardback)
ISBN 978-90-04-41734-2 (e-book)

This book is printed on acid-free paper and produced in a sustainable manner.

Contents

List of Figures and Tables VII
Notes on Contributors VIII

1 Introduction 1
Ray Jureidini and Said Fares Hassan

2 Islamic Ethics, Human Rights and Migration 13
Khaled Abou El Fadl

3 The Living *Fiqh*, or Practical Theology, of Muslim Humanitarianism 28
Abbas Barzegar

4 *Jiwār*: from a Right of Neighbourliness to a Right to Neighbourhood for Refugees 47
Tahir Zaman

5 "Seeking a Widow with Orphaned Children": Understanding *Sutra* Marriage Amongst Syrian Refugee Women in Egypt 67
Dina Taha

6 The Islamic Principle of *Kafala* as Applied to Migrant Workers: Traditional Continuity and Reform 92
Ray Jureidini and Said Fares Hassan

7 Normativity of Migration Studies Ethics and Epistemic Community 110
Sari Hanafi

8 How do Muslim States Treat their "Outsiders"?: Is Islamic Practice of Naturalisation Synonymous with *Jus Sanguinis*? 136
Radhika Kanchana

9 The Obligation to Migrate and the Impulse to Narrate: Soviet Narratives of Forced Migration in the Nineteenth Century Caucasus 154
Rebecca Ruth Gould

10 Experiences of Uyghur Migration to Turkey and the United States: Issues of Religion, Law, Society, Residence, and Citizenship 174
Mettursun Beydulla

11 Arab Immigrants under Hindu Kings in Malabar: Ethical Pluralities of "Naturalisation" in Islam 196
Abdul Jaleel P.K.M.

Index 215

Figures and Tables

Figures

3.1 Five crucial dimensions of human development 37
9.1 Map of Terek province (Riabchenko 1913) 165
10.1 The Xinjiang Uyghur Autonomous Region. Source: Millward 2007, page xx 176

Tables

7.1 Number and percentage of articles by language 128
7.2 Geographical regions of the journals 128
7.3 Types of institutional affiliation 129
7.4 The discipline of the first author 129
7.5 Country of the affiliated institutions 129
7.6 Year of publication 130
7.7 Types of articles 130
7.8 Geographical scope of the articles 131
7.9 Frequency of keywords by language 131
7.10 Methods used (multiple responses) 132
8.1 *Jus sanguinis* in selected muslim-majority states—access to naturalisation in the citizenship policies 141
8.2 Nationality law in the GCC states and the length of residence for naturalisation 146

Notes on Contributors

In alphabetical order.

Dr. Khaled Abou El Fadl

is one of the world's leading authorities on Islamic law and Islam, and a prominent scholar in the field of human rights. Dr. Abou El Fadl holds a BA in Political Science from Yale University, a J.D. from the University of Pennsylvania Law School, and an MA and PhD in Islamic law from Princeton University. He is the Omar and Azmeralda Alfi Distinguished Professor in Islamic Law at the UCLA School of Law where he teaches International Human Rights, Islamic Jurisprudence, National Security Law, Law and Terrorism, Islam and Human Rights, Political Asylum, and Political Crimes and Legal Systems. He is also the Chair of the Islamic Studies Interdepartmental Program at UCLA. Among his many honours and distinctions, Dr. Abou El Fadl was awarded the University of Oslo Human Rights Award, the Leo and Lisl Eitinger Prize in 2007, and named a Carnegie Scholar in Islamic Law in 2005. He was previously appointed by President George W. Bush to serve on the US Commission for International Religious Freedom, and also served as a member of the board of directors of Human Rights Watch. He continues to serve on the advisory board of Middle East Watch (part of Human Rights Watch) and regularly works with human rights organizations such as Amnesty International and the Lawyers' Committee for Human Rights (Human Rights First) as an expert in a wide variety of cases involving human rights, terrorism, political asylum, and international and commercial law. Dr. Abou El Fadl is the author of 14 books and over 50 articles on various topics in Islam and Islamic law.

Dr. Abbas Barzegar

is an Assistant Professor of Religion at Georgia State University (GSU) and a term member of the Council on Foreign Relations. At GSU he co-directs two interdisciplinary research projects: *Civic Approaches to Conflict Resolution in the Muslim World*, and *After Malcolm: Islam and the Black Freedom Struggle*. He received his PhD in 2010 from Emory University specializing on the Sunni-Shiite conflict, Islam in America, and transnational political Islam. In addition to numerous articles and book chapters, he is the co-author of *Islamism: Contested Perspectives on Political Islam* (Stanford, 2009). His work has been supported by The Carter Center, The National Endowment for the Humanities, The British Council, The European Union, The US Institute of Peace, The Mellon Foundation, and the Georgia Humanities Council. His public commentary and analysis can be found in a variety of print and broadcast media outlets, including The Huffington Post, The Guardian, CNN, Aljazeera, and Fox News.

Dr. Mettursun Beydulla
was born in Xinjiang, China, went to Uyghur schools, studied intensive Chinese and graduated from university preparation courses at the Central Nationalities University in Beijing. He received a BA in History from Shaanxi Normal University in Xi'an and an MA in History and a PhD in Social/Cultural Anthropology from Ankara University, Turkey. He researched and taught Uyghur at the American University in Cairo in 2006, and was a visiting scholar in Harvard in 2007. Between September 2008–June 2013, conducted research and taught Uyghur language, literature, and culture at Harvard and MIT. He taught Sociology and Anthropology courses between July 2013 and June 2016 at Fatih University, Istanbul, then taught Uyghur in the Diplomatic Language Services in Arlington, VA during Oct. 2016. He has been teaching Turkish at the ICA Language Service, Arlington, VA since Jan. 2017. His research and publications include: national identity, social and identity change among the Uyghurs; Chinese socio-cultural practices in Xinjiang; Uyghur Diasporas; relations between Xinjiang and Central Asia; the social, linguistic, cultural, religious, political, and institutional history of the Uyghurs and Xinjiang; and pan-Turkic culture.

Dr. Rebecca Ruth Gould
is the author of *Writers and Rebels: The Literatures of Insurgency in the Caucasus* (Yale UP, 2016), which was awarded honorable mention for the Joseph Rothschild Prize in Nationalism and Ethnic Studies, Association for the Study of Nationalities. She is the translator of *After Tomorrow the Days Disappear: Ghazals and Other Poems of Hasan Sijzi of Delhi* (Northwestern UP, 2016) and *The Prose of the Mountains: Tales of the Caucasus* (Central European UP, 2015). Broadly specializing in the Islamic Caucasus, she is a Reader in Translation Studies and Comparative Literature at the University of Bristol. From Fall 2017 onwards, she will be Professor, Islamic World and Comparative Literatures, University of Birmingham. The Harry Frank Guggenheim Foundation, the National Endowment for the Humanities and the Van Leer Institute for Advanced Studies has supported her work. In 2015, she received the Charles Schmitt Prize awarded by the International Society for Intellectual History and the MLA Florence Howe Award for Feminist Scholarship awarded by the Women's Caucus for the Modern Languages Association for her work on Syrian postcolonialism.

Dr. Sari Hanafi

is currently a Professor of Sociology at the American University of Beirut. He is also the editor of *Idafat: the Arab Journal of Sociology* (Arabic). He is the Vice President of the International Sociological Association. He was a member and Vice President of the board of the Arab Council of Social Science (2012–2016). He is the author of numerous journal articles and book chapters on the political and economic sociology of the Palestinian diaspora and refugees; sociology of migration; transnationalism; politics of scientific research; civil society and elite formation and transitional justice. Among his recent books are: *From Relief and Works to Human Development: UNRWA and Palestinian Refugees after 60 Years*. (Edited with L. Takkenberg and L. Hilal) (Routledge). His latest book (with R. Arvanitis) is *Knowledge Production in the Arab World: The Impossible Promise* (2016).

Dr. Said Fares Hassan

currently teaches at al-Azhar University, Faculty of Languages and Translation, Dept. of Islamic Studies, Cairo, Egypt. He received his PhD from UCLA in 2011. He worked as a visiting assistant professor at Georgetown University in 2012; a visiting fellow at the Institute for Islamic Studies (IAIN) Sultan Maulana Hasanuddin, Indonesia in 2014; a visiting fellow at the Berlin Graduate School Muslim Cultures and Societies, Freie Universität, Berlin also in 2014. His publications include *Fiqh al-Aqalliyyat: History, development and Progress* (New York: Palgrave Macmillan 2013) and "Law-Abiding Citizen: Recent *Fatwas* on Muslim Minorities" Loyalty to Western Nations," *Journal of the Muslim World*, October 2015. He has contributed a number of chapters to edited volumes such as *Education and the Arab Spring: Shifting Toward Democracy*, 2016, *Christian-Muslim Relations. A Bibliographical History*, 2016, and *The Encyclopedia of Muslim American History*, 2010.

Dr. Abdul Jaleel P.K.M.

is currently associated with ARI at the National University of Singapore. He received his PhD from Jawaharlal Nehru University, New Delhi. His research on "Hadrami Sayyid Diaspora of Kerala and Singapore: A Comparative Study" is an historical and anthropological examination of diasporic experiences of an immigrant community from the same homeland and how they ended up with diverse socio-political and economic trajectories. On the lines of recent attempts to perceive societies around the Indian Ocean as culturally and economically inter-connected since centuries, it approached immigrant Hadramis in the both places as a maritime community whose trajectories were shaped by both land-based polities and sea-based communities. Thus, the study demonstrated how the Hadrami immigrants worked as one of the prime agents in inducing the similarity of religious traditions in both South India and Southeast Asia. It also attempted to explain the socio-religious factors that facilitated the diaspora to assume a legitimate leadership of host societies, and it signified their faith-based nature, showing the complexities in dealing with a Muslim diaspora that have sanctified notions of the lineage and Sufism. At ARI, his work is focused on the cultural and economic maritime connections of Malabar with other Asian regions. His forthcoming publication is "Religion and Politics in Eighteenth Century Malabar: The Diasporic Writings of a Hadrami Scholar" with Oxford University Press, New Delhi.

Ray Jureidini

Dr. Ray Jureidini has been professor of migration ethics and human rights since 2014 at the Center for Islamic Legislation and Ethics in the College of Islamic Studies at Hamad Bin Khalifa University, Doha, Qatar. His human and labour rights based research and activism centers on migrant labour exploitation, human trafficking, racism, debt bondage and slavery-like practices in the Middle East. After teaching Sociology in several universities in Australia, he spent 6 years at the American University of Beirut from 1999 where he addressed human rights issues concerning migrant domestic workers in the Middle East. At the American University in Cairo from 2005–2011, he became director of the Center for Migration and Refugee Studies and conducted a number of research projects on migrant and refugee issues, including household domestic workers, child domestic workers, and Somali asylum seekers in Yemen, Syria and Turkey. Dr. Jureidini was one of the authors of the Qatar Foundation's 2013 Mandatory Standards for Migrant Worker Welfare and has authored articles on migrant labour, refugees and Islamic ethics and reports on labour recruitment, wages and other migration issues relating the Gulf States. Professor Jureidini is a consultant and advisor on refugee issues, labour recruitment, labour supply chain evaluations and migrant labour reform advocacy.

Radhika Kanchana

Dr. Radhika Kanchana is Research Associate, Centre de Recherches Internationales (CERI) in Paris, France. She received her PhD in Political Science (November 2016) from the Institut d'études Politiques de Paris, with a dissertation titled, "The expediency of the contemporary guest worker migration policies that curb mobility: the Arab-Gulf countries and the Indian migrants." She completed a Master of Research in Comparative Politics (2008) from the Institut d'études Politiques de Paris, a Master of Arts, in International Relations (2004) Syracuse University, USA and a Master of Business Administration, Finance

(2000) from Osmania University in India. Dr. Kanchana's current research interests include the Arab-Gulf region in particular and international migration with focus on states' policy and international law, from the perspective of what they mean to the people experiencing them. Her PhD field research was conducted from 2009 to 2011 in the UAE, Qatar, Oman and Bahrain.

Dina Taha
Ms. Dina Taha is a third year PhD candidate in the Sociology department at York University in Toronto. She is the recipient of the Humanitarian Response Network of Canada research grant and the Ontario Graduate Scholarship of 2017. Her research interests focus on forced migration and gender, critical refugee studies and post-colonial/anti-colonial critiques. Her dissertation explores survival mechanisms of Syrian refugee women in Egypt particularly through marriage to Egyptian nationals. Dina holds a BA in Political Science from Cairo University and an MA in International Human Rights Law from the American University in Cairo. She has extensive experience with feminist and minority advocacy groups such as Nazra for Feminist Studies and Minority Rights Group International. She plays a very active role at the Center for Refugee Studies (CRS) at York University, chairing the Student Caucus and serving as a research assistant for the Refugee Research Network project (RRN) which has been created to mobilize and sustain a Canadian and international network of researchers and research centers committed to the study of refugee and forced migration issues and to engaging policy makers and practitioners in finding solutions to the plight of refugees and displaced persons. Her job description includes monitoring and updating different social media platforms for the network as well as develop a weekly research digest which provides a synopsis of recent research on refugee and forced migration issues from entities associated with the RRN.

Tahir Zaman
Dr. Tahir Zaman is primarily interested in matters pertaining to refugee agency and alternative socio-cultural understandings of refuge during times of mass-displacement. He was awarded a PhD in Refugee Studies from the University of East London in 2013. His work located at the intersections of human geography and social anthropology explored the social and cultural life-worlds of Iraqi refugees in Damascus where he undertook fieldwork in 2010 and 2011. His doctoral thesis was recently published as a book by Palgrave Macmillan in 2016 under the title of "Islamic traditions of refuge in the crises of Iraq and Syria." Dr. Tahir has since worked extensively with a leading peace-building and conflict transformation NGO on considering the role of Syrian Diaspora actors in

responding to mass displacement and contributing towards peace-building. He is a member of the Joint Learning Initiative on Faiths and Local Communities—a platform for academics, policy makers, humanitarians, and development practitioners working on conflict and displacement. Dr. Tahir is also a member of the core design team on a project led by the Overseas Development Institute that seeks to reimagine the humanitarian architecture. His current research interest focuses on the intersections of forced migration, humanitarianism, and social economy.

CHAPTER 1

Introduction

Ray Jureidini and Said Fares Hassan

A principle concern of the authors in this collection of papers is how Islamic ethical and legal traditions can contribute to current global debates on the dilemmas of migration and displacement. Can the Muslim tradition provide an alternative international moral and legal paradigm where others have proven inadequate? Abou El Fadl, in this volume, argues that the Muslim tradition is replete with "powerful virtuous ethical impulses that could make substantive contributions to the field of forced migrants and displacement." The ethics of *mu'ākhā* (brotherhood), *ḍiyāfa* (hospitality), *ijāra* (providing protection and support), *amān* (providing safety), *jiwār* (neighborliness), *sutra* (protection, esp. in case of marriage), *kafala* (to guarantee someone) among others, may provide common ethical grounds with other religious traditions, moral philosophies and social customs that can go beyond the technical applications and procedural standards of international law. The argument that these moral principles or "ethical potentialities and trajectories" are only entitled to fellow Muslims and not applicable to non-Muslims, contradicts the general historical trajectories and normative understanding in Islam. These ethics, according to the authors of this volume, are inclusive and not context-specific. They present "a normative imperative for Muslims that would apply whenever there is an obligation to escape oppression or injustice," and represent "purposeful construction of social and political virtues" (Abou El Fadl, Chapter One).

Unfortunately, post-colonial Muslim scholars have been more occupied with the apologetic discourse of either reinterpreting classical concepts (such as the division of the world into *dār al-Islām* and *dār al-ḥarb*) to relate to the political conceptualization of contemporary nation states, or proving an essential compatibility and reconcilability between Islamic theology and international law. The better task is to turn the moral imperatives inherited from the Islamic tradition into significant theological and ethical engagements with modern discourses on human rights and dignity.

This volume provides scholarly attempts to achieve this task by reviewing questions of migration, residence, naturalisation and citizenship from multi-sided perspectives, thus more broadly defining the Islamic tradition to cover not only theology but to also encompass ethics, customs and social norms, as well as modern political, humanitarian and rights discourses.

1 Movement/Migration

The movement of people—individuals, families, tribes and entire communities—has shaped and transformed the history of humankind. Groups of people have migrated for many reasons: economic, religious, political, as well as for education and cultural exchange. Masses have also migrated to escape conflict, persecution, natural disaster and harsh living conditions. The scholarly field of migration studies has been developing for over a century, primarily in the English speaking West in both colonial and post-colonial contexts, but primarily within established social science disciplines such as Sociology, Anthropology, Politics and Demography, but also in Labour Economics, Industrial Relations and International Relations. Migration studies also include forced migration and refugee studies with a proliferation of university departments and research centers in the last few decades teaching and researching migration issues—but rarely, perhaps never, from an Islamic ethical and juridical perspective.

This is a curious phenomenon since a large proportion of global migration and refugee movements are related to Muslim-majority states—as origin, transit and destination countries (Castles et al. 2014). For example, as of 2015, the majority (65%) of the 21.3 million refugees worldwide were Muslim (including 5.2 million Palestinian refugees). Almost 40 per cent of the 65.3 million classified as forcibly displaced (that includes internally displaced persons), were hosted in the Middle East and North Africa. Excluding Palestinians, around 54 per cent of registered refugees were from 3 Muslim countries—Syria (4.9 mill), Afghanistan (2.7 mill) and Somalia (1.1 mill) (UNHCR 2015). As of June 2016, most Syrian refugees were being hosted by the neighbouring countries of Turkey (2.8 million), Lebanon (1.02 million), Jordan (655,000), and Iraq (230,000). Around 900,000 Syrians filed asylum claims in Europe, while resettlement countries have taken relatively few—USA (18,000), Canada (40,000), Australia (12,000) (Migration Policy Centre, 2016). The GCC states (excluding Oman) have admitted around 620,000 Syrians since 2011, although there are claims of having taken more. The GCC countries do not, however, classify them as "refugees," partly because they are not signatories to the 1951 UN Refugee Convention (see De Bel Air 2015; Jureidini and Reda 2017).

In the same way that it has shaped many communities across the globe, migration also shaped the history of Islam from its very beginnings. Indeed, the question of the legality of Muslims residing in a non-Muslim state was the first of the "juridical" problems facing Muslim minorities.

Hijra in the Islamic tradition has been seen as the starting point of Muslim civilization and set the foundations for an Islamic society. It was one of the defining elements that revolutionized the conception of unity among the nascent Islamic community, not only among the Meccan supporters of Prophet Muhammad, later known as "the migrants" (*al-muhājirūn*), but also between them and the hosting community in Medina, later known as "the helpers" (*al-anṣār*). Unity meant solidarity between the *muhajirun* and the *anṣār.* Thus, Islamic teachings associated with *hijra* have contributed to the ethical principles relating to the treatment of foreign or migrant communities. It is seen as "a source of ethical norms and social behaviour" associated with brotherhood, economic cooperation, protection and social integration.

In modern Arabic *hijra* also means "migration" in a general sense. In Islamic jurisprudence it has a specific meaning, namely, the duty to migrate from a surrounding of unbelief towards a society where Islamic rules are prevalent, following the example of the Prophet and his Companions, who migrated from infidel, polytheistic Mecca towards Yathrib which, with the support of the *anṣār*, was to become the City of the Prophet, the basis of the historical body politic of Islam. So we see *hijra*, before anything else, being discussed by religious scholars as a religious principle to be performed as a duty under certain conditions. Throughout Islamic legal history, a doctrine of *hijra* was established, not only questioning the movement of people but also investigating the movement of converts, traders, and preachers.

More recently, Muslim political groups have referred to *hijra* in other ways. To give just a few examples: (1) in opposition to colonial rule; (2) those leaving Russia and the Balkan states in the 1800s; (3) Indian Muslims moving from British-controlled India to Afghanistan in the 1920s; (4) Muslims emigrating from India to the newly created state of Pakistan. These follow a pattern in that they all discuss whether Muslims were obliged to leave areas ruled by "infidels" (Muslims in medieval Christian Spain, colonialized areas, Russia and the Balkans, India towards Afghanistan or India towards Pakistan, etc.) and if so, under what conditions. These discussions were very closely related to issues of jihad.

In addition, post-World War II Muslim migration to Europe was of great historical importance, as it formed the basis of a fundamental change of concepts in Islamic normative thought. It developed what became known as a reverse *hijra*, that is, an unprecedented number of Muslims emigrating voluntarily from Muslim lands to non-Muslim countries. After the Second World War, with the introduction of the United Nations and the formation of Muslim minority communities in Western Europe, Muslim political, legal and religious scholars reached a new interpretation of the peaceful relations between the Muslim and non-Muslim world, rejecting the traditional dichotomy of *dār al-Islām* (abode or land of Islam) and *dār al-Kufr* (abode or land of disbelief) as anachronistic. This paved the way for an Islamic acceptance for residence, naturalisation and citizenship of Muslims in non-Muslim nation states under certain conditions (such as freedom of religion).

This acceptance became the basis for a new branch of Islamic Law that was developed in the 1990s and 2000s, namely *fiqh al-aqalliyyāt*. In less than two decades, *fiqh al-aqalliyyāt* shifted the legal discourse from *fiqh al-hijra* to *fiqh al-muwāṭana*, the Islamic law of citizenship. However, this does not mean that citizenship, nationality and integration of more than 15 million Muslims in the European Union was accepted by Muslim scholars overall. There are still certain countries, circles and traditions where this is rejected and where Europe continues to be seen as part of *dār* al-*Kufr*. The process of re-interpretation of Islamic thought concerning this vital political issue has not yet been completed. These circles normally allowed Muslim residence in other parts of the world for specific, temporary reasons, but not for the purpose of settling (Ramadan 1999; Aldeeb Abu-Sahlieh 1996).

2 Settlement/Citizenship

Normative ethico-legal discussions include rights in contemporary Islamic ethical thought, including, but not exclusive to, fatwas on migration and refugees. This requires critical, analytical and comparative analyses of the normative ethical frameworks in both Muslim countries and the West. Early discussions of citizenship and naturalisation largely began in the late Ottoman period around issues of conversion to Islam as a precondition for citizenship. A stream of fatwas and debates followed on naturalisation and nationality during the colonial era (especially in North Africa).

Islamic discourse around migration and settlement, along with idealizations of a generalized Islamic community has, however, been historically "burdened" by the jurisprudence around the dichotomy of *dār al-Islām* and *dār al-ḥarb*. This has prevented the development of a deeper understanding of contemporary citizenship within nation states that did not exist during early Islamic history and the foundational texts of the Qur'an and Hadith. From the late Ottoman period, the nation-state has been seen, by those who define the *ummah* as the body politic of all Muslims, as oppositional to or contradicting the conceptualization of a universal Muslim community. Thus, many contemporary questions can be raised as to the application of normative Muslim principles to current practices—such as non-Muslim rights in Islamic states or the naturalisation of Muslims in non-Muslim states.

In the Gulf States, citizenship rights are based on *Jus sanguinis*, or the right of blood; that is, citizenship is granted to offspring if one or both parents are citizens. However, gender issues arise where personal status laws do not give the right for women to confer citizenship to their children or husbands. This is distinguished from the right of citizenship for a person born in a particular country (*Jus soli*, right of soil).

The above issues are addressed by the various chapters in this book that makes for a multidimensional and multidisciplinary set of conceptualizations and empirical research.

3 Background to the Book

The chapters in this book were first presented over three days at an internal seminar, 28–30 January 2018. The seminar was entitled "Migration and Islamic Ethics: Issues of Residence, Naturalisation and Citizenship" and was held at the Center for Islamic Legislation and Ethics (CILE) in the College of Islamic Studies at Hamad Bin Khalifa University, Doha, Qatar.

We sought scholarly papers that would explore multi-dimensional approaches to Islamic ethics as applied to various forms of inward and outward migration, in both contemporary contexts and historically, whether forced or voluntary, and how issues of citizenship, integration and assimilation are/were viewed from an Islamic perspective.

Studies on migration usually takes two directions. One direction is to focus on a geographical region (e.g. Eastern Europe, the Middle East, etc.), analyzing migration patterns, causes and effects that such migration may have on the (re)structure of territories and demographies, and socio-economic and political organization of the region. A second direction is to go thematic with a specific methodological approach, adopting social science theories or relying generally on a humanitarian orientation, or method. Both directions yield qualitative and quantitative results on their own. However, bringing both directions together in one volume and even going beyond them may reveal other ways of thinking about the phenomenon of migration in a Muslim world. If these other ways of thinking are taken into consideration, we will be better informed of the phenomenon, not only in terms of who, why and what happened, and not only in terms of numbers, locations, time and space, but also we can have a perspective on the moral, ethical, emotional and religious factors at play. For example, studying a phenomenon like the impact of the practice of *kafala* (chapter 6) on migration movement from this perspective reveals that it is not only about economic control of the labour migrants or about humanitarian exploitation, but also ethical (e.g. Islamic contractual moral assumptions like that of sound intention) and religious factors (e.g. fatwa issuance) can have an impact on the application of the practice and real life situations.

As editors, we could have asked our contributors to confine their chapters to certain themes or to adopt certain methodological frameworks, but we did not opt to do this. We did not want to provide a regular-analytical text that could have been produced elsewhere. Our objective is to show the over-complexity of the subject matter, and that it cannot be studied only by counting numbers, or providing statistics, or drafting laws, but as every subject dealing with humans, a comprehensive multi-layer perspective and interdisciplinary approach are needed. Such an approach may result in better understanding of the subject under investigation, provide informative analysis, and lead to better workable solutions.

We understand that this approach may result in a volume that seems to lack a unified thinking paradigm, but a closer look will not only reveal the interconnectedness of the chapters but also opens new venues of thinking about the subject among researchers in the field. One anonymous reviewer of the manuscript's original draft noted that the book chapters "collectively, are original to the extent that the new conditions of rapid and uncontrolled migration originating in Muslim countries allowed the contributors to see old events in a new light and state a case that a new condition has developed that requires an Islamic ethics of migration, aside from a global one."

4 Chapters in the Book

The chapters are loosely divided into three themes; the first, addressing theorizations and conceptualizations using contemporary examples, mainly in the treatment of asylum-seekers, refugees and other forcibly displaced; the second, containing empirical analyses of contemporary case studies; and third, historical accounts of Muslim migratory experiences.

After this introductory chapter, the book begins with the chapter by Khaled Abou El Fadl, distinguished professor of Law at the University of California Los Angeles School of Law. We could not have wanted more for an opening chapter to this book than Professor Abou El Fadl's powerful and eloquent overview of Islamic ethics, human rights and migration. He uses the idea of "Islamic moral impulses" as a means for addressing migration and forced displacement issues. These moral impulses are comprised of concepts of counter-*istiḍʿāf*, countering oppression and powerlessness (between Muslims themselves and with "the other") through mobility and accessibility; as well as the ethics of *mu'ākhā* (brotherhood), *ḍiyāfa* (hospitality), and *ijāra* (asylum). The chapter touches on almost all of the issues focused upon in the subsequent chapters, without having been privy to their content—from classic Islamic scholars of the text to contemporary critiques of the sorry state of affairs in global migration and refugee movements, particularly in relation to Muslim migrants and refugees and the responses or lack of responses from the more powerful and affluent states. In a most encouraging passage for further pursuit, Abou El Fadl states:

> The values of brotherhood and hospitality provide fascinating normative precedents that could have been developed by contemporary Muslims into a significant inspirational ideation or an aspirational moral direction. Hospitality and brotherhood, added to migration as a normative response to a state of powerlessness; all of that, plus the ethic of mobility as an essential component of human dignity, is a promising ethical baggage that could be seen as trajectories that could be employed in the purposeful construction of social and political virtues.

In the third chapter, Abbas Barzegar looks at the Muslim practice and discourse of humanitarianism in relation to refugees. He refers to a "theologically informed universal humanitarianism" that he identifies as a "living *fiqh*," invoked by Muslim communities that transcends or overcomes "religious sectarianism, ethno-nationalism and political ideology" that burden contemporary migration crises. Along with the living *fiqh* is Muslim custom (*ʿUrf*) in relation to humanitarian principles and aid. The author provides illuminating examples from his study of Syrian refugees in Turkey in a reflective ethnography of both Turkish and Syrian aid workers, or humanitarian activists.

He asserts that living *ʿurf* practices go beyond the limitations of textual justification set forth by experts and academics. In these social spaces of interaction and encounter among people, practical theology brings in new precepts that may be further explored for potential ethical developments. These provide much needed concrete examples of cooperative ethics and practical solutions to pressing problems faced by the victims of forced displacement and the resultant impact on questions concerning the place of Islam and Muslims in the contemporary world.

In chapter four, Tahir Zaman looks closely at Muslim brotherhood and hospitality by drawing upon his ethnographies of the lived realities of refugees (Palestinian, Syrian, Sudanese, and Iraqi) in countries of asylum, particularly Turkey and Syria (before 2011). He takes the traditional notion of *jiwār*, or neighbourliness, in an understanding of the care and protection of others that transcends the nation state in the sense of independence from state governance over asylum-seekers and with the idea of "self-settlement." In the neighbourhood, "the open-ended possibility of everyday mundane social interactions that take place in parochial spaces generates an ethos that invites the stranger." The Turkish state, it is argued, expresses good intentions but this political intention remains ambiguous and ambivalent in actual everyday life.

Zaman provides an example of how a tradition maintains its ongoing relevancy to the present world through negotiation, adaptation and accommodation. This discursive power allows successive generations to find meanings for themselves. The ethical *jiwār* principle creates a space of acceptability, accessibility, and conviviality, not only to the neighbor next-door, but also generally to the fellow-refugee in need. This example stresses again the internal mechanism of the Islamic tradition to recall its ethical and moral properties and relate them to living practices of people that push against individualization, self-interest and state-interest principles dominating political and philosophical discourses.

In chapter five, Dina Taha provides a sometimes heart-rending account of Syrian refugee widows with children in Egypt who seek and are sought by Egyptian men to marry under the principle of *Sutra*, or "protection marriage." Using three case studies, the author far from presents the women as hapless victims, but provides them with agency by identifying quite different experiences, motivations and actions that take place. Invoking the idea of a Muslim "jurisprudential culture," the analysis of the three case studies is viewed from both feminist and post-colonial perspectives. The examples also provide evidence of how moral virtues can be manipulated and exploited for personal gain.

Chapter six, by Ray Jureidini and Said F. Hassan, takes a more innovative evaluation of the infamous *kafala* system of migrant labour management in the Gulf States. They canvas the traditional historical applications of *kafala* as an Islamic trusteeship mechanism whereby a person acts as a guarantor (*kafīl*), taking responsibility for someone else (*makfūl*)—whether a stranger, an orphan, a debtor or someone who must attend court or a business meeting. From the mid-twentieth century, this system was applied to the management and control of the increasingly large foreign workforce required to develop these countries following the sudden riches that flowed from oil and gas production. The chapter concludes that the human rights and Islamic ethics violations that have received much critical publicity over the past decade has not been so much a function of the *kafala* per se, but the lack of compliance to the traditional principles. A key example is given regarding the fundamental principle that a *kafīl* (guarantor) should not receive any remuneration or profit in that role and that this principle has been sustained as evidenced by fatwas, laws and prosecutions.

In chapter seven, Sari Hanafi conducts a content analysis of 74 recent academic articles in Arabic, English and French dealing with the question of migration and religion in the context of Muslim immigrant communities. Intriguingly, he starts his investigation by positing the controversial questions on the nature of knowledge production of social studies: is it universalistic (i.e. hard core science) or normative (i.e. having morals and conscience)? Where does the social scientist stand? He argues for a dual approach where social scientists, at least in migration studies, combine a Weberian ethic of conviction (defined as liberal, multiculturalist with a neo-enlightenment framework) and an ethic of responsibility. Hanafi aims in this chapter, as well as in his other publications, to establish collaboration between social science and religious ethics where each can be informed by the other. Social scientists combine ethics of conviction and ethics of responsibility, while Islamic ethicists would provide what would be a constant and primordial in Islam that should be taken into account in this normative moment. These different ethics will enter into tension that should be resolved through dialog, mutual learning and beyond a mere legalism or rationalism.

With this conviction, Hanafi examined his collection of articles to prove that a great deal of researchers in social science who deal with migration issues constitute an epistemic community that negotiates both ethics of conviction and responsibility while not necessarily being in conflict with Islamic ethics. By that he means they do not reject revelation, nor do they make mention of it. This resulted in a paradigmatic shift in the policies of migration: from a paradigm that forces migrants into assimilation/integration into another country to a paradigm that acknowledges the migrants' lived experiences, their diversity, and the role of religion in their day-to-day lives.

Chapter eight, by Radhika Kanchana, switches focus from legal and social responses to the questions of migration to Muslim state policies of naturalisation. The objective here is to investigate contemporary Muslim states' practice (18 states) in terms of how "open" is the gate of citizenship to the outsider, considering the impact of Islamic doctrine, existing international norms and contemporary practice. Studying these practices reveals that there is a general similarity in naturalisation provisions toward resident foreigners. Most Muslim states are inclined to the *Jus sanguinis* practice, but they do not take a uniform path. This, however, indicates political considerations in the discrimination or strategy, rather than a rigid formula inspired from religion.

Focusing more on the Arab-Gulf nations' citizenship policies, Kanchana notes the discrepancy between the legal text on the conditions of granting naturalisation and the application in practice. She argues that the policies involve ambiguous provisions, a matter that gives authorities the space to apply them in an instrumental way. To what extent the legal text is Islamic and to what extent the application is ethical are questions that are raised in this debate and still require more in depth investigation.

Chapter nine, by Rebecca Ruth Gould, touches upon one of the basic features of living traditions in Islam—the internal ability to de-and-re-construct meanings and concepts to accommodate with various historical, political and social settings. We see in this chapter an example of "how certain concepts now regarded as foundational to Islam were revived in modernity after having undergone centuries of relative marginalization." Gould takes us on a journey through space and time, demonstrating how the event of the *hijra* of the Prophet Muḥammad in 623–3 AD had turned from an historical moment into a religious doctrine that changed people's world view and the perception of their role in their communities and in the larger society of the *umma*.

Gould examines the *hijra* narrative in the context of the people of the Caucuses, explaining how it shaped the local histories and formed the diasporic identities of Caucasian Muslims forced out of their homes in the nineteenth and twentieth centuries. *Hijra* served as

> a reminder that "salvation lay in going forth for heroic ventures," and as a response to persecution, *hijra* increasingly became a discourse on the condition of being Muslim in a non-Muslim world, and a commentary on the extent to which the Islamic community (*umma*) could be spatially imagined and materially mapped.

The intriguing phenomenon in this context is that "*hijra* doctrine" is not established only through the legal theological narrative but it became part of the literary and cultural history in the Caucasus. The *hijra* literature is found in novels, poetry, autobiography and other literary forms—in official languages and in the vernacular. In the last part of the chapter, Gould turns to a couple of historical novels from the twentieth century to provide readers with another perspective on how the *hijra* story is being acted out repeatedly.

In chapter ten, Mettursun Beydulla informs us about a different *hijra* experience—the Chinese Xinjiang Uyghur Muslim *hijra* to Turkey and the United States. Based on field work and more than 200 interviews conducted between 2013 and 2017 with diasporan Uyghurs in Istanbul, Ankara, and Kayseri in Turkey as well as Washington, New York and Boston in the US, Beydulla demonstrates modes, causes and effects of this forced migration experience. It is a comprehensive treatment focusing upon theological, legal, social and political dimensions not only of the immigrants themselves, but also of both the homeland and host countries.

A particularly salient point in the author's analysis is that the Uyghur refugees' relationships with Turkey and the US can be analyzed within a context of Turkish and US multiculturalism. This implies on the one hand as democracy and tolerance and, on the other hand, exclusion, inferiorization and "otherness." Regardless of their formal status, Uyghurs in the US, and to some degree in Turkey, are considered as "other" and are thereby subject to unfair treatment, being ignored, ridiculed or treated differently. They are not viewed or treated as equals socially or culturally, hence, there is a gap between formal and "substantive" citizenship. As for the relationship of the Uyghur migrant community with their origins, the author's fieldwork showed that they have maintained intense social and emotional bonds to their homeland in Xinjiang.

Chapter eleven, by Abdul Jaleel P.K.M., concludes the volume by reminding us that scholars in the field of migration, especially those studying Muslim migration experiences, should go beyond simple generalizations and taken-for-granted assumptions such as the argument that the process of "naturalisation" of immigrant Muslims in modern nation states should be understood from within the Islamic legal parameters drawn by Muslim scholars in the heartlands of Islam. Conversely, the peripheral context, as in the case of Arab immigrants to the Indian Ocean, can provide a better understanding of the process of naturalisation in non-Muslim lands. In other words, the author argues that the legal-ethical demarcations of habitats by classical Muslim scholars into *dār al-Islām* and *dār al-ḥarb* were mostly de-contextualized general assertions that did not correspond to the real experiences of naturalisation that Islam and Muslims have experienced in these countries.

To prove his case, Abdul Jaleel P.K.M. provides a comparative review of historical and legal critical texts (Ibn Ḥajar's *al-Fatāwā al-Kubra*, al-Maʿbarī's *Tuḥfat al-Mujāhidīn*, al-Makhdūm al-Ṣaghīr's *Fatḥ al-Mubīn*) from both spheres, the heartland (Mecca and Cairo) and the periphery (Malabar). Such a comparative analysis raises the important question of what to focus upon while studying Islam and Muslims as an historical phenomenon. Should it be textual traditions or human practices, the integration of both as part of a discursive tradition, or as a hermeneutical engagement with the Pre-Text, Text and Con-text?

The answer to this question reveals itself in different places in this collection. To explore Islamic Ethics in the context of migration, one needs to engage not only the legal texts or the moral principles, but also the philosophical assumptions, the historical experience and the social setting. It is a multi-layer process that should engage all these elements together to produce a better understanding of migration.

The uniqueness of this book is threefold. First, the authors combine theoretical, legal and philosophical perspectives to the sociological and anthropological approaches that provide grounded, real-life observational analyses to the empirical sites of their subject matter. Second, common to most contributions is the tension between Western thinking paradigms about immigration and the Muslim tradition. There was reference to the plight of Muslims trying to manage with Western thinking paradigms of post-colonialism and their need to look inside to their own tradition that provides healthier alternatives to the problems of migration and displacement. In all chapters, the analyses draw upon the rich scholarship of Islamic ethics that provide a dimension to migration studies that has not been addressed previously. Third, the selection of papers provides a broad geographical coverage with case studies from many corners of the Muslim world, and addressing many specific actors—men, women, religious leaders, political authorities, non-governmental organizations, social and humanitarian activists.

Bibliography

Aldeeb Abu-Sahlieh, Sami. 1996. "The Islamic Conception of Migration." *International Migration Review* 30(1): 37–57.

Castles, Stephen, Hein De Haas & Mark Miller. 2014. *The Age of Migration*. Fifth Edition. New York: The Guilford Press.

De Bel-Air, Françoise. 2015. "A Note on Syrian Refugees in the Gulf: Attempting to Assess Data and Policies." *Gulf Labour Markets and Migration* 11.

Jureidini, Ray and Latife Reda. 2017. "The Convergence of Migrants and Refugees: Western and Muslim Perspectives." *Sociology of Islam* 5 (June 2017): 224–247.

Migration Policy Center. 2016. *Syrian Refugees*. Florence: European University Institute.

Ramadan, Tariq. 1999. *To Be a European Muslim: A Study of Islamic Sources in the European Context*. Leicester, UK: The Islamic Foundation.

United Nations High Commissioner for Refugees (UNHCR). 2015. *Statistical Yearbook for 2015*. Geneva, United Nations High Commissioner for Refugees.

CHAPTER 2

Islamic Ethics, Human Rights and Migration

Khaled Abou El Fadl

I will begin by addressing the issue of migration first from a Muslim perspective. I will then comment about the international law that governs issues of migration, and then come back to what might be termed, "Islamic moral impulses"—what in my view is a tradition that could be developed, but which so far, has not.

1 Normative Impulses

Perhaps a good starting point would be the Qur'anic verse in *Surat al-Isrāʾ* (The Night's Journey) stating that "God dignified human beings and has facilitated to them mobility on earth and the seas, and bestowed bounties upon them and distinguished human beings over much of God's other creations (or creatures)." (Q. 17:70). I have always been struck by the discourse of this verse: the idea that mobility and travel—i.e. the ability to traverse earth and sea, and mobility and access in the form of travel—is perhaps a constituent element in human dignity; and in fact, that the denial of mobility detracts from our dignity as human beings. Mobility implies freedom, and in this context, the Qur'anic discourse can be understood to refer to the freedom to enjoy what God has created and made available to human beings. If human beings are denied the freedom of mobility, does this diminish human dignity? Note that it is not necessarily the actual movement that is necessary for human dignity but the freedom to do so. What is deprecating to dignity is the inability or more precisely, the denial of freedom of movement.

Added to the Qur'anic narrative found in *Surat al-Isrāʾ* is the discourse of *Surat al-Nisāʾ* (The Women), one that easily lends itself to the issue of migration. In *Surat al-Nisāʾ*, the Qur'an addresses those for whom the angels come to arrest their souls and are found in a state of inequity. Then, we have this intriguing inquiry from the Heavens asking what had prevented them from migrating? The Qur'an rhetorically asks those who are in a state of inequity—literally, "*ẓālimī anfusihim*," which means "those who are unjust towards themselves"—"Wasn't God's earth vast and expansive enough for you to migrate?" (Q. 4:97). Critically, according to the Qur'anic discourse, these individuals exist in a state of inequity, and their excuse for living in a state of injustice is that they are oppressed. The reason that these individuals live in a state of oppression is

 | DOI:10.1163/9789004417342_003

that they are powerless. This condition of powerlessness is what Qur'anic commentators refer to as a state of "*istiḍʿāf*"—a state of oppressive injustice due to disempowerment. But per the Qur'anic discourse, the way to address this state of oppressive injustice and powerlessness is through migration.

Reading the Qur'anic verses in *Surat al-Isrāʾ* together with *Surat al-Nisāʾ*, there is a rather fascinating conjunction and a point of normative meeting between the idea of an earth that has been bestowed and granted to human beings in general, and the notion that mobility and travel is an essential or constituent element of human dignity. Oppression is a state in which one is powerless to enjoy the bounties (*niʿam*) of God's creation. A human being is entitled to dignity as a right bestowed by God upon creation, but this dignity is not simply theoretical or abstract; it has a concrete and material essence, or one can say, it is quintessentially deontological in meaning. The dignity of human beings is intimately interconnected with the opportunity to enjoy God's bounties and the freedom of movement and mobility. Accepting or acquiescing in oppression is iniquitous; it is as if passive acceptance of oppression leads one to be unjust towards oneself. Existing in such a state of injustice is morally unacceptable, and importantly, freedom of movement is necessary for the right to dignity and perhaps for a virtuous existence. Of course, the Qur'anic narrative goes on to state that men, women, and children who are truly weak and oppressed, and therefore, without any real means for escaping persecution are deserving of God's pardon because they are not blameworthy (Q. 4:98).

Before proceeding further, we should note that when it comes to the verses about migration in *Surat al-Nisāʾ*, a number of Qur'anic commentators concluded that this revelation was intended to address a particular set of historical events. Some Muslims who had converted at the time of the Prophet in Mecca had failed to join the Prophet and his followers in migrating to Medina. As a result, some of these converts to Islam ended up fighting on the side of the Meccan idolaters against fellow Muslims in the Battle of *Badr*. The revelation in *Surat al-Nisāʾ* was intended to blame those who placed themselves in the deplorable situation of having to fight on the side of idolaters against fellow Muslims by failing to migrate. If the Qur'anic discourse on migration is wedded to this specific historical circumstance, or in other words, if we read these verses as addressing those who converted to Islam but failed to join the Prophet in Medina and as a result, ended up joining the Battle of *Badr* on the wrong side; then these verses are substantially emptied of their normative content because they were intended to address an historical contingency that has already come to pass. But as a number of Qur'anic commentators have noted, even if the occasion for revelation was a specific historical event, by the terms of its own phrasing, the Qur'anic discourse on migration remains normatively pertinent. The Qur'anic narrative on migration is stated broadly and generally, and therefore, seems to be in a form that is non-contextual and to create a normative imperative for Muslims that would apply whenever there is an obligation to escape oppression or injustice (al-Rāzī 1990, 10–13; Quṭb 2007, 744–6).

We should note here that the issue of *hijra* or migration as a normative obligation in Islamic theology and law is complex and layered. Many jurists insisted that there is a permanent and lasting obligation upon every Muslim to migrate from the abode of unbelievers (*dār al-kufr*) to the abode of Islam (*dār al-Islām*). Accordingly, any sojourn to the abode of unbelievers must be temporary and wedded to a specific purpose. However, some reports attributed to the Prophet assert that the obligation to migrate was abrogated upon the defeat of Mecca and its entry into the Islamic fold (*lā hijrata baʿda al-fatḥ*) (al-Hanbali 1996, 114). In other words, according to this genre of hadith, migration was a temporary obligation that expired upon the defeat of the Meccans at the time of the Prophet. This counter tradition to the claimed obligation to migrate from the abode of unbelievers to the abode of Islam continued to be dynamic and viable, as many Muslims who lived in non-Muslim territories continued to seek legitimacy for their status. In other words, while some Muslim jurists insisted that Muslims should permanently reside only in the abode of Islam, other jurists negated this obligation contending that the duty to migrate expired shortly before the death of the Prophet. Nevertheless, apart from the polarizing debate about residing in the abode of Islam, the issue of *wājib al-hijra* or the duty to migrate as a response to injustice, persecution, and oppression remained a tantalizing normative challenge throughout Islamic history. Many Muslim jurists argued that migration remains a normative duty until the end of time, but the obligation is to migrate and reside wherever Muslims may practice their faith freely or what they called "*iẓhār al-dīn*." Others argued that the duty is to migrate from the land of inequity (*dār al-fisq*) to wherever justice reigns (*dār al-ʿadl*). Especially in mystical Sufi orientations, the duty to migrate was interpreted in entirely spiritual and internal terms: *hijra*. In these spiritual theologies, *hijra* becomes an obligation to journey from and abandon the lower base and material self to the higher divine and supernal self. *Hijra* is not a physical residential status but a dynamic and perpetual process of spiritual elevation (Hassan 2013; Abou El Fadl 1994).

In addition to the normative idea of migration as a response to disempowerment and oppression, there are at least two other moral impulses within the Islamic tradition that are important to note in any discussion on Islamic ethics and migration. The two possible ethical norms in the Islamic tradition are *wājib al-ḍiyāfa*, the norm arising from the duty of hospitality, and *muʾākhā* (brotherhood), which is an ethical example set when the Prophet built an effective social brotherhood between migrants of Mecca and the natives of

Medina. I will comment on *ḍiyāfa* and *mu'ākhā* momentarily, but it is worth noting at this point that the Islamic tradition is replete with normative ethical possibilities or what one may describe as ethical potentialities and trajectories. The values of brotherhood and hospitality provide fascinating normative precedents that could have been developed by contemporary Muslims into a significant inspirational ideation or an aspirational moral direction. Hospitality and brotherhood, added to migration as a normative response to a state of powerlessness; all of that, plus the ethic of mobility as an essential component of human dignity, is a promising ethical baggage that could be seen as trajectories that could be employed in the purposeful construction of social and political virtues. I see the moral baggage inherited from the Islamic tradition as containing ethical impulses of virtue that could have been marshalled by contemporary Muslims into significant theological and ethical engagements with the modern discourses on human rights and dignity.

In my view, the Islamic tradition is replete with ethical potentialities that are embedded in complicated and layered historical narratives. These layered historical narratives do not contain a single or a unitary normative trajectory. Indeed, the historical narratives contain numerous normative trajectories that are often conflicting and that exist in tension with one another. Having said this, however, it is undeniable that in the midst of this tension, one finds soundly embedded ethical impulses or virtues, such as hospitality and brotherhood, that are as if an untapped potentiality. These ethical impulses have a moral trajectory or a possible normative power, but only if reclaimed and reconstructed into coherent epistemic interventions and practices in the modern world (Abou El Fadl 2014, iiii-iv). Relying on their own native moral and ethical resources, Muslims could have anchored themselves on virtues such as brotherhood and hospitality in making serious interventions in the contemporary discourses on migration and human rights (Hollenbach 2016; Wilson & Mavelli 2016).

The reality, however, is that far from developing these normative impulses in their own tradition, Muslims in the contemporary, post-colonial age became rather obsessed with the apologetics of proving the essential compatibility between Islamic theology and law, and international law, but not going much beyond that. One often gets the impression that in Islamic normative discussions it as if the reconciliation between the Islamic tradition and the perceived demands of international law is a sufficient moral response to the challenges that confront the international community. There are numerous contemporary Muslim studies that seek to prove that Islamic norms are reconcilable with international legal standards. However, for the most part, in response to the growing problems of forced migration and displaced populations, contemporary Muslims have not leveraged their own ethical tradition in attempting to critique the limitations and exceeding the expectations of international law. Put bluntly, when it comes to forced migration and displacement, anchoring themselves on the moral thrust of their tradition, Muslims could have exceeded existing international law standards.

2 The Inadequacy of International Law

When dealing with forced migration and the displacement of human beings, international law continues to be largely inadequate. So, to argue the point that Islamic ethics or norms are simply consistent with international law is not much of a moral achievement. We know that the Refugee Convention and its accompanying protocol sets the standard for the non-refoulement of forced migrants, but we also know that its coverage is very limited. Article 33 in particular, which is the operative Article in much of the jurisprudence on migrants, provides the following:

> No Contracting State shall expel or return ("refouler") a refugee in any manner whatsoever to the frontiers of territories where his life or freedom would be threatened on account of his race, religion, nationality, membership of a particular social group or political opinion.

The fact is that the Refugee Convention only addresses displaced individuals who have crossed an international border. The Refugee Convention does not cover internal displacement, i.e. people who have been displaced but have not crossed an international border. Moreover, the Refugee Convention simply obligates Contracting Parties not "to refoul," or turn back to the frontiers of territories, those individuals who are threatened on account of race, religion, nationality, social group or political opinion. The protected categories of race, religion, nationality, social group, or political opinion are legalistic and technical. For the most part, Contracting Parties to the Refugee Convention are not obligated to provide anything beyond the duty of non-refoulement. If the reason that someone is threatened falls out of the protected categories of race, religion, nationality, social group or political opinion, then states may, in fact, refoul or send back individuals to areas where their life and safety can be at risk. One should add that under The Convention Against Torture and Other Cruel, Inhuman and Degrading Treatment, there is an absolute prohibition against the refoulement of individuals who are at risk of suffering torture or any of the other enumerated harms. However, the protections afforded by the Torture Convention are narrow, and, in my opinion, are rather insufficient (McArthur & Buchinger 2008).

The obligations of Article 33 of the 1951 UN Convention Relating to the Status of Refugees (Refugee Convention) are severely constrained by the acknowledgement that States can refoul those individuals who threaten a country's national security or its perceived political stability. Thus, in international law, while we often talk about the ideals of voluntary repatriation, local integration, or safe resettlement to a stable country, the durable solutions continue to elude us. Ever since World War II, we have been talking about durable solutions for displaced refugees, whether it be groups of refugees such as Palestinians; Iraqis in Iran; Afghanis in Iran and Pakistan; Syrians in Turkey; Tibetans in Nepal; Filipinos in Malaysia; Angolans in Zambia; Sri Lankans in India; Mauritanians in Senegal; or Rohingyas in Thailand, India, Malaysia or Bangladesh. Solutions continue to elude us because the international jurisprudence that governs displaced individuals—while speaking of the ideals of voluntary repatriation, local integration or safe resettlement—does not have the power to obligate nations to, in fact, provide durable solutions.

What has been occurring is that for some 60 years, the world has taxed the already overtaxed *Office of the United Nations High Commissioner for Refugees* to provide ad hoc solutions to displaced populations around the world, often condemning people to life in camps with tents or makeshift communities, while countries continue insisting on the framework of national sovereignty as the overarching paradigm in dealing with and reacting to the crisis of displaced human beings around the world. One of the critical components missing in International Law is that there is no proportional obligation upon States that create the displacement of migrants, such as the United States or Russia, to take a proportional number of migrants for resettlement. In other words, a country like the United States can create an enormous amount of displacement in Iraq or Afghanistan, but wash its hands when it comes time to resettling refugees, simply throwing the obligation upon other countries such as Turkey, Pakistan, Kenya, Jordan, Lebanon, Chad, or according to the latest statistics, Germany. There are numerous problems with the International legal framework that continues to create a perpetual state of crisis in the world when it comes to dealing with forced migration, whether for political or economic reasons, and other displaced individuals. The problems of forced migration overlap with the exploitation of cheap labour and the trafficking in human beings in complicated and deeply troubling ways. We know that the 1951 Convention and 1967 Protocol Relating to the Status of Refugees came into being post-World War II addressing largely European concerns in the Cold War era. The Refugee Convention protected specific categories of people that are able to be physically present in the territory or port of entry of the host country and that are then able to make an application for non-refoulement. But there is no international standard obligating countries that cause widespread displacement because of political, military, or economic policies pursued by such countries to take responsibility for the population of forced migrants. As it stands, the US, through the invasion of Afghanistan and Iraq, has created a serious refugee crisis. Russia has exasperated the refugee crisis in Syria through its persistent bombardment of populated areas. Saudi Arabia and the U.A.E. have created a refugee crisis in Yemen that is truly horrific, and Israel continues to act with absolute impunity towards the Palestinian refugee crisis. In all of these situations, while there are humanitarian and human rights standards that do apply, and that do condemn offending countries for their acts of aggression, the international law response to forced migration and displacement remains weak at best (Martin & Weerasinghe 2014; Cubie 2017). Ideally, if a country, through its military policies or otherwise, causes forced migrations and displacements, then such a country at a minimum should be held financially accountable for compensating the displaced populations, and should be responsible for providing a safe haven and the safe resettlement of the populations it displaced. Otherwise, powerful countries and governments through aggressive military, political, or economic policies will continue to exacerbate the ongoing refugee crisis in the world. Some states and governments are more responsible than others for creating the current refugee crisis and it is ethically defensible to expect that these states and governments bear the greater burden of solving this crisis (Duarte et al., 2017).

3 Islamic Ethics and Migration

Returning to the issue of Islamic ethics and migration, I think it is fair to say that the Muslim contribution in this ongoing state of crisis has been largely muted and ineffective. In fact, there has been a drift away from the Islamic tradition, which could have enriched international discourses by tapping into the theology of *muʾākhā* (brotherhood), or *ḍiyāfa* (hospitality), or *hijra* (migration) as a response to *istiḍʿāf* (oppression). Indeed, beyond these under-developed normative impulses, there is a well-embedded moral concept of refuge and protected status in the Islamic tradition (Zamān 2017, 19–43; Shoukri 2010; Arnaout 1987). The Qurʾanic text states: "And if any of the unbelievers seek asylum with you (*istajāraka*), grant it to him (*fa-ʾajirhu*) until he hears the Word of God, then escort him to a place where he is secure for they are people without knowledge." (Q. 9:6). Classical Muslim jurists developed extensive discussions on the rights of the *mustaʾman* (person enjoying a protected status) and the status of *amān* (pledge of security or safe conduct) (Bashir 2018, 236–9). Whether asylum can be elevated to the status of an entitlement or right as opposed to a solemn and perhaps sacred privilege is anchored in the ethical tradition of *ijāra* as opposed to the jurisprudence of *amān*. The *muʾjar* or the recipient of *ijāra* was a person who enjoyed a protected status by virtue of a social status as opposed to political or business interest. Although the practice of *ijāra* in the Islamic tradition calls for more extensive historical investigations, the ethical impulse is poignantly represented in a number of traditions from the time of the Prophet. Umm Hanī bint Abī Ṭālib, the Prophet's cousin, made a grant of *ijāra* to unbelievers who were visiting Medina. As the narrative goes, she had a rather public and heated dispute with ʿAlī ibn Abī Ṭālib, her brother, about the validity of this grant of protection. The dispute was taken to the Prophet who ruled in favor of Umm Hanī, making what would become a famous statement providing that the grant of *ijāra* by a single Muslim is binding upon all Muslims. In perhaps an even more famous incident, the Prophet's daughter Zaynab stood up in the mosque in Medina after the morning prayers, and announced that she had given an *ijāra* to her ex-husband, the idolater Abū al-ʿĀṣ ibn al-Rabīʿ, who apparently was present in her house at the time. The Prophet stood up and announced that this is the first that he has heard that Ibn al-Rabīʿ was in Zaynab's home, and that Zaynab had granted him protection. However, the Prophet announced that as Zaynab had granted Ibn al-Rabīʿ this status, her *ijāra* must be respected. Reportedly, on this occasion, the Prophet made a proclamation that has for long engaged and stimulated the ethical thinking of Muslims. Reportedly, the Prophet said words to the effect that the commitments of one Muslim is binding upon all (*dhimmatu al-muslimīn wāḥida*), and that a grant of protection by the weakest in society is binding upon even the strongest (Al-Jawzī 1992, 257; Al-Ṭabari 1387, 348; Guillaume 1955, 317).

The above mentioned traditions on *ijāra* are often cited in classical juristic discussions on *amān* or the granting of safe conduct. In fact, relying on the Zaynab and Ibn al-Rabī precedent, Ḥanafī jurists and some others held that a guarantee of safe conduct can be granted by any member of society and it is valid and effective against all (Al-Dawoody 2011, 133). However, one suspects that the tradition of *ijāra* connoted a moral virtue of hospitality and kindness towards strangers or aliens that is broader in its ethical import than *amān*. The Qur'anic verse quoted above advising Muslims to grant unbelievers safe conduct so that they may hear the word of God (Q. 9:6) was interpreted by Muslim jurists as the legal basis at the heart of the jurisprudence of *amān*. However, this verse uses a derivative of the word *j.w.r.* which means to protect, aid, or honor. In the Muslim tradition, the word *jiwār* has a diverse set of meanings that contain far reaching moral implications (Ibn Manẓūr 1997, 414–5). A *mujāwir* was a client who adhered to the service of a sanctuary, and such clients enjoyed a sacrosanct status (Bashir 2018, 50; Al-Ghunaimi 1968, 11–13). Servants of shrines or Sufi lodges were known as *mujāwirs* (*mujāwir* sg./ *mujāwirun* pl.) and at least until modernity this class of individuals enjoyed a protected status. Moreover, the rights of neighbors, or neighborly rights and privileges, is known as *ḥaqq al-jiwār* or *ḥaqq al-jār*, which continues to be an important normative category at least in non-urban or less urbanized Muslim cultures.

The ethical impulses that one finds permeating the Islamic tradition if transformed into inspirational ideological concepts, or even beyond this, if articulated into systematic legal conventions and treaties between Muslim nations, could have coalesced to become an influential institution in modern international practice. The concept of freedom of movement as a necessary element for upholding human dignity; the right to escape oppression through migration; this coupled with the traditions of hospitality and brotherhood (which is analogous to the French concept of fraternity); in addition to neighborly rights and the sanctity of visitors create a powerful normative universe that could become the basis of inspired activism and practice. To the extent that ideals can inspire and influence human activity, one can rightfully expect that Muslims tap into their own rich normative tradition to improve upon the universal standards that humanity sets for itself. Unless one believes in strict historical materialism and does not credit ideas with the ability to at least in part direct and shape human activity, I think we are justified in asking whether contemporary Muslims have been able to co-opt, adapt and negotiate their own moral traditions in helping to shape the humanitarian standards that exist in the world today. I think it is fair to say that the entire genre of "human rights thinking," or "thinking about virtue ethics" is premised on an aspirational modality. All thinking about human rights standards as well as the discipline of virtue ethics seeks to change conduct through persuasion and influence. If one abandons the task of hoping to persuade and influence the way people conduct themselves, then there would be no point to scholarly narratives beyond the strictly descriptive and non-evaluative. However, because I do believe that ideals do matter, in much the same way that ethics and legal standards matter, I do not believe that it is overly naïve to hope that Muslims would be able to tap into the power of the ethical trajectories embedded in their own tradition to achieve a greater measure of justice for the human community.

Before commenting on Muslim countries in the modern context, I should briefly address the issue of *dār al-Islām* versus *dār al-kufr* or *dār al-ḥarb* (abode of Islam as opposed to the abode of infidels or the abode of war). Even before the rise of ISIS and its so-called Caliphate state, some modern commentators have continued to argue that the major obstacle to Muslims embracing an inclusivist participatory paradigm towards the world community is their persistent influence of the polarity of the abode of Islam, which exists in opposition to the abode of infidels or the abode of war (Lewis 2006). According to this point of view, it is the continued impact of this dichotomous and exclusivist perspective upon Muslim thinking that has obstructed the ability of Muslims to make normative commitments to democracy, human rights and humanitarian standards. Although this is a larger issue that cannot be adequately addressed in this context (Abou El Fadl 2014, 203–270), I will say that I do not believe that the historical legacy of *dār al-Islām* or abode of Islam versus any other abode as a significant obstacle to the development of a moral response to the issue of displacement in the modern age. For the most part, I do not see it as a significant obstacle because I think that *dār al-Islām* is an ambiguous category, endlessly discursive in nature, and endlessly negotiable. In my reading of the tradition, much of what is written on *dār al-Islām* in the classical period correlates to or parallels the medieval discourses on Christendom, or in the case of Judaism, the discourses on Jews and Gentiles (MacCulloch 2014; Hall 1997). There were historically embedded ideological and political categories that helped pre-modern subjects negotiate the realities of their existence. However, those who study the history of the Crusades and the complex and non-dogmatic Muslim response to the Crusades, and those who study the rise and fall of Muslim dynasties and the rise of the Ottoman Empire ought to be struck by the historically discursive and persistently negotiable nature of a designation such as *dār al-Islām*. The least one can say is that it was no less negotiable and no less resistant to broad generalizations than the history of the idea of Christendom or the categories of Jew and Gentile. Moreover, one should note that Muslims have found it sociologically easy to migrate from Muslim countries to non-Muslim countries if that meant attaining a greater degree of dignity and a greater degree of justice. In the modern age, while Saudi muftis continued to issue *responsa*, prohibiting Muslims from migrating or residing in the abode of infidels, and by infidels they mean the West, such fatwas do not seem to have made much of an impact in stemming the flow of Muslim migrants to Western countries. The alleged or presumed continued impact of the abode of Islam upon the Muslim mind is nothing but a projected myth—*dār al-Islām* has become a nuanced, highly problematized category in the Muslim mind and has been so for centuries. It is disingenuous to suggest that *dār al-Islām* has survived as a coherent category not only through the vestiges of medieval history, but also colonialism, World War I and II, the Arab Revolt, the breakup of the Ottoman Empire, the rise of nation-states, and even dramatic and traumatic modern events such as the Iraq/Iran war and many others.

Overcoming the hold of a stereotypical dichotomous division of the world over the Muslim imagination is not the challenge that Muslims must overcome in the modern world. The real challenge is for Muslims to re-interrogate and rediscover their own rich tradition and adapt it to meeting the moral challenges of the age. For instance, the very idea of *dār al-Islām* coupled with the Qur'anic narrative describing Muslims as but a single nation or *umma* (Q 21: 92; Q 23: 52) could have inspired Muslims to overcome, or at least mitigate the worst pitfalls of nationalism, ethnocentrism, and racism. Muslims could have co-opted and leveraged the moral impulse behind *dār al-Islām* into an ethic of civility, fraternity, and decency towards one another. Indeed, the utter failure of projects such as the Muslim World League in mitigating the draconian harshness of national territorial borders or in alleviating the suffering of displaced people—especially displaced Muslim populations in other Muslim countries, is living proof of the ineffectiveness of a concept such as *dār al-Islām* upon the modern Muslim imagination. I do not say this because I wish to deconstruct the concept of *dār al-Islām* as perhaps intimately interconnected to the notion of a single *umma* or indeed to a Muslim fraternity or *muʾākhā*. Rather, I say this because it does take a certain amount of incredulous mythological thinking to continue ignoring the socio-historical realities, and insist that Muslims do in fact adhere to conceptual categories found in medieval texts written for a different time and place.

Unfortunately since the colonial era, Muslim countries have first emulated Western countries in adopting vulgar forms of stark nationalism in which they drew strict territorial boundaries vis-a-vis one another. But then Muslim countries lagged behind Western countries that have reached a point of what some have called a "post-nationalist paradigm." In other words, the West has successfully managed to reach a post-nationalist reality in which they diluted the national borders between various Western countries. It is true that this post-nationalist reality is racially and ethnically contingent—the rise of the ideology of a unified Europe was accompanied by the rise of the racist thesis of the clash of civilizations and the triumphalist, albeit racist, thesis of the "European miracle" and the West against the rest (Schmidt 2004; Pagden 2009; Jones 2003). But the reality is that one can be an American citizen and travel all over Europe without a visa, and one can also be a British citizen and travel all over Europe without a visa. Moreover, it has become as if an article of faith that an act of aggression against a single Western country is an attack against the rest. It is not an exaggeration to say that in the contemporary world, despite the differences in languages, cultures, economic systems, and religious beliefs, there is a basic and fundamental moral unity of purpose and fate among White Europeans. Trying to make sense of this post-nationalist unity of fate and purpose, some have even resorted to describing it in terms of the largely incoherent category of the "Judeo-Christian tradition," as a distinctive sociologically and anthropologically shared reality (Cohen 1971; Topolsky & Nathan 2017). The irony is that while orientalist scholars continued to refer to the Muslim world as a single unit and to attribute to this unit a tribal-like mentality of allegiance and affiliation, it is really the White Western world that developed a common sense of solidarity and cultural affinity. Whether one accepts that the Western sense of solidarity is in reality racially based or not, many believe that the West has formed a common sense of purpose over shared normative values such as democracy, liberty, freedom of speech and the like.

Muslims meanwhile have deconstructed the concept of *umma*, and deconstructed the concept of brotherhood (*ukhuwwa*), and largely ignored their tradition of *ḍiyāfa* or hospitality in rather ironic and paradoxical ways, to become more zealously defensive of the paradigm of nationalism and nationalist borders, even amongst Muslim countries themselves in ways that have made them lag morally behind Western countries. We should recall in this context the *kafala* system in Gulf countries that continues to be directly responsible for very widespread abuses against labour (Human Rights Watch 2009). Far from being consistent with the ethics of *ḍiyāfa*, *mu'ākhā*, or *ijāra*, the *kafala* system has institutionalized structural abuses against migrants and displaced people. Some countries such as Saudi Arabia and the U.A.E. have become habitual offenders in the unconscionable practices of human trafficking and modern-day slavery (Mahdavi 2009). Moreover, in oil-rich Gulf countries, the *kafala* system has become inextricably interwoven with a racist outlook in which the Western White man occupies the upper height of the racial hierarchy. In oil-rich Gulf countries there is a strict racially stratified cultural outlook in which the White European and American male occupies a distinct place of superiority and privilege. It is as if many Muslim countries imported and internalized the racial outlooks of their former White colonizers in ways that have effectively hampered their ability to rehabilitate and develop their own natively-based ethical contributions towards migrant workers and displaced human beings.

If one wants to understand the hold of territorial nationalism over the Muslim imagination, one needs to go no further than evaluating the status of the Hijaz since it came under Saudi control in the early 20th Century. The Hijaz, the place of the holy cities of Mecca and Medina, is a cultural and moral heritage for all Muslims of every school, sect, and creed. Yet instead of having some semi-independent sacred status such as the Papal states or a status of shared Muslim governance, the Hijaz is treated strictly from within a territorial nationalist paradigm. It is considered part of the nationalist territory of the sovereign state of Saudi Arabia, and it would be absolute sacrilege for any Muslim country to demand a role in the shared governance of the holy sites (Abou El Fadl 2014). My point is that the status of the Hijaz is emblematic of the fact that it is not the native ideals of *dār al-Islām* or the single *umma* that holds sway over the modern Muslim imagination but the imported principles of vulgar territorial nationalism. Some of the nationalist practices of Muslim countries have been nothing short of shocking to the conscience. For instance, the way Egypt has dealt with the displacement of Bedouins in Sinai or the Palestinians of Gaza, or the way that the United Arab Emirates and Saudi Arabia have dealt with displacement in Yemen is a course of a pattern of practice that is not just offensive to modern concepts of humanitarian law and human rights, but even to the most basic principles of the Islamic tradition. The conduct of the Egyptian, Emirati, and Saudi governments towards displaced and destitute Palestinians and Yemenis respectively evidences not just a gross disregard of human rights and humanitarian standards but also the flouting of Islamic ethical precepts with rather disquieting impunity.

4 Conclusion

We should not end on a despondent note. The aspiration is that Muslims would investigate their own moral tradition to help construct humanitarian paradigms that elevate international moral trajectories rather than simply acquiescing and rubber-stamping vague doctrines produced by nation-states in search of their own national interests. The Muslim tradition is replete with powerful virtuous ethical impulses that could make substantive contributions to the field of forced migrants and displacement. Among these ethical impulses are critical concepts of counter-*istiḍʿāf*—countering oppression and powerlessness through mobility and accessibility, first and foremost between Muslims themselves; and then second, between Muslims and "the other"; as well as the ethics of *muʾākhā* (brotherhood), *ḍiyāfa* (hospitality), and *ijāra* (asylum). These are ethical concepts that could easily find common ground with other religious and faith-based traditions, in a way that challenges and elevates, rather than simply apologetically rubber-stamping modern international law. It is perhaps not too audacious to hope that Muslims take their own ethical tradition seriously enough by deploying it in the service of alleviating and removing human suffering, especially when it comes to what the Qurʾan poignantly describes as *al-ghārimīn wa fī sabīli Allah wa ibn al-sabīl* (those who are burdened with debt and the wayfarers in need) (Q. 9:60).

Acknowledgements

I am very grateful to my wife, Grace Song, and my student and research assistant, Zezen Zaenal Mutaqin, for their invaluable feedback and assistance.

Bibliography

Abou El Fadl, Khaled. 1994. "Islamic Law and Muslim Minorities: The Juristic Discourse on Muslim Minorities from the Second/Eighth to the Eleventh/Seventeenth Centuries." *Islamic Law and Society* 1(2): 141–187.

Abou El Fadl, Khaled. 2014. *Reasoning with God: Reclaiming Sharīʿah in the Modern Age*. Maryland: Rowman & Littlefield.

Al-Dawoody, A. 2016. Islamic Law of War: Justifications and regulations. New York: Palgrave Macmillan.

Al Ghunaimi, M.T. 2013. *The Muslim Conception of International Law and the Western Approach*. Springer.

Arnaout, G.M. 1987. *Asylum in the Arab-Islamic Tradition*. Geneva: Office of the United Nations High Commissioner for Refugees, International Institute of Humanitarian Law.

Bashir, Khaled Ramadan. 2018. *Islamic International Law: Historical Foundations and al-Shaybani's Siyar*. S.l.: Edward Elgar Publishing.

Cohen, A.A. 1971. *The Myth of the Judeo-Christian Tradition: and other Dissenting Essays*. New York: Schocken Books.

Cubie, Dug. 2017. *The International Legal Protection of Persons in Humanitarian Crises: Exploring the Acquis Humanitaire*. Oxford: Hart Publishers.

Duarte, Melina, Kasper Lippert-Rasmussen, Serena Parekh and Vitikainen, Annamari. 2018. *Refugee Crisis: The Borders of Human Mobility*. Taylor & Francis.

Guillaume, A. 1955. *The Life of Muhammad: A Translation of Isḥāq's Sīrat Rasūl Allāh*. Oxford: Oxford University Press.

Hall, D.J. 2002. *The End of Christendom and the Future of Christianity*. Eugene: Wipf and Stock Pub.

al-Ḥanbalī, Abū al-Faraj ibn Rajab. 1996. *Fatḥ al-Bārī Sharḥ Ṣaḥīḥ al-Bukhārī*. Vol. 1. *Maktabat al-Ghurab'ā*.

Hassan, Said Fares. 2013. *Fiqh al-Aqalliyāt, History, Development and Progress*. New York: Palgrave Macmillan.

Hollenbach, David. 2016. "Religion and Forced Migration." In *The Oxford Handbook of Refugee and Forced Migration Studies*, edited by E. Fiddian-Qasmiyeh, G. Loescher, K. Long, and N. Sigona. Oxford University Press.

Human Rights Watch. 2009. *"The island of happiness": Exploitation of migrant workers on Saadiyat Island, Abu Dhabi*. New York: Human Rights Watch.

Ibn Manẓūr, Al-Imām. 1997. *Lisān al-ʿArab*. Vol. 2. Sader.

al-Jawzī, Jamāl al-Dīn Abū al-Faraj ʿAbd al-Raḥmān ibn ʿAlī Ibn. 1992. *Al-Muntaẓam fī Tārīkh al-Umam wa-l-Mulūk*. Vol. 3. Beirut: Dār al-Kutub al-ʿIlmiyya

Jones, Eric. 2003. *The European Miracle: Environments, Economies and Geopolitics in the History of Europe and Asia*. Cambridge University Press.

Jones, R. 2017. *Violent Borders: Refugees and the Right to Move*. Verso Press.

Lewis, B. 2006. *What Went Wrong?: the Clash between Islam and Modernity in the Middle East*. Harper Perennial.

MacCulloch, D. 2014. *Christianity: the First Three Thousand Years*. Penguin Books.

Mahdavi, P. 2011. *Gridlock: Labor, Migration, and Human Trafficking in Dubai*. Stanford University Press.

Martin, S.F and S. Weerasinghe. 2014. *Humanitarian Crises and Migration: Causes, Consequences and Responses*. Routledge.

Mavelli, Luca and Erin Wilson. 2017. "The Refugee Crisis and Religion beyond Conceptual and Physical Boundaries." In *The Refugee Crisis and Religion: Secularism, Security and Hospitality in Question*, edited by L. Mavelli and E. Wilson. Rowman & Littlefield International.

Nathan, E. and A. Topolski. 2017. *Is there a Judeo-Christian Tradition? A European Perspective*. Berlin de Gruyter Mouton.

Nowak, Manfred and Elizabeth McArthur. 2008. *The United Nations Convention against Torture: A Commentary*. Oxford University Press.

Pagden, Anthony. 2009. *Worlds at War: The 2500 Year Struggle Between East and West*. Random House.

al-Rāzī, Fakhr al-Dīn. 1990. *Al-Tafsīr al-Kabīr*. Vol. 11. Beirut: Dār al-Kutub al-ʿIlmiyya.

Quṭb, Sayyid. 2007. *Fī Ẓilāl al-Qurʾan*. Vol. 2. Cairo: Dār al-Shurūq.

Schmidt, Alvin. 2004. *The Great Divide: The Failure of Islam and the Triumph of the West*. Regina Orthodox Press.

Shoukri, A.M. 2011. *Refugee Status in Islam: Concepts of Protection in Islamic Tradition and International Law*. I.B. Tauris.

al-Ṭabarī, Ibn Jarīr. 1387. *Tārīkh al-Ṭabarī*. Vol. 2. Egypt: Dār al-Turāth.

Zaman, T. 2017. *Islamic Traditions of Refuge in the Crises of Iraq and Syria*. New York: Palgrave Macmillan.

CHAPTER 3

The Living *Fiqh*, or Practical Theology, of Muslim Humanitarianism

Abbas Barzegar

1 Introduction

Global refugee and migration flows stemming from recent economic, social, and political conflicts in the greater MENA region have become a pressing global priority for governments, NGOs, and civil society networks alike. Practitioners in these sectors are faced with competing pressures ranging from the delivery of urgent humanitarian relief and providing sustainable development solutions to counter increasingly erratic Islamophobic practices by European and American governments and media outlets. Over the course of the last three years, I have conducted ethnographic and policy research aimed at better understanding the ways faith-based humanitarian organizations operate, specifically Muslim ones, in this complex multi-sector landscape. I have explored both their logistical capacity to tackle these problems as well as the ethical and moral discourses that undergird their operational culture. In this paper, I analyze the ethical practices that emerge organically in these spaces to better understand the emergence of a distinct discourse. Provisionally, I refer to this discourse as a type of "non-secular universal humanism," that seemingly binds an otherwise incompatible set of actors together in a quest to overcome the truly impossible challenge of providing humanitarian care to forcibly displaced migrants across the MENA region and the Mediterranean corridor to Europe.

In doing so, I argue that this emerging discursive tradition, and the practices it enables, provides Muslim ethicists with a rich repository of existing customs (*ʿUrf*) from which they can derive normative solutions and ethical positions that can address the range of complex issues engendered by the forced migration crisis. These challenges include increased sectarian division, rights to national citizenship, and presumed conflicts between humanitarian law and Islamic law. Thus, this paper proceeds in two broad sections. First, following Talal Asad's logic of understanding the living practice of Islam as a "discursive tradition" (Asad 1996), I analyze the ways in which secular, nationalist, and religious discourses converge in the practices of Muslim

 | DOI:10.1163/9789004417342_004

humanitarian organizations dealing with the challenge of forced migration. For this analysis, I draw upon fieldwork in Turkey among organizations such as Deniz Feneri (Lighthouse) and IHH (Humanitarian Relief Foundation) as well as upon institutional literature from Islamic Relief Worldwide that addresses migration and conflict. In doing so, I demonstrate the pervasiveness of non-secular humanistic discourse in the Muslim humanitarian sector as an emerging customary practice in global Muslim civil society. Then, in the second section I discuss how a normative Islamic ethics of universal humanism can be derived from this discursive tradition and its attendant practices by developing an integrated approach to modern methods of humanistic inquiry and Islamic ethical development. In the former, I draw upon the work of Tariq Ramadan, and in the latter, I posit the use of *ʿUrf*. When taken together, this synthesis creates the concept of a "living *fiqh*," a term I employ to refer to the day-to-day Islamic discursive and material practices that underwrite the pervasive ethic of non-secular humanism found in the Muslim humanitarian sector.

The key feature of this approach prioritizes an empirically grounded understanding of the operative, embedded discourses, concepts, and categories that enable actors "on the ground" from secular, Christian, and Islamic backgrounds to work together in the quest to serve the needy, over and above the often abstract theological and textual justifications set forth by academics, public intellectuals, and traditional clergy (*ʿulamaʾ*). I argue that in these spaces and sites of social interaction, encounter, and cooperation, interesting examples of practical theology can be mapped and further explored for their potential ethical development.

The outcome of this analysis supports the positions of critical thinkers such as Talal Asad who argue for a nuanced understanding of the forces of secular logic in the post-modern period as well as moral philosophers such as Tariq Ramadan who demand that the only viable theological and ethical framework for Muslims and their secular counterparts around the world must be grounded in real-world contexts. If mapped, debated and engaged with responsibly, the discourses that emerge in the spaces of "living *fiqh*" that I have outlined above promise to provide much needed concrete examples of cooperative ethics and practical solutions to pressing problems faced by the victims of forced displacement and the resultant impact on questions concerning the place of Islam and Muslims in the contemporary world.

2 Turkish, Syrian, Muslim, Human

The non-descript border town of Kilis, located in southern Turkey sits just forty miles north of the war-ravaged metropolis of Aleppo. An otherwise forgotten stop on an ancient trading route, Kilis found itself at the center of sectarianism, imperialism, and geopolitical rivalry. Between 2012 and 2016, the city of 90,000 swelled to just over a quarter of a million as countless displaced Syrians fled their homes to find shelter, medical treatment, and sustainable life anywhere they could. Kilis, with its streams of humans in transit, miles of aid convoys, and overpopulated tent cities provides a useful, if callous, space to witness the emergence of non-secular humanism.

After spending an afternoon with Mahmood, a local philanthropist in his late fifties who upon first glance one would assume is a day labourer, I asked him about what kind of Islamic literature he read when he was younger. Mahmood's story was an illuminating one. I was attempting to get a sense of the intellectual motivations that drove this successful and wealthy businessman to dedicate the majority of his time and energy tending to the care of some 106 women and children whom he had housed in various locations in the city. He told me, counting off the names on his fingers, "Ḥassan al-Bannā, Sayyid Quṭb, Ayatollah Khomeini, Ali Shariati, Mawdūdī, Muhammad Iqbal… they all had it right, they said the same thing, and we got it wrong. But, Mawlana [Rumi] had it a 1000 years before them: *Insān, Insān*!" *Insān*, or simply mankind, was a refrain that I heard continuously among aid and development workers in the Turkish-Syrian context, but to hear it in this formula has made me think more carefully about what my interlocutors meant when they talked about humanity, or humans. In one sentence, Mahmood had managed to combine a vast and complex range of contemporary Islamic political thought and conclude that the aim of these projects was an essentially humanistic one. But the human here was clearly not the human of western liberal secularism, nor could I say that it was the human of some rarified Islamic theological vision. The humanitarian imperative for Mahmood was as self-evident as it was universal. For Mahmood, the rights of his guests (*misafirim*)—the term used for displaced Syrians in Turkey both legally and colloquially—were not grounded in a formal legal institution or charter, such as the international human rights regime. Rather, the rights and entitlement of those he cared for were simply ontological, yet simultaneously divinely ordained.

Mahmood's use of the term guest has larger implications, however. Turkey's President Erdogan, for example, during a Ramadan dinner in the summer of 2015 repeated a motif he had long expressed to justify his policy on hosting Syrian refugees:

> I pray this may be the last Ramadan you observe away from home. You are *Muhājirūn* for us. We, as *Anṣār*, try to take care of our *Muhājir* brothers with the love, enthusiasm, excitement of Medina. In our culture, a guest means prosperity, honour and joy. You have brought prosperity to us. You have honoured us with your presence. ("President Erdogan Shares" 2015)

Many Turkish Muslim activists and some of their Syrian counterparts imagine their relationship as a parallel to the Prophet Muhammad's flight (*hijra*) from persecution in Mecca to refuge and solace in Medina. The story is a foundational element in Islam's grand narrative. The themes of the *Muhājirūn* and *Anṣār* pervaded virtually every conversation I had with faith based Turkish aid agencies.

Mahmood and I had this conversation in the courtyard of an old residential building that now doubled as a makeshift charity headquarters. This is where Mahmood hired a cook to prepare daily meals for his guests, received donations and supplies, as well as hosted volunteers and guests such as us. The doorway boasted a large banner belonging to Humanitarian Relief Foundation (IHH), the leading Muslim aid agency in Turkey, familiar to most of the world for its role in the Gaza Freedom Flotilla in 2010. Although Mahmood worked in tandem with IHH, his efforts to help those in need in his hometown were of his own volition and that of his close network of colleagues and friends. IHH, however, with its central offices in Istanbul was, like most aid agencies, keen on demonstrating its presence as far and wide as possible. So, when it found an implementing partner in the person of Mahmood, it was quick to offer basic food provisions in exchange for a formal partnership.

At IHH headquarters in Kilis I was met by volunteers who, with good cause, were deeply suspicious of my presence. I asked for an interview and the group reluctantly accepted after my Turkish hosts insisted on my trustworthiness. I was given a twenty-two-year-old volunteer who participated in daily deliveries to the Aleppo countryside. He had himself only recently arrived in Kilis from a small town north of Istanbul. I asked how he and his fellow aid workers managed to conduct their work inside Syria. My question, in fact, had been a purely logistical one. He responded however with something far more existential. He told me, "IHH has a paid staff of 500 and volunteer force of 5000 that works harder than the staff. Every day we wake up and have 70,000 orphans to feed." He continued and reminded me of the Qur'anic imperative to care for orphans, doing so with a tone of voice and body language suggesting that he lamented why something so obvious must even be explained. Like Mahmood, the young IHH volunteer understood his work as a natural outgrowth of a self-evident Islamic humanitarian ethic.

The rhetoric of the volunteers and workers in Kilis differed drastically with that of Huseyin Oruc, the deputy director of IHH. When I inquired about the role of Muslim NGOs in the conflict he quickly corrected me and insisted that I refer to his organization as a strictly humanitarian one engaged in mainstream aid and development work. He considered the classification of IHH as a faith-based group a deliberate attempt to undermine their work; that is, he interpreted such a description as relegating IHH to a second-tier organization. He did make it clear, however, that what distinguishes IHH from others is their expressly political posture. In addition to advocating for taking the unique position of being both an aid agency and a human rights advocacy organization, he described IHH's position on international humanitarian law as particularly strident. He argued that IHH considered human rights, especially those of the basic entitlements of food, shelter, and safety as absolutely inviolable. IHH takes the position then that no politics or economics can or should stand in the way of the delivery of these basic services. This is the logic, he explains, that allows IHH activists and volunteers to weather the danger of war zones such as Syria to deliver aid, or to challenge the military blockade of Gaza, or to help broker local cease-fires in conflict zones around the world.

Yet, in the offices of IHH in Istanbul, one is hard pressed to find any reference to Islamic culture or thought. Rather, the décor resembles something one would expect from any mainstream international aid agency: large maps of the world, pictures of women and children in need, images of their services, and so forth. Is it the case the IHH deliberately conceals its Islamic orientation for the purposes of strategic maneuvering in the Turkish and international political space? It is, of course, no secret that IHH is connected to global Islamist networks and its rank and file is deeply connected to the Islamist governing party, the AKP. So why wouldn't the group simply announce its Islamist leanings overtly? I am inclined to suggest that the answer to such a question lies somewhere in the observation that humanitarianism and the notion of humanity itself has become such a vacuous rhetorical currency in global politics that a group like IHH can appropriate it and give it any meaning it deems worthwhile. In this way, the Islamist vision of humanity that we see articulated casually among aid workers seamlessly weaves into global secular discourses of humanitarianism yet retains its vernacular and colloquial religious character in local vernacular. contexts.

Other large aid agencies such as *Deniz Feneri* and *Mahmood Hudayi Vakfi*, also based in Istanbul with operations around Turkey, share IHH's sense of humanitarian urgency but are much more open at higher levels of the organizations to express their overtly Islamic orientations. These groups' visions for humanitarian aid is also much more grounded in a sense of Turkish identity.

Members from both of these groups told me on separate occasions, for example, that when doing their work they often recall the words of the medieval Turkish Sufi poet and saint, Yunus Emre (d. 1320): "We love all created beings, for the sake of the ultimate creator." Likewise, the directing manager of Deniz Feneri was eager to express to our group of visitors over lunch that charity and stewardship were integral parts of Turkish Islamic identity. He also recounted a story of an Ottoman sultan—which one and when it doesn't matter of course—who spread bread crumbs and grain on the snowy hilltops of the eastern Anatolian mountains in the dead of winter so that it could be said that even the birds were cared for under his dominion. The story is a reinvention of an early Islamic tale where the Umayyad Caliph ʿUmar ibn ʿAbd al-ʿAzīz is said to have done the exact same thing. Today there is even a charitable organization that actually feeds birds in winter in the Kurdish regions of eastern Turkey. The repetition and reinvention of this tradition, and others, speaks volumes to the imagined community that contemporary aid workers inhabit.

The narrative motifs of Islamic charity, civilization, and history surfaced in all of my conversations with aid workers and volunteers. It was clear that these were sincere discursive commitments on the part of the practitioners—that this was the world they created and occupied. It allowed them to be fully Turkish, Muslim, and human simultaneously. I argue that this discursive matrix enables a culture of non-secular humanism that underwrites a range of humanitarian and civic practices that challenge conventional paradigms of national identity as well as those of reified theological or sectarian identity. Muslim ethicists can draw upon and expand these discourses to augment a powerful resource for an emerging and transnational Islamic ethics of civic and humanitarian engagement.

3 Islamic Relief Worldwide and Non-Secular Humanism

Islamic Relief Worldwide (IR) is the leading independent Muslim humanitarian NGO headquartered in North American and Europe. Established in 1984 by Dr. Hany Al-Banna it now boasts a global reach, operating in dozens of countries around the world with an annual operating budget reaching nearly half a billion dollars. Although Islamic Relief and its various branches have been accused of having connections to organizations such as the Muslim Brotherhood or other Islamic revivalist and politically oriented organizations, it has consistently gained the trust of the conventional aid and development sector. Islamic Relief representatives are often the sole voice representing the Muslim humanitarian sector in leading think tanks, international organizations, and policy forums such as the German-led Partnership for Religion and Development, The Overseas Development Institute, and the UN Inter-Agency Task Force on Religion and Development. Given their wide reach and credibility across multiple sectors, Islamic Relief aid teams are often found on the front lines of the world's most pressing humanitarian crises. I argue that Islamic Relief can operate in these fragile and otherwise polarized contexts largely due to its religious-ideological orientation, which is deeply rooted in a vision of Islamic values and ethics but also seamlessly intertwines with a global ethic of universal human rights and citizenship recognized by the international community.

Here, I briefly review the way in which this espousal of a non-secular humanism is expressed in Islamic terms through two Islamic Relief publications that bear directly on the question of regional instability, migration and conflict in the MENA region. The first text is a small pamphlet entitled, "The Rights of Forced Migrants in Islam" which outlines the way in which the organization approaches the subject of forced migration from an Islamic humanitarian perspective (Kidwai 2014). The second, "Working in Conflict: A Faith Based Toolkit for Islamic Relief" is a conflict transformation manual taught at various levels of the organization's operational and administrative teams (Salek 2015). IR's development of this manual is in line with the increasing tendency among humanitarian actors, including faith-based organizations such as World Vision and Mercy Corps, to take a more active role in the transforming conflict scenarios that precipitate many of the crises they are asked to manage. What we find in both texts is an expression of IR's worldview that simultaneously affirms its commitment to universal, liberal, and ultimately secular conceptions of human rights as well as a faithfulness to Islamic concepts of community and human fraternity.

IR's brief pamphlet on forced migration attempts to "nurture the theological discourse on the issue of forced migration protection in Islam" in light of the fact that Muslim countries play a key role in hosting displaced peoples (Kidwai 2014, 3). From the outset of the text we find that the subject of forced migration is positioned as both a particular problem in the contemporary moment and universal feature of human history. The pamphlet begins:

> Forced migration has been a core element of the human experience throughout history. The Islamic tradition is rich with stories of forced migration and teaching on the importance of providing protection from those seeking refuge. (Kidwai 2014, 4)

The text proceeds to discuss migration in the context of pre-Islamic prophetic history, reminding readers that figures such as Ibrāhīm (Abraham), Mūsā (Moses) and of course Muḥammad were all forced migrants.

The pamphlet proceeds to equate concepts such as asylum with the idea of "security" (*amān*) whereby the author states that it is universally agreed upon that Muslims are obligated to provide refuge to those in need, whether "Muslim or non-Muslim, and is not dependent on political, civil, social cultural religious or economic characteristics of the fleeing person (Kidwai 2014, 11). Foundational principles of the international humanitarian regime such as the right to non-discrimination and the right to freedom of religion are also discussed through recourse to Qur'an, *Tafsīr*, and *Ḥadīth* traditions. Through these discursive practices, Islamic Relief participates in and contributes to the emergence of the culture of non-secular humanism visible in other contexts of faith-based humanitarianism.

The IR conflict toolkit provides a useful explanation of its continuing effort to balance Islamic ethics and values that are typically applied to the Muslim community in particular with a wider sense of how these ideas merge with a secular, humanistic framework. IR is explicit about its approach:

> It is important to emphasize that we do not intend to work only with Muslims, or to engage in *daʿwah* (proselytising for the Islamic faith) through our work. These tools are equally valid for use with non-Muslim communities and we actively encourage readers to redesign these appropriately. We do not advocate for a particular school of thought or make judgements about sectarian differences. Our goal is to better understand the Islamic values that motivate us to alleviate suffering, and how these values unite us across our cultural and theological differences. This toolkit aims to refer to sources across the spectrum of Islamic thought, to inspire readers to develop understanding of the connections across the Muslim world about how we are encouraged to transform conflict towards peace. (Salek 2015, 1.7)

Throughout this text, IR begins with the particularities of Islamic principles and slowly merges them with universal concepts. For example, the following description of *Tawḥīd* [*tawhid*], or the Islamic concept of monotheism, is seamlessly blended with the idea of the unity of humanity:

> *Tawhid* (unity and oneness) lies at the heart of the Islamic tradition and refers to the state of unity, oneness and uniqueness of God (*Allah*). *Tawhid* further encompasses the integration and connected nature of a

> diverse humanity as emerging from one Divine source of creation. (Salek 2015, 1.14)

The authors draw upon the well-known Qur'anic verse, "People, we created you all from a single man and a woman, and made you into races and tribes so that you should recognize one another (49:13)" to justify this appeal to the sanctity of human diversity as a feature of Islamic faith and practice.

The theme of universal human sanctity is also expressed through an elaboration on the concept of *Fiṭra* [*Fitrah*]:

> *Fitrah* (sacredness and dignity of human life) recognizes the fundamental goodness of all people at birth: "We create man in the finest state (*Q 95:4; see also 2:30–34, 17:70*)." Because of *fitrah* all human life is sacred and its dignity (*karama*) is to be preserved: "...We decreed to the Children of Israel that if anyone kills a person—unless in retribution for murder or spreading corruption in the land—it is as if he kills all mankind, while if any saves a life it is as if he saves the lives of all mankind Q 5:32." (Salek 2015, 1.16)

The blending of the theological concepts of *Tawḥīd* and *Fiṭra* with humanistic, secular sensibilities is indicative of an emergent, but stable tradition and custom of what I propose to refer to as the "living *fiqh*" of the Muslim humanitarian sector. Indeed, the theological concepts found in the discourses of Muslim humanitarian organizations is not merely rhetorical; in concrete situations of humanitarian relief, organizations such as IR provide aid in a neutral, unbiased way, without recourse or pretense to proselytization, sectarian bias, or ideological association.

The emergence of a non-secular humanistic discourse in the tradition of Islamic Relief's humanitarian work is perhaps most poignantly illustrated in its sublimation of the *Maqāsid al-Sharīʿa* (aims and objectives of the *Sharīʿa*) into the concept of human dignity. As we have seen above, IR has steadily found symmetry between foundational Islamic principles such as *Fiṭra* and *Tawḥīd* and those of human rights and dignity that are pervasive in the conventional aid community. Figure 3.1, taken from the Islamic Relief "Toolkit," however, provides a powerful image of how this discursive operation unfolds in context. Taken from the section on policy, the five traditional categories of the *Maqāṣid* (faith, life, intellect, posterity, wealth) are presented here in a floral, circular pattern reminiscent of Islamic geometrical motifs and couched within a discursive framework of "human development" and "human dignity." The image is accompanied by a set of columns with bullet points, which outline

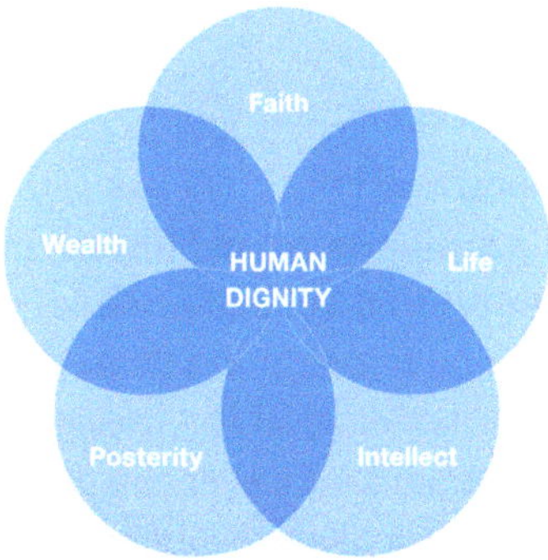

FIGURE 3.1
Five crucial dimensions of human development

various dimensions of each of the *Maqāṣid*. These characteristics include language and parlance traditionally found in the aid and development sector but adapted here under the rubric of Islamic ethics and values. For example, "humanitarianism" is categorized under "life," while "environment" is found under "posterity." This integration of Islamic humanistic values and those traditionally associated with a secular, human rights framework is among the chief characteristics of the emergent non-secular humanistic discourse found throughout the Muslim aid and development sector. As I argue in more depth in the next section, these discourses provide a stable ground through which a new tradition of normative ethics and law may be realized by Muslim ethicists and legal practitioners.

4 Context (*Wāqiʿ*): Tariq Ramadan's Call for a Socially Derived Normative Ethics

My argument that an emergent non-secular universal humanist, but simultaneously Islamic, ethic occupies a distinct space in the political and moral imagination of Muslims in the current political moment is confirmed by observers of political Islamic formations elsewhere. Indeed, as Halim Rane argues, the "*maqāṣid*-contextual approach" of Islamic oriented parties both in and out of the Arab world have enjoyed more electoral success than their predecessors, precisely because they have focused less on an utopian ideology that stresses "*sharīʿa*" and more on universal human values and practical programs of social reform (Halim Rane 2012–13). These examples include the election of the Nahda Party in Tunisia, the overwhelming success of the AKP in Turkey and the Prosperous Justice Party in Indonesia. Such an observation seems to corroborate my ethnographic claims that the living traditions of Islamic humanitarian practices undergird a new space of Muslim civic engagement whereby an ethics of global citizenship are cultivated inextricably with a sense of global Islamic revival. Islamic ethical and legal thinkers would benefit by engaging these existing practices as sources of practical ethics and law.

In advocating to derive a living *fiqh* from pre-existing spaces of Muslim civic engagement, here specifically those found in the Muslim humanitarian sector, I call for a coherent integration of social sciences and Islamic normative ethics. As we have demonstrated thus far, Talal Asad's methodological and theoretical concept of understanding Islam as a "discursive tradition" has enabled us to analyze social and cultural contexts through an anthropological framework. In doing so, we have identified examples of a living *fiqh* whereby Muslims engage humanitarian work with universally informed moral and ethical principles that are coterminous with their interpretations of Islamic theology and law.

In our current case, I posit that Muslim humanitarian practices can inform emerging Islamic legal and ethical approaches to civic engagement, democratic culture and global citizenship by virtue of the fact that existing custom (*ʿUrf*) of Muslims in these spaces has now come to prioritize humanistic principles that transcend national, ethnic, sectarian, and ideological affiliations. At the same time, these practices are thoroughly fused with the larger aims and objectives (*maqāṣid*) of Islam and *Shariʿa* and thereby have become part of the customary understanding of Islamic truth by millions of Muslims around the world. These practices, which are informed by subtle interpretations of Islamic ethics, provide the "data" or living texts that can help ethicists and legal thinkers better determine norms and guidelines to develop timeless Islamic solutions to contemporary and particular problems.

To further make the case that the social scientific observation of Muslim practices should be used as a source of Islamic normative thinking, I now turn to Dr. Tariq Ramadan's notion of context or *wāqiʿ* to serve as the hermeneutical bridge needed to integrate the largely disconnected realms of *uṣūl al-fiqh* and modern social sciences. Here, I draw upon Ramadan's call to not only integrate, but to center *wāqiʿ* or context based knowledge as a primary source in determining contemporary Islamic ethical practices. I do so to then (re)introduce the principle of *ʿUrf* as a source of Islamic law that grounds the notion of living *fiqh* within a broader tradition of both contemporary and historical Islamic hermeneutics.

Ramadan begins his discussion about *wāqiʿ* with a reminder that among the many divine mandates of the Qur'an is the continual invitation to ponder and analyze the existing universe as an unfolding revelation of God's truth in and of itself. He argues that this element "affects all the areas of human knowledge about the created Universe: a Universe that is both a gift and a "sign" fraught with meaning and its Creator, as we have seen, keeps inviting "those who are endowed with insight" to observe, study, and analyze it in all its dimensions (Ramadan 2008, 104). From this vantage point, Ramadan encourages the ethicist to move beyond the conventional modern tradition of using scientific reason to "prove" the truth of revelation and rather engage in a deep understanding of the human culture, tradition and art as an equally valid source of augmenting Islamic ethical and legal norms. By elevating the truth found in the social sciences to that of the natural or empirical sciences, he enables thinkers to contextualize the interpretation of Islam in the contemporary moment as part of a continuation of tradition, rather than a break from it.

To accomplish this, however, Ramadan must differentiate between the two broad types of interpretive conclusions used in Islamic legal judgements: *qaṭʿī* (certain, definitive) and *ẓannī* (speculative). He argues that one realm of the social sciences attempts to identify the underlying universal principles and laws that undergird human behavior historically:

> The constants in the various legislative models, relations to power, domination structures, the relationship to politics, the historical behaviors of the rich and the poor, and symbolic expressions, match logical patterns and causality principles that may be verified even though those are not exact and scientifically definitive. The laws underlying the diversity of phenomena remain operative and universal and in this respect they are similar to the *qaṭʿī* category as to their qualification. One cannot, in the social sciences, deny or overlook the presence of constants explaining human behavior patterns. (Ramadan 2008, 107)

Ramadan is less concerned, however, with this area of the social sciences because despite significant levels of debate, in his opinion the quest for generalizable principles in the social sciences is similar to that in the natural sciences. What is more challenging is understanding society, social norms, and human behavior in particular and concrete historical moments that are fluid, subject to change, and politically contested.

The challenge of deriving principles for Islamic ethics that are contextually grounded is due to the highly speculative (*ẓannī*) nature of these interpretative conclusions. Acknowledging the inconclusive nature of contextual readings of cultural norms and social change, Ramadan argues that human reason and "constant *ijtihād*" defined as an "autonomous critical approach" can serve as guides to support navigating this complex interpretative space. Precisely because they are speculative and require the rigorous reflection of human reason, they demand particular attention. I quote Ramadan at length:

> The Book of the Universe and the social sciences that unfold there open the doors of the *zannī* that requires human reason to perform a constant *ijtihād* (autonomous critical approach) to identify enduring or/and changing causality principles, the various relationships to cultures and/or customs, symbolical and/or imaginary projections, and the like. A vast field thus opens for the exercise of human rationality, and it is by no means less important because it contains less certain knowledge than the exact or experimental sciences: on the contrary, it is because of the need to be in direct contact with the lived reality and with human behavior (in its diversity in worldly time) that specific attention must be paid to the social sciences as a whole. What they teach us about humankind, about indeterminate elements in groups and in human behavior, in value systems and in cultures—although this is *zannī* (open to interpretation) or rather *all the more so* because it is *zannī*—is essential to any intellectual exercise striving to remain faithful to the ethical meaning of the revealed Book. It is indeed in this field of the *zannī* that jurists elaborated the main part of their reflections: at the heart of diversity, of the nonorganic, the seemingly unorganized, they tried—by deduction as well as by inference—to suggest ways of respecting faithfulness to the global, and invariably positive, message of scriptural sources. The social sciences, the many specializations in the observation and understanding of reality, play the same part and it would be unthinkable—and quite illogical and absurd—to cut oneself off from those fields of knowledge because they offer nothing "certain" or because behaviors, or even "moral categories," appear there as indeterminate or contradictory. (Ramadan 2008, 107–8)

Ramadan's insistence that context-specific *zanni* interpretations of human behavior and culture provide a basis for ethical and legal determination may seem broad and inconclusive to some critics who then argue that no concrete solution to pressing social problems is made by such an intervention. Such a criticism is, in part, correct but ultimately misguided.

It is the case that the call to rely upon *ijtihād* or human reason is open ended and categorically inconclusive. However, Ramadan's call to rely upon these tools aims precisely to urge that Muslim ethicists—to phrase it in my own words—embrace and determine the course of their own tradition, to develop it, to curate it. In advocating an open-ended, *zannī* approach to using the social sciences as a source of law, Ramadan is encouraging contemporary scholars to follow in the footsteps of Islamic civilization's great thinkers, rather than simply mimic them. He concludes: "the first Companions, as well as early scholars, confident, as we said, in the Revelation's global message and intimately familiar with their natural environment, never refrained from including the latter in their legal elaborations" (Ramadan 2008, 108). Ramadan's call therefore is one of actionable intelligence—a call to intervene in and reform the ethical stagnation that plagues many quarters of the Muslim intellectual milieu. In order to address the overwhelming ethical, social, and political challenges posed by the forced migration crisis, it is imperative that Muslim thinkers in the contemporary moment develop conceptual frameworks that are both theologically and practically viable. In the remainder of this essay, I argue that *ʿUrf* (customary practice) is a conceptual tool that can satisfy the multiple demands faced by Muslim ethicists today.

5 The *ʿUrf* of the Non-Secular Humanism

I close this essay with a (re)introduction of the concept of custom (*ʿUrf*) as a means through which contemporary Muslim ethicists may consider concretizing the existing practices of non-secular Islamic humanism found in the Muslim aid and development sector into a normative Islamic ethical tradition. I also argue that *ʿUrf* provides an intellectual basis to allow for the project of deriving norms from the lived context (*wāqiʿ*). Taken together, I posit that the complex challenges of sectarianism, ethno-nationalist citizenship, and political ideology can be mitigated by developing the emerging custom (*ʿUrf*) of non-secular Islamic humanism found in the Muslim humanitarian sector into a viable normative Islamic ethical tradition.

As part of a multi-generational effort of reformist theology, Muslims have developed contemporary interpretations of *fiqh*, *akklāq*, and *Shariʿa* that are intended to better enable Muslims ways to navigate the complex social space of religious and political identity in the era of the modern nation state. As part of this conversation, it has long been argued that classic Islamic ethnical formulations of political community remain at odds with modern concepts of citizenship and equality. Critics and reformists alike point to structures such as the *jizyā* system of non-Muslim taxation or concepts such as *al-walāʾ wa-al-barāʾ*, which encourage communal solidarity and repudiation of non-Muslims as examples of the incompatibility of Islamic political ethics and modern norms of universal humanism. While most of this discussion takes place in the abstract and theoretical, I use the practice of Muslim humanitarianism as a site to explore how contemporary practices of Muslim communal solidarity intersect with the international norms of neutrality and impartiality. I argue that, contrary to the alleged tension between Muslim identity and modern universal humanism, the practice of Islamic humanitarianism is embedded in and embodies a rich discourse of non-liberal, universal humanism grounded in a deep discursive and performative tradition of Islamic ethics. I argue that this non-secular humanism constitutes a source of *ʿUrf*, or custom, that can be considered a site through which contemporary Muslim practices can serve as a basis for sustained ethical cultivation.

As noted by a range of scholars such as Hashim Kamali, Anver Emon, Gideon Libson, and Ayman Shabana among others, while it is well known that although custom is not formally recognized as a source of law, Muslim jurists and theorists have consistently incorporated it into their determination of law and ethics (Emon 2006; Kamali 2005; Shabana 2010; Libson 1997). In the modern period, *ʿUrf* has played a central role in the revival and reformation of Islamic ethics in a range of contexts. As Ayman Shabana, whose research provides a useful overview of the subject's treatment in classical and modern scholarship notes:

> *ʿUrf*, as well as similar legal principles such as *maslaḥah*, was an important legal tool that Muslim reformers invoked in their efforts to work out a comprehensive methodology to bridge the gap between the past and the present on the one hand and legal theory and practice on the other. (Shabana 2010, 41)

Indeed, the writers of the late Ottoman *Mejelle* and leading modern Muslim intellectuals such as Rashīd Riḍā and Muḥammad Amīn Ibn ʿĀbidín (d. AH 1252–1836 CE) looked to *ʿUrf* as one of the main mechanisms through which the practice of *ijtihād* could be used to address a range of emerging social problems and questions. The prolific scholar, Mohammad Hashim Kamali, likewise has given special attention to the depth and nuance of *ʿUrf* as a source of Islamic jurisprudence. He points to the broad utility, even democratic nature of *ʿUrf* in that it: 1) requires broad but not uniform consent; 2) depends on popular affirmation, not just a decision by the *mujtahids*; 3) is changeable in light of differing times and circumstances; and 4) depends on gradual acceptance over time (Kamali 2003, 375–76). The two different types of *ʿUrf*: approved (*ṣaḥīḥ*) and disavowed (*fāsid*) also provide a mechanism through which cultural practices are identified as compatible with emerging norms and positive principles or should be discarded as unacceptable (Kamali 2003, 376).

The precedent of taking custom seriously throughout Islamic civilization and history is indicative of a strong tradition of independent thinking and practice among jurists and ethicists that seemingly strengthens over time. Here I draw upon the work of the scholars mentioned above to outline some of the textual sources and genealogies of custom as an authoritative tradition in order to augment the authority of Ramadan's call to ground contemporary judgements in living context (*wāqiʿ*).

The strongest explicit support for custom as a source of law seems to have come from the pen of Muḥammad ibn Aḥmad al-Sarakhsī (d. 490/1097) who mentioned custom as a source of law when discussing the conditions of a jurist's capacity for independent reasoning: "if a *mujtahid* is familiar with the *Qur'an* ... and with the Sunna, and if he is an expert in *qiyās* and knowledgeable with regard to the custom" (Lisbon 1997, 138). In this instance al-Sarakhsī seems to suggest that custom is on par with the foundational sources of Islamic law. That al-Sarakhsī mentions custom instead of *ijmāʿ* as might be expected is representative of a larger and deeper tradition among jurists to equate the two. In most cases, custom was sublimated into other sources of law and hermeneutic tools. For example, Mālikīs would assume the custom of Madina as a standard part of the Sunna and Ḥanafīs would often use the principle of preference (*istiḥsān*) to incorporate local custom into law and ethics.

By the post-classical period, custom seems to have become a very normative feature of the Islamic legal landscape. Ibn Nujaym (d. 970/1563), for example, notes:

> Know that the consideration of custom and usage reappears frequently in law in many cases, so much so that they [viz., the jurists] have transformed it into a legal source, and they said in the uṣūl literature, in the chapter on the abandonment of literal meaning: the literal meaning is abandoned on the basis of an indicator found in inferential methods of inquiry and in custom. (Lisbon 1997, 141)

As Gideon Libson notes, this trend to close the gap between practice and theory on the role of custom continued into the late Ottoman period, where it was codified in the *Mejelle* as a source as authoritative as revelation itself: Article 45 reads "Whatever is dictated by custom is as if dictated by Scripture" (Lisbon 1997, 154). Although few would accept this logic or find a viable route to apply it, the fact remains that custom is one of the richest sources of Islamic ethical and legal thinking available to contemporary jurists and ethicists.

In closing, however, I would like to highlight another feature of utilizing custom as a source of law that I find important for the contemporary conversation on legal reform: the demand of autonomous and independent juristic discernment. Most sources of law are textual. Aside from the Qur'an and Sunna, even the precedents found in *qiyās*, *ijmāʿ*, and the *qawāʿid* are deeply rooted in a textual tradition that often positions the jurist or ethicist in a secondary or tertiary role in arriving at a conclusion. While this is not actually the case in practice given that scholars always apply their own thinking to a problem, textual fidelity often obfuscates and hides the amount of independent thinking taking place in the way a scholar approaches a problem. Reliance on custom, however, demands that jurists engage in an autonomous act of discernment. Custom demands a sound, but ultimately subjective, analysis of a fluid and dynamic social context, echoing Ramadan's discussion above about the incorporation of the social sciences and humanities in contemporary Islamic thinking.

In the past, this process seems to have been less controversial than it may be today. A concise statement that sums up how simple, yet powerful, *ʿUrf* actually is has been attributed to Imām al-Ghazālī: "Custom is that which is established in a man's mind by virtue of logic and the sound mind accepts it (Libson 1997, 141)." It is interesting to note that the criterion for "logic" and "sound mind" here are not elaborated upon or discussed in detail. In fact, much of the legal literature on custom assumes it to be self-evident which essentially empowers and entrusts the jurist to come to their own conclusion on the subjects. This conclusion, however, was determined by the wider sense of what the community considered acceptable, appropriate, and viable. The pervasive legal maxim (*qawāʿid fiqhiya*), "*al-ʿāda muḥakkama*" (custom is binding), which underwrote a range of legal discussions, was often justified in the saying of Ibn Masʿūd, which was also cited as a Prophetic *ḥadīth*: "That which the Muslims see as good is considered good by God." Here, again, we see a position for Muslims to understand custom as self-evident, binding, and legally sound.

6 Conclusion

The "living *fiqh*" of Muslim humanitarianism that is non-secular and also non-sectarian should be understood as a rich repository of practical custom (*ʿUrf*) through which Muslim ethicists can develop concrete normative positions, which can help bridge the presumed gulf between secular humanism and the classical Islamic tradition. That is, rather than creating a theological justification from classical sources to *justify* or *persuade* practitioners of the potential for an integrated Islamic and secular ethics, the normative traditions emerging in the Muslim humanitarian sector offer a repository of discursive resources that are already operative in social life and thoroughly entangled in both Islamic and secular traditions. The ethicist's position becomes then, not one to convince or argue for a potential normative stance, but merely to augment it. In a sense it is to provide a "reverse reification" of existing practices in order to ensure that they are not treated as merely anecdotal or happenstance, but rather supported by legitimate hermeneutical traditions. For such a reverse reification to take place and remain viable, Muslim ethicists need to draw upon intellectual practices grounded in classical Islamic traditions as they formulate their positions. Here, I have suggested that they draw upon practice of *ʿUrf* to do so.

The contemporary challenges of the forced migration crisis for Muslim ethicists and scholars are staggering. The MENA region and its immediate environs are plagued by internecine and sectarian feuds in fragile political contexts where foundational problems of citizenship, identity, and citizen rights continue to evade resolution. In the midst of this turbulence, the transnational Muslim aid and development sector, through its continued engagement with universally recognized principles of humanitarian engagement, has developed a living tradition of customary practice that prioritizes the unconditional rights of beneficiaries over and above considerations of nationality, religion, or sect. As we have seen, the discursive environment that enables these practices is firmly grounded in Islamic discourses, texts, and traditions, leaving no question as to their compatibility with the historic tradition of a multitude of Islamic civilizations and cultures. It has been my argument that Muslim ethicists, jurists, and intellectuals will recognize that the belaboured discussions and questions surrounding the relationship between the *Sharīʿa* and issues such as citizenship and human rights can be rejuvenated in this dynamic and largely understudied social space. Such an agenda of intellectual practice promises to not only answer theoretical questions of law and ethics entertained by Muslims in the modern period for generations, but also provide ethical and moral guidance to help arrive at a shared vision for resolving a humanitarian crisis that promises to remain with the global community for generations to come.

Bibliography

Asad, Talal. 1996. *The Idea of an Anthropology of Islam*. Center for Contemporary Arab Studies, Washington D.C.

2015. "President Erdoğan Shares Fast Breaking Dinner with Refugees at Midyat Accommodation Center," *Presidency of the Republic of Turkey.* Retrieved from: <https://www.tccb.gov.tr/en/news/542/32770/president-erdogan-shares-fast-breaking-dinner-with-refugees-at-midyat-accommodation-center.html>. Accessed May 17, 2018.

Emon, Anver. Dec. 2006. "Conceiving Islamic Law in a Pluralist Society: History, Politics and Multicultural Jurisprudence." *Singapore Journal of Legal Studies*, 331–355.

Kamali, Mohammad Hashim. 2005. *Principles of Islamic Jurisprudence*. Islamic Texts Society.

Kidwai, Sadia Najma. 2014. "The Rights of Forced Migrants in Islam." *Islamic Relief Worldwide*. Birmingham.

Libson, Gideon. 1997. "On the Development of Custom as a Source of Law in Islamic Law." *Islamic Law and Society* 4(2), 131–155.

Ramadan, Tariq. 2008. *Radical Reform: Islamic Ethics and Liberation*. London: Oxford University Press.

Rane, Halim. 2013. "The Relevance of a *Maqāṣid* Approach for Political Islam Post-Arab Revolutions." *Journal of Law and Religion* 28(2), 489–520.

Salek, Lucy. 2015. "Working in Conflict: A Faith Based Toolkit for Islamic Relief." *Islamic Relief Worldwide*. Birmingham, UK.

Shabana, Ayman. 2010. *Custom in Islamic Law and Legal Theory*. New York: Palgrave Macmillan.

CHAPTER 4

Jiwār: from a Right of Neighbourliness to a Right to Neighbourhood for Refugees

Tahir Zaman

1 Introduction

Traditions as on-going "arguments extended through time" (MacIntyre 1988) allow us to move beyond the meta-narrative of the nation-state and find much needed space to begin thinking differently. The understanding that these arguments are on-going means they remain unresolved and open—the future is not the past repeated. We now live in a world wherein mobility stratifies and is a material mark of difference between people. For displaced people standing at the threshold of a sedentarist world created by the nation-state, religious traditions provide a powerful vernacular and idiom that allows them "to create a past" for themselves which will legitimate them in a way where just being themselves in the present will not allow them to do (Shils 1971: 133).

For Talal Asad (1986, 14), readings of what constitutes Islamic tradition and practice must be understood on its own terms. It cannot be disentangled or disembodied from the living practices of historically and socially located communities and their institutions—it is a discursive tradition wherein "each successive generation [of Muslims] confronts its particular problems via an engagement with a set of on-going arguments" (Haj 2009, 6). In conversation with David Scott, Asad tells us:

> A tradition is in part concerned with the way limits are constructed in response to problems encountered and conceptualized. There's always a tension between this construction of limits and the forces that push the tradition onto new terrain, where parts or all of the tradition ceases to make sense and so needs a new beginning. And looked at another way: with each new beginning, there is the possibility of a new (or "revived") tradition. A new story about the past and future, new virtues to be developed, new projects to be addressed. (Asad cited in Scott 2006, 289–90)

Thinking of ways in which traditions are susceptible to re-calibration and re-assemblage rather than simply a continuity of well-rehearsed beliefs and practices holds open the distinct possibility of traditions to transform and move in new directions. A brief survey of refugee populations across the world today reveals that mass displacement crises are perhaps this generation's immediate "particular problem." More than half (53%) of the 14.4 million refugees registered with the UNHCR came from three countries: Syria, Afghanistan and Somalia (UNHCR 2014, 9). This number excludes the 5.1 million Palestinians who are displaced and receive assistance from UNRWA. Similarly, Muslim-majority countries account for four of the top five countries that are hosting refugees (ibid.).[1]

The response to this movement of displaced people has been characterised by ambivalence, ambiguity, and even paradox on the part of majority Muslim states. It is in this encounter between settled resident populations and the arrival of the newly displaced who are often co-religionists, that a "sedentarist metaphysics" (Malkki 1992, 31) positing the nation-state as the moral container for people, culture, and politics is called into question. Here, the dissonance of contemporary Islamist approaches to the Muslim other is laid bare for all to see. In what follows, I draw on the Turkish state response to on-going Syrian displacement and the Syrian state's response to the earlier displacement of Iraqis (2005–11) to illustrate how the sedentarist logic of the nation-state impedes practices of conviviality that emerge from the lived realities of encounter between those already resident and those who newly arrive.

2 Dissonance—between Hospitality and Exclusion

In the case of the Turkish response to the Syrian displacement crisis, the AKP cleaves to the exclusionary logic of the nation-state. On the one hand, Islamic rhetoric is mobilised to express solidarity with the displaced. In May 2013, following a car-bombing in the Hatay province bordering Syria, Prime Minister Recep Tayyip Erdoğan openly mobilised religious symbolism in reference to displaced Syrians: "My siblings in Reyhanlı should serve as *anṣār* to the *muhājirūn* who fled from the brutality of al-Assad. They should fulfil the same duty, they should also open their homes exactly like it happened at the time [of the Prophet]" (*Hurriyet Daily News*, May 24, 2013). On the other hand, displaced

1 The numbers should be taken as a conservative estimate as they do not include refugees who have spontaneously self-settled in urban locations and have not availed themselves of the protection and assistance available under the aegis of the UNHCR.

Syrians are readily configured as an available pool of exploitable labour. Access to the labour market in Turkey reveals the contradictory positions taken by the Turkish state towards Syrian refugees in its clumsy attempts to reconcile an ethical position (its religious narrative of hospitality) with a political position (state interests). Such dissonance has led some commentators to characterise the AKP as following policies of urban neoliberalism with Islamic traits (Karaman 2013). Two years after the bombing in Hatay, the Minister of Work and Social Security, Faruk Çelik, was taking a less generous stance in relation to Syrians right to work, stating: "It would be unfair to take away their [local Turkish] jobs and give them to refugees" (*Reuters*, 07 August 2015). By January 2016, there was another volte-face as the AKP government announced it would be opening up access to the labour market for Syrian refugees following an agreement with the European Union wherein Turkey agreed to stem the movement of migrants out of Turkey in exchange for $3.3 billion and favourable European entry visa requirements for Turkish citizens (*Reuters*, 11 January 2016).

The unprecedented numbers of Syrian, Iraqi and Afghan asylum-seekers transiting through Turkey and across the Aegean since the summer of 2015 indicates that the Turkish state has hitherto been reticent in responding to the protection needs of self-settled urban refugees. This has been partially addressed through Article 91 of the 2014 *Foreigners and International Protection Law* that makes specific reference to the idea of temporary protection recognizing the collective character of displacement crises. Invoking temporary protection measures to deal with the mass influx of refugees into Turkey has meant theoretically, for Syrians at least, more straightforward access to secondary rights pertaining to education, healthcare, and the labour market.

The temporal nature of such protection should be considered in light of the fact that where refugees are directly administered by the Turkish state they are in camps located close to the Syrian border—emphasising that the primary concern for the Turkish authorities is on *managing* displaced people rather than *protecting* them. Temporary protection provides a bulwark against full local integration of the displaced and encourages repatriation to Syria. Following outbreaks of anti-Syrian sentiment and violence in cities with a large Syrian population in August 2014, the Turkish state predictably reverted to doing what states faced with a large foreign displaced populations often do—encampment. The response also draws attention to the conflicting narrative of a universal hospitality anchored in the ethics of religious responsibility and the imposition of conditionalities on hospitality by the Turkish state, which privileges first and foremost a territorialized understanding of rights sanctioned by the nation-state. The Mayor of Gaziantep from the AKP, Fatma Şahin, declared:

> People took refuge in our city to protect their lives and their families after the civil war in Syria. It wasn't their choice but an existential necessity. They took refuge with their neighbours they saw as a safe port. *Being neighbours is a sacred relationship according to our beliefs*. We are making massive efforts to *enable them to live on their own land* in peace. We want our Syrian brethren to *have a place where they can live in Syria*. [Emphasis added] (Kutahyali 2014).

Such statements underscore the degree to which religious ideas are subordinate to the "national order of things" (Malkki 1995) whereby the practicable solution to a mass-displacement crisis is the common-sense approach of having the refugees *return home* where they supposedly belong. The ambiguities and contradictions of temporary protection expose the arbitrary character of the decision-making process on the part of local authorities as they struggle with the tension between conditional and unconditional hospitality. The emphasis on neighbourliness as being a "sacred relationship" should not go unremarked upon. As we have seen, the AKPs treatment of neighbourliness is characterised by ambiguity and ambivalence. It is mobilised at both local and national scales—the Syrian refugee as a physical neighbour and Syria as a neighbouring country. In what follows, I will outline an Islamic discourse of neighbourliness and its practice. *Jiwār*, interpreted not only as a right and obligation to protect the stranger, but also as a social pattern of cohabitation, equips people with tools to negotiate and manage conflict in their own interests unencumbered by the spatial ordering and management projects of the state. It allows for the self to be constituted through relationships and opens up space for a nurturing and care of relationships between residents and new arrivals alike. The argument here is that proximity through everyday interaction renders the racial, ethnic, and linguistic particularities that construct the citizen, as "unremarkable" (Gilroy 2004, 40).

3 Islamic Readings of Neighbourliness

In the Islamic imaginary the loss of social and material capabilities through being made an exile is a fate worse than penury—it speaks of a poverty of relationships (Rosenthal 1997) or what has been described in refugee studies as "social disarticulation" (Cernea 1996). This we find encapsulated in Arabic loan words that have found their way into proximate languages. For instance, the word for a person living in poverty in Urdu is the same as that for the stranger in Arabic—*gharīb*. Similarly, a popular proverb in Damascus warns of the fate that lies in store for one forced to leave his home: *yallī byitlaʿ min dāru ʾall miqdāruh*—the one who leaves his home, lessens his value.

Nonetheless, the stranger cuts an ambivalent figure in Islamic tradition; standing in for a wide array of characters from students, traders, ascetic dervishes, pilgrims and forced migrants. While exile for the stranger may be accompanied by poverty, the response towards the stranger from those who are "in place" is often welcoming. *Ahlan wa-sahlan*—an oft-heard expression in the Arabic speaking world is more than simply a welcoming phrase. As al-Ghazālī (Sherif 1975, 83) observes it is the sound of awkwardness and barriers being removed: a welcome that finds "room in the heart and in the place." Literally, it is an invitation for someone to be at ease as if they were at home with their family. The word *sahl,* it should be noted, is also in reference to fertile plains to be contrasted with the inhospitable terrain of the desert dominating the landscape of the Arabian Peninsula. Good treatment of strangers was thus a highly regarded custom of pre-Islamic Arabian culture such that those who demonstrated kindness and generosity to strangers were lauded with the title of *maʾwā al-gharīb*—refuge of the stranger (Rosenthal 1997, 68). This favourable disposition towards the stranger was further institutionalized by Qurʾanic and Prophetic injunctions, which encouraged generosity and good conduct toward strangers.

In particular, the bolstering of the pre-Islamic tribal practice of *jiwār*—the granting of protection and assistance to the one seeking refuge, illustrates the central importance of hospitality toward the stranger. While *jiwār* was largely granted for a limited period it was not uncommon for the one granting, the *mujīr,* to extend the scope of protection and assistance such that the one claiming protection, the *mustajīr,* would be integrated fully into the fold of the clan of the *mujīr* (Shoukri 2011, 5)—drawing attention to the fluid understandings of both belonging and kinship. The *mujīr,* both before and after the advent of Islam, could grant protection and assistance to the *mustajīr,* and the clan to which the *mujīr* belonged was obligated to respect this decision without hindrance. The granting of *jiwār* carried much resonance in the Arab world in which Islam emerged. In providing *jiwār,* the guarantor and the clan he belonged to accumulated symbolic capital which raised the prestige and honour of the clan (ibid., 4–7). However, alliances between clans also pre-empted the possibility of *jiwār*. This understanding of *jiwār* as protection can be contrasted with a more contemporary reading of protection wherein the nation-state alone has monopolised the right to grant asylum.

An examination of the biography of the Prophet Muhammad reveals that *jiwār* was fundamental in securing the prophetic mission before the *hijra*—the collective migration of the nascent Muslim community from Makkah to

Madina. The granting of *jiwār* to the Prophet by al-Muṭʿim ibn ʿAdiy and its recognition as legitimate by the Quraysh following the Prophet's return from al-Ṭāʾif is an indication of the importance that Arab society attached to the custom of *jiwār*. The political gravity of the context in which al-Muṭʿim granted protection and assistance to the Prophet cannot be understated given that the Prophet's overtures to the notables of al-Ṭāʾif was deemed tantamount to sedition by the Quraysh leadership (ibid., 25–26).

It is following the *hijra* we begin to see a codified Islamic position on the concept of *jiwār* to develop beyond that of protection and assistance but also as a code of conduct governing social patterns of cohabitation. The significance of the Prophet's *hijra* lay not only in the act itself as a spiritual journey of self-renewal and religious re-birth but perhaps just as important was its material and social implications—the response it engendered. Securing sustainable livelihoods for displaced people was equally a concern at the time of the Prophet as it is today. The *muhājirūn* (The name given to the forced migrants from Makkah) who had sought refuge in Madina found themselves at an economic and social disadvantage, having been forced to abandon much of their wealth in Makkah. Previously they had been accustomed to earning their livelihood through commerce. In Madina, they had to re-adjust to the demands and mainstays of the local economy—craft and agriculture. Many had left their friends and families behind in Makkah and felt alienated in their new surroundings. How did this community of believers respond to the challenges of hosting a displaced population? The response of the *anṣār* (Literally, *the supporters*: this is the name given to the people of Madina who pledged allegiance to the Prophet Muhammad and gave refuge to the exiled Muslims from Makkah) has been celebrated in the Qurʾan and held forth as an example for future generations (Qurʾan, 59:9). Despite the apparent generosity of the *anṣār*, it was deemed necessary to legislate for a system guaranteeing the *muhājirūn* a means to earn a living and make a contribution to society. In contemporary parlance, a durable solution facilitating local integration was founded. Within the first year of the *hijra*, the Prophet established a contract of brotherhood: the *muʾākhā* , between 45 men of the *muhājirūn* and an equal number from the *anṣār* promoting mutual support between the pairings in matters of material assistance, care, advice, and even extending to inheritance rights (though this latter provision was later to be abrogated).

Here, hospitality is not immutable but transformational. To use Derrida's (2000) felicitous phrase, the *mastery of the house* is ceded in order to transform both host and guest into something different—into neighbours or kin. The concept of *jiwār* should thus be correctly recognised as a right of neighbourliness—one recognised as both a "moral and legal right" (ʿAbd al-Rahim

2008, 19) underpinned by the Qur'an and the example of the Prophet. Generally speaking, a neighbour was considered to be anyone (Muslim or otherwise) residing within a radius of forty houses in any direction. Indeed, the Prophet explained that one's neighbour has rights whether they are Muslim or not. He said:

> The rights of a neighbour are that, if he falls sick you visit him, if he dies you follow his funeral procession, if he asks you for a loan you lend to him, if he is in need you assist him, if good befalls him you congratulate him, if misfortune befalls him you console him, that you not build your house up above his, blocking out the breeze, and that you not afflict him with the aroma of your cooking pot without offering him some.[2]

In his discussion on the duties owed to the neighbour recorded in *The Revival of the Religious Sciences*, al-Ghazālī recalls the oft-cited tradition in which the Prophet emphasized the rights of the neighbour to the extent that his companions were left with the distinct impression that the Prophet may commend the neighbour to be included as a rightful heir to an inheritance (al-Ghazālī 2005, 675).

What value then does an Islamic reading of neighbourliness hold for us in contemporary times? How are such rights of neighbourliness for the newly arrived to be balanced against the rights of more long-standing neighbours? Today, there is little doubt that the production of locality and relational ties therein are so heavily shaped by the collective efforts of the apparatus of the nation-state whose citizenry is pitted against a referent migrant other. However, this simple binary occludes how the nation-state operates concomitantly with the interests of capital. Those who possess adequate levels and compositions of capital are arguably looked favourably upon by agents of the nation-state. In the context of Western Europe, for instance, anti-immigration raids or border profiling practices are rarely carried out on white middle class males who may have overstayed beyond the terms stipulated on their visa. Yet, localities with longstanding histories of migration from Africa and Asia, whose residents include citizens and non-citizens alike, are the target of state policies that seek to produce a "hostile environment" for migrants and the communities they reside in (Jones et al., 2017).

---

2 Although the authenticity of this hadith is contested by some scholars, it is important to acknowledge that understanding of the rights and obligations that underpin neighbourly relations are broadly recognised as part of a discursive tradition (al-Zabīdī 1994, 6: 308–309).

Thus, we can see that beyond neighbours being recognised as citizens by the nation-state there are also those who occupy a range of differentiated legal statuses contingent on their migration histories: there are those who enjoy a right to residence granted through having educational or labour mobility; some who may have been granted a temporary protection status; and yet others who enjoy no recognised status—effectively illegalized. Such statuses do not necessarily correlate with duration of stay but may nonetheless shape the production of neighbourly relations. Illegalized migrants, for instance, may find it difficult to access and navigate certain spaces of the city wherein they are made visible to agents of the nation-state. Yet, the presence of people with differentiated legal statuses living cheek by jowl to produce localities and alternative socialities offers an opportunity to move beyond sedentarist assumptions underpinning the distribution and allocation of resources through the nation-state. This emphasis on propinquity and presence as the seat from where rights are located opens possibilities for the stranger to become familiar. This allows us to understand the practice of *jiwār* not only in terms of protection, as discussed above, but also more broadly in terms of conviviality.

4 Practices of Conviviality (and Its Impediment)

It is instructive to think about neighbourhoods as both centrifugal and centripetal flows rather than territorially bounded. In her seminal sketch of her local high street in Kilburn, Doreen Massey (1991, 28) observes that "what gives a place its specificity is not some long internalised history, but the fact that it is constructed out of a particular constellation of social relations, meeting and weaving at a particular locus." This quality of "throwntogetherness" (Massey 2005) is at the heart of what characterises a neighbourhood. The bodies carrying social relations themselves are arriving from other places at different times on journeys that may not yet be complete. The neighbourhoods in which they arrive can thus be thought of as "the contemporaneous existence of a plurality of trajectories; a simultaneity of stories-so-far" (ibid.: 12). Here, the open-ended possibility of everyday mundane social interactions that take place in parochial spaces generates an ethos that invites the stranger. Empathy towards the other emerges as a by-product of this "situated multiplicity" mediated by the coming together of bodies, matter, and technology (Amin 2008: 19).

This explicit acknowledgement and accommodation of difference lies at the heart of conviviality as an integral aspect of civic formation in public space—however fleeting and momentary (Amin 2008). Conviviality—let us be clear—requires work and maintenance. This work, however, cannot be derived from unequal hierarchical relationships. It is work that demands everyday practices of support, reciprocity, and narratives of friendship. Conviviality is not to be located in a premeditated collaboration that seeks to endorse a cosmopolitanism from above (think of state instigated policies of multiculturalism), but rather it is about being affected by the condition of the world to create a "cartography of togetherness" (Rolnik cited in Nowicka & Vertovec 2014, 347). The openness of possible encounter borne out of this "thrown-togetherness" and the ethical response it engenders cultivates a culture of neighbourliness. This ethical impulse is at one and at the same time a learned and an instinctive response to a given situation. In paying attention to one's relationships, virtues are disciplined and care of the self is practised (Zigon 2014, 21). That is not to say this relational ethic is always positive—as we all know tension and conflict between neighbours is commonplace. The point being emphasised here is there is an explicit acknowledgement of the other; an encounter negotiated between the one who is present and the one who arrives. This encounter does not happen outside of the sedentarist logic championed by the nation-state. In fact, this encounter witnesses the collision of two very different geographical imaginaries—producing ambivalence or even dissonance.

Through a broadly consistent refusal to grant refugees the right to work, governments ensure that the responsibility to provide welfare for refugees falls squarely on the shoulders of international organizations. Refugees come to regard local integration as a dim prospect; buttressing the logic of the host state, which opposes integration in favour of creating a more vulnerable refugee population that is able to induce greater financial resources from the international community to share the cost of hosting refugees. It also marks the refugees as recipients of aid that the local population is not entitled to. Entitlements bestowed through the auspices of the state were a point of contention between marginalized communities on the peripheries of Baghdad. The bureaucratic labelling of Palestinians as "guests" by the state was adopted in public discourse in Iraq. A popular Arabic proverb has it that the stranger should be well-mannered—*Ya gharīb kun adīb*! Likewise, Palestinians in Iraq were expected to know their place and show gratitude for the hospitality shown to them rather than challenge the stratification that placed them below the status of citizen. Fatima, a 40-year-old housewife from Mosul, told me:

> Whenever there would be a problem between us and our neighbours or someone, they'd remind us we are Palestinians living in Iraq. They'd say things like *Inta nazīl wa dabchu ʿala saṭḥ* [you're a guest and you dance on

> my roof]. It's an old Iraqi proverb that means you think you're better than us; that you don't even have respect for your hosts.

Top-down interventions to manage populations by the state in this way do little to nurture practices of neighbourliness. Negotiating the encounter with difference is done so from a distance produced by the nation-state that exacerbates feelings of suspicion and mistrust. Shared histories and collective memories of earlier migrations remain, however. In the camps of Southern Damascus kinship ties already existed not only with Palestinian Iraqis that had fled Iraq in the earlier phase of the crisis but with relatives that had settled in Damascus following the *nakba* of 1948. Here is Fatima again. This time relating her experience of being a refugee in Syria:

> Dealings with Palestinian Syrians are good. They've supported us and I don't feel like a foreigner around them. This is a Muslim Arab country, so I don't have the sense of *ghurba* [exile and alienation]. It's only that my wider family is far from me that I feel like that I'm away from home. There are so many similarities here and with our lives in Iraq; food, language [...] yes, there are some differences but it's not great. I feel like that we're all Palestinians together here.

Fatima immediately associates the largely positive interactions she has with Palestinian Syrians with not feeling foreign. Linking the two is the fact that she is in a Muslim Arab country and as such has an understanding of how social relations are structured and mediated. However, one cannot ignore that she refers exclusively to Palestinian Syrians rather than Syrian society at large. As with Syrian refugees in Athens, access to the city was limited. Palestinian Syrians in Damascus were largely concentrated in Mukhayyim al-Yarmūk.

For others forcibly displaced from Iraq, the sense of *ghurba* was more tangible. This is particularly the case for men who are expected to be bread-winners in their households. The liminal space that refugees occupy; the ambivalent position of the state toward Iraqi refugees generally, designating them as guests and the issuing of fixed term residency status of 2–3 months, adds to this sense of *ghurba*. This feeling of alienation may not initially stem from relations with the host population but rather the bureaucracy of state and surrogate state (Slaughter & Crisp 2008) that marks them as other, which in turn creates a distinction for the host population. Here Abū Yasīn recognizes the effect this has on refugee and host community relations, narrating fears of an uncertain future:

> It affects [you] even at the level of the people, and not the State. People get to know that this house is not a Syrian or Palestinian Syrian house. So, social interaction isn't entirely harmonious. Some people like Iraqis; I mean I get on well with my neighbours. But, how do they deal with you? You're not an *ibn al-balad* [...] Up 'til now, I consider myself a guest, a visitor here temporarily and then leaving. I don't have any expectation of permanent residence.[3]

The use of the expression *ibn al-balad* is telling. Literally meaning "son of the land," the term belongs to a category of terms used to highlight autochthony and difference between those who belong and those who fall outside the community. The term *ibn al-balad* fell into popular usage around the nineteenth century at a time in which local populations were coming to terms with the challenges of first having Turco-Circassian and then European colonialists occupying the same social and geographical space (El-Messiri 1978). In contemporary usage the term refers to someone who is legitimately entitled to the resources and welfare of the state and denotes belonging. Rights and citizenship are the bedrock on which the edifice of integration rests. For Abū Yasīn, it is the nation-state that produces the anxiety, creating a sense of alienation. There is also ambivalence in the language that the state employs with respect to Iraqi refugees. At one and the same time, they are *shaqīq* (full brothers) and *ḍuyūf* (guests), which points to a more temporal stay. Oscillating between the two categories refugees and host communities struggle to balance unconditional hospitality—as a *shaqīq* the refugee is transformed into *ibn al-balad*. Yet, the interventions of the Syrian state and humanitarian agencies transform the refugee into a guest constrained by the limits of hospitality. By affirming only negative rights and deflecting the burden of welfare responsibility onto international humanitarian organizations, the Syrian government in tandem with the UNHCR and UNRWA established a parallel system of welfare protection that in fact marks refugees as others. This is contrary to the UNHCR's own guidelines on refugee protection in urban areas, which aims to "reinforce existing fully authorized delivery systems, whether they are public, private or community based" (UNHCR 2009a).

3 Author's interview. Damascus, 18 November 2010.

5 Mapping Togetherness

The right of neighbourliness, which at various times the Prophet granted or was granted, emphasises relational understandings of rights. They are less rights residing in individuals, but rather rights possessed by the Other who seeks recognition (Soroush 2000, 62). Al-Ghazālī notes that there are four kinds of neighbour; each with a corresponding set of rights. The non-Muslim neighbour who has the claim of neighbourliness rights over you; the Muslim neighbour who has the additional claim of Islamic brotherhood; the non-Muslim relative, who is also a neighbour, has both the right of neighbourliness and the rights due from kinship. Finally, the Muslim neighbour who is also kin enjoys all three claims of rights (Sherif 1975, 100). Everyday encounters are littered with reference to real or imagined kin relationships. Fictive kin relationships continue to be a prominent feature of propriety in the Arab and wider Muslim world. Suad Joseph (1996, 200) observes that through the idiom of fictive relationships expectations of a set of moral or ethical practices is re-called in dealings with the stranger to produce a "learned grammar of sociability" (Buonfino and Mulgan 2009, 16). This we find in everyday colloquialisms that are liberally sprinkled in languages spoken by Muslims—*kolay gelsin! yiʿṭīk alʿāfiyih! khasté nabāshī!* for whenever we find someone having done a kindness or worked on our behalf.

The cartography of togetherness delineated by the nation-state recognises only those already resident as citizens or those whom the nation-state has admitted onto its territory. The production of spatialities that this cartography seeks to map cannot simply be reduced to those already resident. We must recognise that for those the nation state seeks to make invisible, for whom a clear legal relation to the nation state has not been established, an alternative sociality is constantly being cultivated—a mobile commons that privileges socio-cultural relations rather than a legal relation. It is in this world that various categories of people on the move exist. In spite of their uncertain legal statuses, people on the move inhabit and construct along with resident others a "world of knowledge, of information, of tricks for survival, of mutual care, of social relations, of services exchange, of solidarity and [a] sociability that can be shared" (Hardt & Negri 2011, 190). In the following sections, we will consider how "cartographies of togetherness" are imagined, inscribed, and interpreted through an Islamic ethic of neighbourliness. Here I draw on observations from a number of research sites: Calais, Athens, Damascus, and Urfa.

The so-called "Jungle" in Calais meets the criteria for what Isin and Rygiel (2007) describe as "abject space." Despite refugee life being "rendered invisible and inaudible" by the state, spaces like the "Jungle" become sites for politics rather than spaces of abjection. This subtle difference they argue suspends the logic of the nation-state and in so doing makes acts of resistance possible (ibid., 184–5). A practical ethic has produced what Africa, a long term-resident calls "a wonderful place" where he not only has neighbours but has "made six thousand persons [sic] my brothers." (Afrika et al. 2017). This, he says makes him "a rich man" adding "and because of that I sleep in safety" (ibid.). This practical ethic is founded in reciprocal relations where "respect with a little smile [...] can solve everything here in the Jungle—everything. Because they [refugees] are looking for respect" (ibid.). The main avenue of the Calais "Jungle" was lined with Afghan and Eritrean restaurants. The proprietors of the restaurants, themselves refugees and migrants, did not simply organise the space of their establishments for the purpose of dining. They recognised the needs of their fellow travellers and permitted residents of the camp to stay at the restaurant, socialise with other residents, share information about possible routes out of Calais, and charge their mobile phones. Warmth, conversation, and cups of tea were at close hand for the residents of the camp biding their time in these eateries. Here, we find a contemporary *mu'ākhā* among residents, contrasted with life outside of the "Jungle" in the cities of France where interaction is often hostile—particularly with police.

To overcome the diminution of social and material capabilities, human activity is re-interpreted through a solidaristic narrative of religion. Being a refugee is de-stigmatized and moves beyond the totalizing discourse of humanitarian and refugee law; mapping an alternative cognitive space in which she is located (Bauman 1993, 148). Thus, while social space may be constructed through a knowledge of propinquity, the learned grammar of sociability or a cultural capital embodied as an Islamic habitus permits refugees to read exile in Muslim majority countries as familiar and as home. ʿĀrif, an Iraqi refugee I met in Damascus in 2010, told me:

> For Iraqis to leave Iraq it was hard. No one wanted to leave Iraq; they needed a safe place to go. I found my belief in Islam makes it easier for me to think about being a refugee. It's a hard thing to do, to leave your home, but I know that my Prophet did the same, and he was a refugee. If we think about it, in Islam we see that borders are not important. There are no nationalities. The differences are with language. All the land belongs to God and you can find a place to live and work wherever you go.

An Islamic narrative allows refugees to re-imagine their migration. As ʿĀrif reminds us: "all the land belongs to God," i.e. territorial sovereignty belongs to God rather than the state. Everyone has the right to move freely without hindrance—borders have no place under this schema. The Islamic narrative demands that the stranger is entitled to "find a place to live and work wherever [she goes].'

Here we must also acknowledge that urban contexts are increasingly central to the spontaneous self-settlement of refugees as they seek out secure places to live and work (Pantuliano et al. 2012). Exploring hospitality extended to forced migrants in the case of Greece, Katerina Rozakou (2012) contrasts the outsider perspective of the state, INGOs, and international agencies administering to the needs of asylum-seekers with that of a more culturally grounded approach located in relations of solidarity between activists and migrants in the city. On the streets of Athens, Rozakou (ibid., 574) observes, forced migrants are "attributed the power and agency that they typically lack in other aid contexts [...reversing] established hierarchies between the citizen and the noncitizen, the indigenous and the stranger." However, hierarchical relations linger which privilege "profoundly cultural" understandings of what it means to be host and guest (ibid.). This then is the contradictory tension ever present in host-guest relations. As Derrida (2000, 14) reminds us: "*Hospitality can only take place beyond hospitality*, only by deciding to make it come from beyond, by surmounting hospitality which paralyzes itself on the threshold where it is" (emphasis added).

The so-called "European refugee crisis" which saw over a million people journey across the Eastern Mediterranean into Europe from 2015 onwards has helped produce new socialities that attempt to move beyond hospitality and towards neighborliness. In the city of Athens, migrants, refugees and some local residents worked together to create and maintain autonomous housing collectives or squats to welcome those who had been made immobile by the European Union. In the absence of support from the formal humanitarian architecture and the state, refugee residents of squats drew on collective and personal memories of both the village and the *hāra*—the urban neighbourhood street wherein understandings of conviviality, mutual aid, and neighbourliness are integral to longstanding socio-cultural traditions. This vernacular of solidarity resonated and was made intelligible to local Greek activists who themselves had extrapolated practices of mutual aid found in the village in response to the crisis of austerity imposed by the Greek state and the European Union—underscoring a "recontextualisation of village-hood" to locate horizons of solidarity in the city (Rakopoulos 2016, 143).

This remains a partial horizon. Accommodation for self-settled refugees is limited to very few neighbourhoods from 59 municipalities of the city. While these neighbourhoods are conveniently located in the city centre and border onto other neighbourhoods densely populated by migrants, it would be a stretch to suggest that the recently arrived refugees are connected to the city. One resident of the Acharnon School squat told me, "the squat is great, we live like a real community here. My family is here. My friends are here. It's like a small village." When I asked whether there was much interaction with the neighbours he replied, "there's nothing to do, we don't really know anyone out there. We spend most of our time smoking *argileh* in here."

A shared sociability is clearly circumscribed here. The degree to which encounter and interaction is possible for the residents of the squats is thus heavily contingent on the networks of volunteers and activists choosing to visit and contribute their time and resources at the squats. This can be attributed in part to a lack of connectivity with the economic life of the neighbourhoods where the squats are located. While the squats were arguably conceived as an iteration of the mobile commons, their relational sense of place remains hemmed in rather than being centrifugal and allocentric. Opportunities for residents to reach out to other neighbours are limited and constrained to the physical space of the squat where activists and volunteers *arrive* to help meet the evident and urgent needs of residents.

Notions of *karam* or hospitality and generosity remain integral to Arab and wider Islamic culture (Chatty 2014). In everyday relations forced migrants in the urban context of the Middle East are able to maintain dignity or *karāma* as they negotiate their experience of exile—hospitality accounts for little if there is no dignity.[4] While the prestige of the host is enhanced through acts of generosity (Chatty 2014, 36; Shoukri 2011, 10), the refugee is able to retain a dignity through everyday neighbourly interactions, which is often made inaccessible through a securitized humanitarian gaze. A religious narrative on conviviality takes us beyond hospitality by transforming the guest into a neighbour.

Refugee-led community development responses are integral to opening up spaces for everyday neighbourly interactions. These home-like spaces emphasise relational aspects of home (Taylor 2015) where protection and security is found within ties of fictive and actual kinship rather than with international NGOs and agencies. They are not only spaces in which material resources are accessed but familiar welcoming places wherein refugees are recognised as being more than just a case number—they are friends or part of a larger family. They are quotidian everyday spaces, rather than spaces that are explicitly labelled as religious, in which the *potential* to facilitate and maintain

4 A commonly cited tradition of the Prophet states that among those who will not be exonerated on the Day of Judgement is he who reminds recipients of his charity to them. See also the Noble Qur'an 2:264.

relationships with both guest and host communities is nurtured. They are convivial "spaces where recognition as well as contestation and conflict can take place" (Dikeç 2002, 244). Iraqi, Palestinian, and Syrian refugees I have worked alongside over the past six years have all established self-help initiatives rhizomatically connected to transnational networks of self-reliance. (Examples include Beit ISP and al-Rābita al-Falastiny fī al-ʿIrāq in Damascus [Zaman 2016], and ad-Dar in Istanbul: <http://www.addarcenter.org/>) From the security of these home-like spaces opportunities emerge for the refugee to be both host and neighbour. A Syrian participant in the city of Urfa in Turkey echoed exilic experiences of Iraqi and Palestinian refugees I had met in Damascus; signalling the salience of neighbourly visits as a barometer of meaningful relationships:

> I like it when they (Turks) treat us equally and not as "poor" refugees. When they visit and invite us to their homes—I feel normal and equal to them. I'm not made to feel like a refugee. It's great when people call on you like this. Visiting people's homes like this means we have proper relations.

6 Conclusion: the Right to Neighbourhood

The recovery and foregrounding of the concept and practice of *jiwār* invites us to reconsider the distribution of rights and entitlements. It calls for an interrogation of where the *ummah* is located and challenges us to think beyond the constraints of methodological nationalism. The discursive move towards relations of neighbourliness complicates binaries of citizen and non-citizen. The concomitant shift away from notions of deserving and undeserving brings less audible voices into the discussion. It asks us to reconsider rights and obligations in light of those who are present.

Echoing the growing literature in critical urban geography on the "right to the city" (Lefebvre 1967, Purcell 2003, Harvey 2003, Marcuse 2010), the right to neighbourhood puts forward the case of enfranchising inhabitants of cities rather than simply national citizens, a right of neighbourliness serves to protect the wellbeing, dignity and integrity of all those resident (temporarily or otherwise) in a neighbourhood, including those who arrive as strangers. It protects the neighbourhood against the caprice of a neoliberal nation-state that serves to defend the interests of those close to its centre. The right to neighbourhood upholds not only social, cultural and political rights but economic rights also. Lefebvre (1967, 158) provocatively labelled the right to the city "a cry and a demand" and it has been a clarion call for the left since. Peter Marcuse writes "the demand is of those who are excluded, the cry is of those who are alienated; the demand is for the material necessities of life, the aspiration is for a broader right to what is necessary beyond the material to lead a satisfying life" (Marcuse 2009,190). At a time where there is an increased enclosure of public space in the city, there is heightened anxiety around the growing trend for those who are excluded, alienated, and dispossessed to be corralled into "abject spaces [...] where their existence is rendered invisible and inaudible" (Isin and Rygiel 2007, 184).

The politics of propinquity (Amin 2004, 38) I am advocating here is far from parochial. It does not serve to exclude those on the margins. Rather, social distance between self and Other are compressed and boundaries are recognised as spaces to cross rather than bound. It understands an individual, a neighbourhood, or a city to be part of a greater whole. Relationships are configured radially. It is useful here to think of a concentric circle spiralling outwards, or of a matryoshka doll—the spaces in between are not void but thick with meaningful relationships producing "multiple geographies of affiliation, linkage and flow" (ibid.).

The cultural geographer, Thomas Tweed (2006, 97) asserts that those who ascribe to a religious worldview are guided by "autocentric" and "allocentric" reference frames. The former can be equated with a concern for the care of the self, whereas the latter refers to concern with that which is external to oneself. These reference frames enable those who ascribe to religious beliefs and practices to orient themselves temporally and spatially by placing their bodies within homes, homelands, and the cosmos. For those cultivating a virtue ethic modelled on the Prophet Muhammad, geographies of affiliation flow outwards beyond any circumscribed boundaries of the nation-state. In encountering the stranger as a neighbour, virtues as learned, habituated dispositions take on transcendent meanings that brings the believer closer to the love of God, as the Muslim ethicists would have it. Thus, simultaneously providing both an autocentric and allocentric reference frame.

Bibliography

ʿAbd al-Rahim, M. 2008. "Asylum: a moral and legal right in Islam." *Refugee Survey Quarterly* 27(2): 15–23.

Afrika et al. 2017. *Voices from the Jungle: Stories from the Calais Refugee Camp*. London: Pluto Press.

Amin, A. 2004. "Regions Unbound: Towards a New Politics of Place." *Geografiska Annaler B* 86: 33–44.

Amin, A. 2008. "Collective culture and urban public space." *City* 12(1): 5–24.

Asad, T. 1986. *The Idea of an Anthropology of Islam*. Centre for Contemporary Arab Studies. Occasional Paper, Washington, DC: Centre for Contemporary Arab Studies.

Buonfino, A. and G. Mulgan. 2009. *Civility Lost and Found*. London: Young Foundation.

Cernea, M. 1996. "Understanding and preventing impoverishment from displacement: reflections on the state of knowledge." In *Understanding Impoverishment: the Consequences of Development Induced Displacement*, edited by Christopher McDowell. Oxford: Berghahn.

Chatty, D. 2014. "Iraqi refugees in the Arab Muslim world: Ottoman legacies and Orientalist presumptions." In *Managing Muslim Mobilities: between Spiritual Geographies and the Global Security Regime*, edited by A.H. Fàbos and R. Isotalo, New York: Palgrave Macmillan, 21–38.

Derrida, J. 2000. "Hospitality." ANGELAKI. *Journal of the Theoretical Humanities* 5(3): 3–18.

Dikeç, M. 2002. "Pera Peras Poros Longings for Spaces of Hospitality." *Theory, Culture and Society* 19(1–2): 227–247.

Al-Ghazālī, Abū Ḥāmid. 2005. *Iḥyā' 'Ulūm al-Dīn*. Beirut: Dār ibn Ḥazm.

Gilroy, P. 2004. "Multiculture in times of war: an inaugural lecture given at the London School of Economics." *Critical Quarterly* 48(4): 27–45.

Haj, S. 2009. *Reconfiguring Islamic Tradition: Reform, Rationality, and Modernity*. Stanford, CA: Stanford University Press.

Hürriyet Daily News. "Turkish PM calls on Reyhanlı locals to resist 'provocations.'" *Hürriyet Daily News*, May 24, 2013. Available online at: <http://www.hurriyetdailynews.com/turkish-pm-calls-on-reyhanli-locals-to-resistprovocations.aspx?pageID=238&nID=47526&NewsCatID=341>.

Isin, E.F. & K. Rygiel. 2007. "Abject spaces: frontiers, zones, and camps." In *Logics of Biopower and the War on Terror*, edited by C. Masters & E. Dauphinee. Basingstoke: Palgrave Macmillan, 181–203.

Jones, H., Gunaratnam, Y., Bhattacharyya, G., Davies, W., Dhaliwal, S., Forkert, K., Jackson, E. and Saltus, R. (2017). Go Home? The Politics of Immigration Controversies. Manchester: Manchester University Press.

Joseph, S. 1996. "Gender and family in the Arab world." In *Arab Women: between Defiance and Restraint*, edited by S. Sabbagh. New York: Olive Branch Press, 194–202.

Kagan, M. 2011. "'We live in a country of the UNHCR': The UN surrogate state and refugee policy in the Middle East." Research Paper No. 201, UNHCR New Issues in Refugee Research. Geneva: Policy Development and Evaluation Service UNHCR.

Karaman, O. 2013. “Urban neoliberalism with Islamic characteristics.” *Urban Studies* 50(16): 3412–3427.

Kutahyali, R.O. 2014. “Syrian refugees under attack in Turkey,” Al-Monitor, August 14, 2014. Available online at: <http://www.al-monitor.com/pulse/originals/2014/08/kutahyali-syrian-refugees-under-attack-turkey-gaziantep.html>.

Lefebvre, H. 1996/1967. “The Right to the City.” In *Writings on Cities*, edited by E. Kofman and E. Lebas. London: Blackwell, 63–184.

MacIntyre, A. 1988. *Whose Justice? Which Rationality?* Notre Dame, IN: Notre Dame University Press.

Malkki, L.H. 1992. “National geographic: the rooting of peoples and the territorialisation of national identity amongst scholars and refugees.” *Cultural Anthropology* 7(1): 22–44.

Malkki, L.H. 1995. “Refugees and exile: from ‘refugee studies” to the national order of things.” *Annual Review of Anthropology* 24: 495–523.

Marcuse, P. 2009. “From critical urban theory to the right to the city.” *City: Analysis of Urban Trends, Culture, Theory, Policy, Action*, 13(2–3): 185–197. doi: 10.1080/13604810902982177.

Massey, D. 1991. “A global sense of place.” *Marxism Today* 35(6): 24–29.

Massey, D. 2005. *For space*. Sage Publications: Thousand Oaks, CA.

El-Messiri, S. 1978. *Ibn al-balad: a concept of Egyptian identity*. Leiden: E.J. Brill.

Nowicka, M. & S. Vervotec. 2014. “Comparing convivialities: Dreams and realities of living-with-difference.” *European Journal of Cultural Studies* 17(4): 341–356.

Pantuliano, S., V. Metcalfe, S. Haysom, and E. Davey. 2012. “Urban vulnerability and displacement: a review of current issues.” *Disasters* 36(S1): S1–S22, doi: 10.1111/j.1467-7717.2012.01282.x.

Rakopoulos, T. 2016. “Solidarity: The Egalitarian Tensions of a Bridge-Concept.” *Social Anthropology* 24(2): 142–151.

Reuters. “Turkey will not give Syrian refugees right to work—labour minister.” *Reuters*, 07 August 2015. Available online at: <http://uk.reuters.com/article/uk-turkey-syria-refugees-workers-idUKKCN0QC1UH20150807>. Accessed 30 March 2016.

Reuters. “Turkey plans to introduce work permits for Syrian refugees, minister says.” Available online at: <http://uk.reuters.com/article/us-europe-migrants-turkey-idUKKCN0UP0QP20160111>. Accessed 30 March 2016.

Rosenthal, F. 1997. “The stranger in medieval Islam.” *Arabica* 44(1): 35–75.

Rozakou, K. 2012. “The biopolitics of hospitality in Greece: humanitarianism and the management of refugees.” *American Ethnologist* 39(3): 562–577.

Scott, D. 2006. “The Trouble of Thinking: an Interview with Talal Asad.” In *Powers of the Secular Modern: Talal Asad and his Interlocutors*, edited by D. Scott and C. Hirschkind. Stanford, CA: Stanford University Press, 243–303.

Sherif, M.A. 1975. *Ghazali’s Theory of Virtue*. Albany: State University of New York Press.

Shils, E. 1971. "Tradition." *Comparative Studies in Society and History* 13(2): 122–159.

Shoukri, A.M. 2011. *Refugee Status in Islam: Concepts of Protection in Islamic Tradition and International law*. London: I.B. Tauris.

Slaughter, A. and J. Crisp. 2008. "A surrogate state? The role of UNHCR in protracted refugee situations." In *Protracted refugee situations*, edited by G. Loescher, J. Milner, E. Newman and G. Troeller. Tokyo: United Nations University Press, 123–140.

Soroush, A. 2000. "The sense and essence of secularism." In *Reason, Freedom and Democracy in Islam: Essential Writings of 'Abdolkarim* Soroush. New York: Oxford University Press, 54–68.

Taylor, H. 2015. *Refugees and the Meaning of Home: Cypriot Narratives of Loss, Longing and Daily Life in London*. Basingstoke: Palgrave Macmillan.

Turton, D. 2005. "The Meaning of Place in a World of Movement: Lessons from Long-term Field Research in Southern Ethiopia." *Journal of Refugee Studies* 18(3): 258–280.

Tweed, T.A. 2006. *Crossing and Dwelling: a Theory of Religion*. Cambridge, MA: Harvard University Press.

UNHCR. 2014. *Statistical Yearbook 2014*. Geneva: UNHCR.

UNHCR. 2009. *UNHCR Policy on Refugee Protection and Solutions in Urban Areas. Geneva:* UNHCR.

al-Zabīdī, Murtaḍā. 1994. *Itḥāf al-Sāda al-Muttaqīn bi-Sharḥ Iḥyā' 'Ulūm al-Dīn*. Beirut: Mu'assasat al-Tārīkh al-'Arabī.

Zaman, T. 2016. *Islamic Traditions of Refuge in the Crises of Iraq and Syria*. New York: Palgrave Macmillan.

Zigon, J. 2014. "Attunement and fidelity: two ontological conditions for morally being-in-the-world." *Ethos* 42: 16–30.

CHAPTER 5

"Seeking a Widow with Orphaned Children': Understanding *Sutra* Marriage Amongst Syrian Refugee Women in Egypt

Dina Taha

1 Introduction

Egypt currently hosts more than 200 thousand refugees registered by the UNHCR all living in urban communities. More than half, around 120 thousand are from Syria[1] (ECHO Factsheet: Egypt, 2018) arriving after 2011. Fleeing one of the worst humanitarian crises since World War II, Syrians arrive to an economically troubled country and a politically polarizing atmosphere, where they face a lack of opportunities and a high cost of living. Some Syrian women in Egypt have drawn the attention of media, religious leaders, and advocacy groups by marrying Egyptian men soon after arriving (Hassan 2015; Geha 2013). Social media campaigns such as *Laajiat Lasabaya* (*Lājiʾāt la Sabāyā*)[2] or "Refugees, not spoils of war" (also rendered on their Facebook page as: Refugees…Not Spoils) were ignited as a reaction to this practice in Egypt, as well as Lebanon, Jordan and other Arab countries where such marriages have been facilitated, encouraged and organized through different channels such as marriage brokers, social media and religious organizations (Barkan 2012).

This paper is part of a broader study that I conducted for my fieldwork in Egypt during the summer of 2017 where I interviewed thirty-three Syrian refugee women who escaped the conflict in Syria and married Egyptian men post 2011 once they settled in Egypt. It highlights a recurring notion that I came across during many of the interviews—*Zawāj al-Sutra* (Protection or Shelter Marriage). In such cases, the man is motivated to marry a widow, especially that of another man who died because of war, with the intention of providing her and her children with livelihood and emotional support. Such a practice

1 The rest are mostly from east Africa or Iraq (ECHO Factsheet: Egypt, 2018). These figures don't include Palestinian refugees (see for instance: Palestine refugees: locations and numbers, IRIN, 2010).

2 More information about the campaign available at: <https://www.facebook.com/Lajiaat.Lasabayaa>.

was arguably recurrent throughout Islamic history where many have suggested it was encouraged in the Islamic tradition.

Muslim scholars' increased interest in the ways *Shariʿa* cultivates ethics and virtue beyond the legally binding provisions in the modern era is arguably novel, compared to pre-modern scholars (Katz 2015, 26). Some factors can be traced back to the impact of modernity and its repercussions on the emergence of a modern (human) subject, as well as the formation of the nation-state and codified law, particularly personal status law, in many Muslim majority countries on the relationship between Islamic jurisprudence and Islamic ethics (ibid., 25). This interest in incorporating ethical questioning due to modern dictates, as argued by Tariq Ramadan, [should] change the foundation and nature of Islamic legal reasoning, requiring a more holistic approach and an understanding of the theory of knowledge "that generates meaning and the ethical questions generated by social, scientific, and intellectual development" (Ramadan 2017, 15). Thus, formulating legal rulings to govern forced migration, a phenomenon that emerged at the end of the second world war and the prevalence of the nation-state as the dominant form of political governance, requires sufficient mastery over the field of knowledge that religious rulings are based upon, including an understanding of the higher ethical objectives of *Shariʿa* (*Maqāṣid*).

I approach the phenomenon of *Sutra* marriage from an anti-colonial theoretical framework which seeks to analyze and use local cultures as a tool to resist "the everyday devaluation, denial and negation of the creativity, agency, resourcefulness and knowledge systems" of non-Western cultures (Dei 2012). Among the pioneers of Postcolonial Feminism, Gayatri Chakravorty Spivak and Chandra Talpade Mohanty in particular have (re)developed the theories of Frantz Fanon and Edward Said towards the creation of Postcolonial/Anti-orientalist critical approaches of knowledge production to challenge Western hegemonic ways of knowing. Mohanty asserts that portrayals of Third World women as victims contribute to further marginalizing those women (Mohanty 1984). Anti-colonial frameworks, however, do not attempt to deny the existence of victimhood and victimizing dynamics in the Global South; rather, they seek to challenge essentialized understandings of binaries such as victims or agents.

My objective from offering an anti-colonial reading of this case study is twofold: first, by shedding more light on the complexity of the woman refugeeness through addressing women's multidimensional and complex forms of oppression and autonomy in the Global South, I aim to offer Islamic scholars and jurists a critical language that responds to the often-orientalised feminist and human rights advocates' characterizations of gendered relations in non-Western contexts. Second, an anti-colonial feminist perspective showcases the need for having a "gendered" approach to Islamic fatwas. A gendered approach can be traced whether in offering a "meaningful and healing" solution to refugee women, and Muslim women in general, or in revisiting and assessing the complex power dynamics that defines conjugal relationships of the kind being addressed here.

Moreover, in response to the changing nature of global mobility and in commitment to the anti-colonial principle that seeks to destabilize Eurocentric hegemonic ways of knowing, the article also seeks to pose questions that push the debates surrounding the ethics of migration today. Particularly, Can *Sutra* marriage be considered an ethical and moral response to the gendered forced migration? Can it be regulated to echo calls for gender equality and gender empowerment? Who sets the rules about principles and notions of international humanitarianism? How can we include cultural diversity, including gender, ethnicity, and sexual orientation in ethics of migration? And whose voices should be included in these discussions?

Hence, this is not an ethical, legal, or jurisprudential paper *per se*, but offers important sociological insights to jurists in issuing fatwas that are better informed about contemporary realities, gender discourses and forced migrants' experiences. Sociology "as the study of the individual, society and the relationship between structures and group processes" (Castles 2002) should assist jurists, particularly with regard to understanding human mobility, in grasping the societal dynamics of forced migration. A particular contribution relevant to this study is introducing issues around identity (re)formation and the effect forced migration might have on traditional gender roles in the modern (and post-modern) world order as well as critiquing notions such as victimhood and exploitation from both gender and forced migration perspectives.

I start by positioning this practice in Islamic jurisprudence and the role played by the jurisprudential culture in defining *Sutra* marriage and its parameters. I then critically engage with a sample of contemporary fatwas in order to trace the jurisprudential perception to *Sutra* as grounds for marriage and *Sutra* marriage as a tool for shelter and aid to Muslim (women) refugees. Next, I relate the stories of three women to unfold the different trajectories and the mixed experiences that *Sutra* marriage has taken with different Syrian refugee women in Egypt. I seek to address these marriages from the women's perspective in a way that goes beyond assessing them morally, but to expose the gaps between the fatwa's opinion, vision and advice and the application, especially given the vulnerable status of many forced migrants. Finally, and using an anti-colonial lens, I conclude with a discussion of (a) how the narratives discussed pose theoretical and conceptual challenges to some central feminist concepts such agency and gender roles, and (b) some avenues through which sociological research can offer Islamic jurisprudence a deeper understanding of the experiences, and consequently the needs of some marginalized groups such as refugee women in Muslim societies.

2 *Sutra* Marriage in the Islamic Jurisprudential Texts and Cultures

The term "*Zawāj al-Sutra*" has been used by both media and advocacy groups to mean different things, including marrying rape victims (Barkan 2012; Natour 2016). In the fatwas below, three meanings of *Sutra* marriage emerge. First, *Sutra* in the general sense means providing *'Iffa* or chastity and modesty. In that sense, marriage is considered as a means for the gratification of sexual needs and procreation (Mir-Hossein 2003). Second, *Sutra* can be perceived as a means for providing relief for rape victims (or women who committed adultery and then repented). Third, *Sutra* can be used in the sense of providing shelter, livelihood support and protection for widows and divorced women.[3] The last meaning is the primary concern of this paper.

Keeping the above in mind, I turn to examining four fatwas that I was able to authenticate from the Fatwa Center website. The Fatwa Center is a scientific Islamic portal affiliated with the Ministry of *Awqāf* and Islamic Affairs in Qatar. It is concerned with answering questions related to the Muslim faith, worship, transactions, ethics, behavior, and other matters.[4] The small sample size of the selected fatwas goes back to the rigorous verification process. During this verification process I was committed to the following criteria: (1) excluding any fatwas that did not mention the name and the credentials of the *Muftī* (jurist) or the body of jurists responsible for issuing the fatwa; (2) excluding any fatwas mentioned on social media or blogposts due to the overrepresentation of fabricated fatwas, fake news, unauthenticated post-sharing about Islamic scholars issuing controversial fatwas surrounding Syrian refugee women in particular;[5] (3) excluding fatwas that were acquired orally, no matter how prevalent they

3 In the nineties, the notion of *Sutra* marriage started to gain cultural association with Muslim war victims and refugee women. It began with Bosnian women in the late 90s followed by Iraqis and recently Syrians.

4 More information about the fatwa center available at: <http://fatwa.islamweb.net/fatwa/index.php?page=aboutfatwa>.

5 For instance, a fake news was disseminated among different media portals that the Saudi Scholar Muḥammad al-ʿArifī issued a controversial fatwa allowing what they referred to as Jihād al-Nikāḥ. More information available here: <https://www.youtube.com/watch?v=JL1Nl7MyWPk>.

were. The latter contained fatwas acquired through personally asking a scholar or those propagated during Friday sermons. This criterion also excluded fatwas mentioned by some of my respondents during the interviews.

Most references relied on two avenues to justify and encourage *Sutra* marriage for widows and divorced women. The first is by citing historical incidents where the prophet himself or his companions were eager to marry widows and divorced women (see for instance, AlHamoud, 2011). A second avenue was through citing religious texts from Qur'an and *Sunnah* that encourage Muslims to protect each other, especially the most vulnerable like the poor, widows and orphans[6] and emphasize the reward for taking care of them. For instance, it is reported on the authority of Abū Hurayra that the Prophet said: "*Whoever removes a worldly grief from a believer, Allah will remove from him one of the griefs of the Day of Resurrection. And whoever alleviates the need of a needy person, Allah will alleviate his needs in this world and the Hereafter. Whoever shields [or hides the misdeeds of] a Muslim, Allah will shield him in this world and the Hereafter. And Allah will aid His slave so long as he aids his brother*..." [al-Nawawī *40 Hadith, no. 36*]. In another report, the Prophet said, "*One who cares for widows and the poor is like those who fight in the way of Allah or those who spend their days fasting and their nights praying.*" [al-Bukhārī *Adab al-Mufrad,* chapter "*The Virtue of Those Who Care for Orphans*"—Agreed upon hadīth]. A third report states that Umm Saʿīd bint Murra al-Fihrī related from her father that the Prophet, may Allah bless him and grant him peace, said, "*I and the guardian of an orphan will be in the Garden like these two (His two fingers).*" [al-Bukhārī *Adab al-Mufrad,* chapter "*The Virtue of Those Who Care for Orphans*"]

In all the four fatwas below, the notions of *Sutra* (covering, protection or sheltering) and *'Iffa* (chastity and modesty) were referenced explicitly or implicitly as "noble" grounds and a reason for marriage. The fatwas address cases involving widows, refugee women, or other vulnerable cases such as rape victims and women who lost their virginity due to unlawful intercourse. Following is a brief summary of each fatwa.

2.1 *Fatwa (1): Marrying with the Intention of Providing Chastity*[7]

In this fatwa, the inquirer is referring to some Facebook pages that facilitate the marriage of Syrian women living in Egypt. He expressed his wish to provide

6 In Islamic fiqh, an orphan is someone who has lost their father or both parents before the age of maturity.

7 The script of the fatwa was taken from: <http://fatwa.islamweb.net/fatwa/index.php?page=showfatwa&Option=FatwaId&Id=235441> (last accessed May 2018).

chastity (*'Iffa*) to a Syrian sister and asked whether this wish and intention are permissible and if the *muftī* (jurist) has any advice for him. The fatwa responds by confirming the permissibility of marrying a Syrian Muslim woman. In fact, it encouraged the inquirer to do so because the intention of providing her with chastity as well as emotional support in her hardship is an act that will be rewarded generously.

2.2 *Fatwa (2): Marrying a Widow with Orphans*[8]

In this fatwa, the inquirer seeks guidance for his intention to marry a widow as a second wife but planning to keep it a secret from his first wife. He explained that he sought this marriage in order to take care of her orphaned children but then changed his mind last minute after realizing that his intentions weren't "pure." He came to the conclusion that he can support the orphans without the marriage or the secrecy. The fatwa responded by describing sheltering a widow and her orphans through marriage as a good deed that would be rewarded. It encouraged him to be honest with his first wife but clarified nevertheless that he is not obliged religiously to inform her.

2.3 *Fatwa (3): Marrying to Cover a Sin*[9]

In this fatwa, a woman was asking about the legal and religious obligation on a man she was in a relationship with and with whom she lost her virginity. She mentioned that he has always expressed his loyalty to her and his desire to eventually marry her, but his family ended up opposing the marriage. The woman is asking the *muftī* to encourage the man to take responsibility for his actions. The fatwa started by condemning both the man and the woman for their behaviour and asserted that even though the man is not religiously obliged to do so, he "should" marry her with the intention of applying *Sutra* to her and he would be rewarded for his deed. The fatwa quotes the hadīth "*Whoever shields [or hides the misdeeds of] a Muslim, Allah will shield him in this world and the Hereafter…*"

2.4 *Fatwa (4): Marrying a rape victim*[10]

In this fatwa, the man states that after proposing to a girl, she asked to meet him privately and confessed that she was raped at 17 and that she hasn't told

8 The script of the fatwa was taken from: <http://fatwa.islamweb.net/fatwa/index.php?page=showfatwa&Option=FatwaId&Id=66438> (last accessed May 2018).

9 The script of the fatwa was taken from: <http://fatwa.islamweb.net/fatwa/index.php?page=showfatwa&Option=FatwaId&Id=63748> (last accessed May 2018).

10 The script of the fatwa was taken from: <http://fatwa.islamweb.net/fatwa/index.php?page=showfatwa&Option=FatwaId&Id=7994> (last accessed May 2018).

anyone including her parents. He is asking for a religious opinion whether to marry her. The fatwa responds that, under the condition that he can trust that she is telling the truth, he should pray *Istikhāra* (the prayer of seeking guidance from Allah) and weigh in her religious devotion before he moves on with the marriage. The *muftī* stresses that there is no objection in marrying her especially that what happened to her was beyond her control. The fatwa also encouraged him, whether he decided to marry her or not, not to disclose her secret to anyone and also cites the hadīth "*Whoever shields [or hides the misdeeds of] a Muslim, Allah will shield him in this world and the Hereafter...*"

From the above fatwas, one can notice that they are motivated to a large extent by the *muftī*'s assessment of advancing the women's interest. Each fatwa encouraged an action based on the assumption that it will provide emotional support to the woman during hardship, when it encouraged the inquirer to be honest with his first wife, even though he is not obliged to, or when it advised the inquirer not to disclose the rape victim's secret. On the other hand, recalling the relationship between Islamic jurisprudence and advancing virtue and ethics, there were also common issues between the fatwas and their understanding of the woman's best interest, which create dilemmas for the contemporary understanding and application of social justice, especially for vulnerable groups such as uprooted refugees. First, the fatwas place a huge weight in their rationale and verdict on the "pure" intention of the man without identifying accountability measures to protect the women from future potential abuse. Second, they frame the marriage decision-making, or lack thereof, almost solely in the hands of the man and his discretion. Third, and most importantly, they portray the woman as a one-dimensional character lacking any depth or any form of varied experiences, agency or preferences. That is to say, the fatwas do not pay diligent attention to the individual women's circumstances. For them, a rape-victim and the widow, a woman who lost her virginity and a refugee, all have the same needs and are the same woman—"the" woman. This woman is often portrayed as the victim who needs to be saved (by "the" man).

In the following section, I try to add a "face" to "that woman" in the above fatwas while focusing on the experience of the refugee woman. In doing so I demonstrate that different women have different approaches and understanding of *Sutra* marriage; and in many occasions, defy the "victim" image that underlies the rationale and the verdict of many jurisprudential texts that address marriage and spousal rights.

3 *Sutra* Marriage: Stories from the Field

Three women that I came across during my fieldwork: Maha, Marwa and Nour[11] presented three interesting and variant trajectories to what they themselves labelled as *Sutra* marriage. The three women are Syrian refugees who arrived in Egypt after 2012 and settled in the city of ʿĀshir min Ramaḍān (or of *Al-ʿĀshir* for short), a newly industrial but suburban city in *Sharqiyya* governorate and is considered to be part of greater Cairo. The three women had children from previous marriages and they all referred during their interviews to *Sutra* or *Sutra* marriage. Marwa and Nour are siblings and they are in close acquaintance with Maha. Despite all the commonalities, their stories present three different understandings and outcomes to their marriage experiences.

4 *Maha*: Killing Two Birds with One Stone

Maha was in her 40s. She grew up in Damascus (commonly referred to as *Shām*) in a well-off area. Unlike many of the Syrian women that I have interviewed, she went to law school where she met her first husband and got married after a "powerful" love story. When she got divorced, she refused to marry for 11 years because most suitors requested that her children stay behind with her family, which she firmly refused. After arriving to Egypt in December 2012 and settling within the relatively large Syrian community in the city of *Al-ʿĀshir*, like many of her counterparts, marriage proposals started to pour in. When I asked her if she was seriously considering marriage to an Egyptian and her motivation behind this marriage, her response was mainly focused on emotional and social support that results from having a male figure in one's life in an Arab country.

D: But you weren't opposed to the idea of marriage?
M: No, because the situation was really tough to be honest. After my siblings left (to Saudi Arabia) and my parents are old and all my siblings are married, I thought that I have to get married.
D: And how did you generate income (before marriage)?
M: My parents
D: Oh, so you didn't need marriage for financial reasons but socially and emotionally.

11 Pseudonyms were used to keep the participants identities anonymous.

M: I am very romantic, and there was a love story with my first husband, so it was a tough situation because 10 years… it is like they say "emotional drought" …. God bless my children.
D: So, when you got married you didn't feel obliged to?
M: I had to get married. Like they say marriage is Sutra.
D: What do you mean marriage is Sutra?
M: I found that without (marriage) many men crossed the line with me. It is protection and support for me later on. And my kids too need a father.

Of course, I was intrigued by the concept of *Sutra* so I asked her to expand a little bit on her interpretation of its meaning and how she would explain the Egyptian men's eagerness to marry Syrian women. Her response reflects not just a conscious understanding of the realities and driving forces of this notion but also a sense of control of the situation. That is, in this kind of marriage, she is also offering something in return not merely waiting to be saved or protected.

D: … you mentioned that many (Egyptian men) wanted to marry you. Did you ask them why?
M: They say they want to apply Sutra to my children. They don't say it explicitly, but we get it.
D: So what do they say?
M: They don't say that "exactly." Of course, they appreciate our tidiness, cleanliness, and beauty. But in some cases, they say it explicitly, like in Marwa's case: so that he would protect her (apply Sutra) and her children and receive reward (religious oblation). Of course, it's not just for that (the oblation) but it's also for himself. It's like killing two birds with one stone. On the one hand, he would receive a huge reward that he raised her kids and on the other, she is Syrian. She is going to make him happy and pleased. That's the opinion of all of them (the Egyptian men) because they have witnessed similar experiences before their eyes and they have noticed our different nature (compared to Egyptian women). For example, with my husband, his friends would tell me: you switched him 180 degrees. Even his kids…

Overall, Maha's marriage seemed to be a positive experience. Despite being a second wife and going through a few hiccups due to the first wife's resistance, she expressed on multiple occasions that she carries respect to her current husband, that she has fallen in love with him and that she was trying hard to get pregnant for the second time with him. In fact, when asked explicitly about her marriage experience in Egypt compared to that back home in Syria, she enthusiastically concluded that she is better off with her Egyptian husband and that in general Egyptian husbands are better than Syrian ones largely due to cultural and social habits.

5 Nour: "Tasting a New Fruit in the Market"

Nour was the youngest. She was 25 years old when her husband got killed in Damascus a year and a half before our interview. She and her daughter were, hence, forced to catch up with her family in Egypt a few months later after ill-treatment at her in-laws' household. Just a few months after arrival, a family friend introduced them to an Egyptian man who is married with kids but was searching for a Syrian widow to apply *Sutra* to. They had the religious marriage[12] three weeks after they first met. She noticed a change in her new husband's treatment and aloofness after the first month of their marriage that ended up with separation just four months into the relationship. Despite her young age, her negative experience and feeling of being used, Nour still demonstrated a sense of agency and responsibility in both her decision to marry soon after arriving to Egypt and her desire to remarry again after the failure of the first attempt. Her justifications reflected deep self-awareness of her social position and she was able to identify the best options and alternative to make the best out of the situation.

D: So he told you he is married and he wanted to marry again in secret?
N: Yes
D: And what was your impression?
M: That his wife will eventually know by time. Nothing can be hidden
D: Didn't you think, why would I be a second wife? I want to be a first wife?
M: No
D: Why?
M: Because I have special circumstances, I am not a normal girl.
D: Don't you think that this is lowering one's standards?
N: Dear, it's not us. It's the world around us that forces us (to think and act this way). Even if you are convinced, the society around you won't be convinced.

12 So she would be his lawful wife religiously but socially she still stays with her parents until they prepare for the wedding and the new place. This facilitates his visitation and them getting to know each other. Having sex would be lawful but is socially frowned upon. If they separate, she is considered divorced but there are usually no documents to prove the marriage and divorce.

D: You are right

N: Excuse me, I'm sure your study showed you, but most of our society is not like that. Even if you convince yourself.

D: Do you mean that you might be convinced with one thing but the society obliges you to another?

N: Exactly. So why would I bother/pressure myself. If I wanted to marry a single man, no one would want my daughter [...]

D: Oh so you mean you don't care if you are a first or a second wife as long as your daughter is with you?

N: Yes dear. Excuse me but for women like us we don't think about ourselves, we think about our children. When you buy anything for the house do you think of yourself or your son? [...] In my country, I had my rights and I was able to manage. Here I am in a strange country. Why would I work and humiliate myself, meet this and meet that, the good and the bad? No, I apply Sutra to myself and my daughter and find a human being who is honest and straightforward and offers me a decent life. I'm not saying that I want a car and a big house. Middle ground. A decent life....

For Nour, she knew there are social restrictions that are not just present due to her gender and social status: a widow with a child, but also due to her forced migration status and being in a foreign country. She was convinced that a woman's "natural path is to eventually get married." Her forced migration status, however, have turned this natural path, which might now comprise more limited and slightly different options given her current social status, into a solution, an opportunity, and even, one might argue, an advantage because of her gender. Based on her rationale, other solutions such as working, as a hairdresser, which was her job before she married her first husband, would keep her away from her daughter and expose her to a relatively foreign culture hence making her prone to exploitation and "humiliation" as she described it. For her, marriage was the "safe" or the "decent" option, if not the obvious one in her situation, especially given that her child was her priority. She expressed her dissatisfaction with the idea of Egyptian men seeking a Syrian woman *per se* and described some of them as "wanting to try the new fruit in the market."

During our conversation, we were both trying to figure out the reason why her ex-husband called the marriage off. She hesitantly confessed that, after a lot of insistence from him and despite the traditions, she agreed to have sex with him once closer to the end of the first month. Soon after, his treatment and attitude started to change which later escalated to the separation. We debated a few theories to try to make sense of the situation. The "trying the new fruit in the market" explanation was obviously the first and the most depressing amongst the potential explanations, especially after adding the intercourse factor. His care about his first family and fear from destroying it was also another explanation. A common theme amongst all the potential explanations is that it seemed that *Sutra*, unlike the coming story, was not a strong enough reason for this marriage to survive. In fact, basing this marriage solely on *Sutra* created a fragile relationship, despite any noble intentions.

6 Marwa: "He Gave Me the Choice and I Chose *Sutra*"

Like her younger sister, Marwa's husband was killed in the war five years ago and soon after she moved with her parents to Egypt in 2012. Marwa seemed to be more resourceful and demonstrated higher ability to act on her own than her sister, despite having two kids and growing up in the same context. As soon as she arrived in Egypt, she searched for a job and was able to move among, and often fight for, a few decent office jobs that seemed to bring her great satisfaction. She had two experiences with *Sutra* marriage, one of which was incomplete. In this case, despite her father's refusal, the Egyptian man, who was also motivated by the religious oblation from supporting orphans, promised her a monthly allowance for her kids. Three months in, however, he asked her hand in marriage again, hoping that his commitment over three months would make a good case for him. After being turned down for the second time, he withdrew his commitment and she had to search for a job again. In the second story, she meets her current husband who constantly reminded her and her family that he is doing this for the children. In fact, before they met each other in person, over the phone, he gave Marwa the choice between *Sutra* (here implying *Sutra* through marriage) and just financial support by giving a monthly allowance to her children. She picked the first without hesitation. In the excerpt below, Marwa was describing her conflict between agreeing to marry her husband whom she initially refused because of his looks and between what *Sutra* would bring her and her kids:

D: … and what were you looking for in a husband? Did you care about love?

M: Yes, I did care, but I cared more about commitment and religious devotion. I cared about Sutra too.

D: What is the meaning of Sutra?

M: In my opinion, Sutra means a man… when you say "that's it!" no one is going to harass me, no one is going to impose themselves on me. That's it! I am with this man and so I can rest mentally.

D: Do you mean because he is going to be your support and back bone?

M: Yes... however up until that moment I wasn't sure how I felt. I was destroyed but at the same time I had the motivation because of my children [...] Of course my dad didn't allow me to come outside and meet him when he came the first time. I stayed inside and then my husband said I just want to see the kids I don't want to see her. I am here for the kids

D: Oh so he was referring to sheltering orphans?

M: Yes, and he didn't request to see me and my dad really appreciated this gesture. He spoke with the children and gave my daughter money, like allowance, and brought them sweets and he didn't see me despite coming from a long distance. And then my father wanted to see him for a second time and of course I saw him that time but at this time I didn't really approve of him.

D: Why? His looks?

M: Yes, he wasn't good looking. Can you believe that? I was concerned about the looks! But now despite all the problems between us I think he has a peaceful face and he has nice hair too. So I started to see his good looks now.

D: After marriage?

M: Yes... slowly through his good treatment and concern about us. Even until now. Yesterday I was asking him about something and he said are the kids comfortable with it or not? I told him: "but I am not comfortable," so he responded: "I married you for the kids."

D: Does that make you happy or upset?

M: Sometimes it makes me happy and sometimes upset depending on the context.

Marwa, unlike her sister, didn't reject the idea of working to support herself and her kids. In fact, she met her husband because she was searching for a job. She has proven resilience and skill in acquiring jobs and expressed deep satisfaction with her "printer, computer and very nice office." However, despite trying it and experiencing the satisfaction resulting from it, when given the option, she still preferred marriage over working. When her current husband's first wife asked her: "didn't you think about me? What would happen to me when my husband marries a second wife." She simply replied: "No, to be honest, I didn't think about you" implying that was already in a much worse situation and needed to take care of her own self first. Marwa, like Nour and Maha, used her agency to assess the situation and her social position within it and took the decision that best served her interest, which extended in the three cases to their children's interest.

7 Discussion

The trajectory of the three marriages, despite the common label of *Sutra*, had to do a lot with the man/husband's circumstances, understanding and real reasons behind the marriage. In Maha's case, both the husband and the wife were honest with each other about their intentions and need for intimacy. In such case, *Sutra* had served as a bonus that reinforced a second marriage against a resisting first wife and has potentially worked as a social justification for the husband who was a public figure. In Nour's case, while it is hard to speculate the ex-husband's real intentions, *Sutra* and the religious oblation was not a strong enough reason for the marriage to survive. The husband's theoretical and moral understanding of *Sutra* marriage and his attempt to apply it clashed with his "other" social life and probably conflicted, in his mind, with modernist social dictates of the nuclear monogamous family. In Marwa's case, on the other hand, *Sutra* was the glue that kept the marriage together thus far. The husband's clear vision of marrying her for the sake of her orphaned children played a major role in giving both the husband and the wife a reason to keep going, despite all the problems as Marwa clarified. It was even a reason for Marwa to fall in love with her husband later on in the marriage and for him to hold on to this marriage despite his first wife's constant call to get a divorce.

The above stories point to the major role the husband and his understanding (or misunderstanding) of *Sutra* marriage play in determining the success of the marriage. That said, the women on the other hand demonstrated substantial control in making and calculating the initial decision to get married. That is to say, for the three women, the decision to marry using the rationale of *Sutra* had its mitigating social pressures, some stemming from patriarchy and others stemming from the uprootedness and their forced migration status. I argue here that they all point to the fact that those mitigated social structures particularly gender and refugeeness can offer the refugee women an advantage and an ability to manoeuvre traditions to serve their best interest. In other words, facilitated but not entirely determined by the religious *Sutra* rhetoric, their labeled "vulnerable" and "victim" status created by social factors, namely, their refugeeness, gender, ethnicity: Syrians (compared to other sub-Saharan refugees such as Sudanese, Eritreans and Somalis), and social position as widows/divorced-with orphaned children had provided them with an opportunity and a solution that are not usually available to other displaced demographics in the same context. This statement complicates notions such as agency, victimhood, vulnerability and exploitation to both the contemporary liberal feminist and humanitarian discourses and to the justifications on which many of the *Sutra* marriage fatwas are built.

7.1 *Liberal Agency and Moral Agency*

Agency in liberal feminist literature and imagination is understood ultimately as the resistance to forms of domination and the capacity to realize one's own interest against custom (Mahmood 2001). What I sought to demonstrate through my respondents' narratives is that while a deeper look into those women's testimonies reveals a strong resemblance to the above definition, especially regarding the pursuit of one's interest, this notion of liberal agency captures only a thin layer of those women's experiences. In other words, restricting ourselves to such definition of agency sharply limits our understanding of those women's subjectivities and experiences that were formed by and within non-Western liberal cultural contexts.

The three cases above reveal that the women were still able to utilize relational autonomy[13] and agency–in its liberal sense, to pursue their interest. A major fracture to this rhetoric, however, is that those women still prescribed themselves to the traditional marriage institution and many other "patriarchal" discourses. That was manifested in *Maha*'s statement: "a woman without a man is like a tree without leaves"; *Nour*'s conviction that the woman's ultimate path is to get married; or *Marwa*'s decision to choose marriage over monthly financial support when given the choice by her future husband. Here, the post-structuralist Foucauldian concept of Subjectification that was later taken by Judith Butler in her gender analysis, is particularly helpful. Subjectification draws attention to power (and norms in Butler's analysis) as both subordinating or constraining and enabling. In other words, the modes that allow and create agency are in fact the products of power operations (they didn't exist before the dominance of this power). Personal preferences and gender roles are social constructs dictated to a large extent by culture, upbringing and other social forces. For instance, *Nour's* conviction that marriage is the natural path to any woman has helped form her options and preferences and shaped her understanding of marriage as "the decent" option for her situation. It has also

13 Relational autonomy is the label that has been given to an alternative conception of what it means to be "a free, self-governing agent who is also socially constituted and who possibly defines her basic value commitments in terms of inter- personal relations and mutual dependencies" (Christman 2004, 143). Recognizing relational autonomy as an analytical tool helps us see those women as aware of their social position, aware of the social transaction or the mutual benefit created by this form of marriage.

helped set her priorities when it came to her obligations to her daughter as well as her understanding of love and intimacy.

This is not to deny the patriarchal and unjust conditions, such as fear from harassment or distress about personal safety, that underlie those women's socio-cultural milieu and shape their preferences and decision to marry. Rather, I want to pick up on Saba Mahmood's argument which sought to problematize a question that has dominated scholarship, such as: "how do women contribute to reproducing their own domination, and how do they resist or subvert it?" (Mahmood 2001, 255). Here, I would like to recall the anti-colonial critique that challenges the assumption that the desire to freedom from subordination is universal and innate to human nature (ibid., 256). I argue that the decision/desire to marry for those women is determined by a complex web shaped by: (a) explicit/liberal understanding of agency and weighing one's interest against custom; (b) societal patriarchal dictations that re-articulate marriage as the decent and almost the only solution; and (c) those women's moral agency. Such moral agency does not particularly aim to enhance one's material interest or status but rather to "attain a certain kind of state of happiness, purity, wisdom, perfection, or immortality" (ibid., 210). In short, those women have perceived marriage as an agentive act not just in terms of promoting their socio-economic interest or to manoeuvre social structure but also as a moral and virtuous act that complements their existence and understanding of their femininity and gender–which, recalling Butler (1990), should not be understood as having an inner core or a value independent from the social.

7.2 *Marriage, Intimacy and the Nuclear Family*

Another conceptual challenge that the narratives of those women have imposed on liberal scholarship is the *reconceptualization of the notion of marriage*. While not challenging the idea of marriage as an institution *per se*, many of the women have posed important challenges to some of the core principles of marriage as understood in a postmodern world. At first glance, and consistent with the point made above about the multi-layered understanding and embodiment of agency, one could identify some pragmatic motives behind such challenges such as preferring and pursuing a polygamous marriage for reasons such as wanting to be only part-time wives which gives them more time for their children. Some others have also refused to register the marriage officially and limited it to a customary contract for some calculated reasons such as simplifying any potential separation especially in the event that they wanted to leave the country. However, beyond those pragmatic motives and throughout the narratives, one is able to trace malleable meanings of intimacy, romantic love and the nuclear family which pose challenges to the simplistic explanations of gender inequality in non-Western, particularly in this case Islamic, cultures.

For instance, despite her negative experience, *Nour* was actually pleased with her ex-husband's interest in applying *Sutra* to a widow and her orphaned children. As a researcher, I was astonished by the fact that she would be happy that someone is marrying her out of apparent charity. She clarified that she appreciated his honesty and noble intention and she was convinced that love, an important factor still, is a gradual process that will come later. When I reflected back on my astonishment, I could trace in my rationale elements of a colonized understanding of intimate relations that are often explained through convictions about the nuclear family as well as individualized perceptions, commercialized romantic expressions and monopolized affections. This malleable understanding of marriage and gender identity should not be understood merely in terms of strategic malleability, but that it also "emerges *because of* her traditionally ascribed gender identity not *despite of* it" (Taha 2017, 117).

7.3 *Reimagining Contemporary Jurisprudence*

So far, I have spent time arguing for reimagining the meanings of agency, family and marriage to understand the cultural complexity of those women's consciousness and articulation of autonomy, intimacy and gender roles. Now I want to direct the attention to how the above accounts and analysis are helpful to contemporary Islamic jurisprudence, particularly in two main ways. First, as was evident in the previous section, it destabilizes the orientalised portrayal of Third World refugee women, particularly Muslim refugee women, as passive victims of a primitive patriarchal legal system, here namely *fiqh*.[14] Rather, the women's accounts show how social restrictions and structures that produce vulnerability due to gender and forced migration have simultaneously opened new spaces and opportunities to, and have been utilized by, this social group. Moreover, the accounts offer refugee researchers tools to explore new areas and new meanings for notions such as shelter and resettlement. Thus, while the latter might not necessarily be used in explaining the rational of a religious verdict, it still provides the jurists and Islamic scholars with a common "language" with feminist and human rights advocates to engage in a meaningful debate on gender dynamics, gender rights and gender-based violence in Muslim societies.

That said, as a postcolonial feminist myself, my objective from this paper is not by any means to deny forces of social oppression to women in Islamic, as

14 Almost always confused with and is known as *sharia* in the West.

well as other, cultures. There is some extensive work by specialized ethicists who identify areas of moral and ethical dilemmas surrounding *Sutra* marriage, particularly from the male-perspective and as a product of patriarchal forces (see for instance, Al-Khatib 2018). Rather, a second benefit from revisiting notions such as agency, marriage and victimhood from a critical sociological perspective to contemporary Islamic Jurisprudence is to offer jurists a deeper sociological understanding of the realities of women and particularly refugee women in Muslim societies. Recalling Ramadan's argument about the imperative of mastering the field of knowledge for which a fatwa is being developed, the process known as *Ijtihād*, or "when legal scholars working in the field of social affairs produce an informed opinion (fatwa) on a given subject where the texts are either open to interpretation or silent" that is both scripturally and ethically informed (Ramadan 2017, 14), should particularly benefit from such analysis. Hence, I would like to conclude by highlighting a few sociological insights that are relevant to this case study:

- *Understanding the larger forces and explanations that pushed the refugee women to marry in the first place.* Refugee women have been often portrayed in sociological and anthropological studies as weak victims of war and violence and "thus in great need of protection from male family members or from foreign humanitarian aid workers" (Young and Chan 2015). It is important to recognize that accepting this perception uncritically would lead to consolidating oppressive and marginalizing forces that continue to determine the experiences and the social position of women in Muslim countries in general and Muslim refugee women in particular (Hajdukowski-Ahmed, Khanlou, & Moussa, 2008). That said, it is also important to recognize the patriarchal elements that shaped those women's understanding of *Sutra*. For instance, the three women agreed that marriage offers them a shield against sexual harassment. Harassment could be due to their gender, uprootedness, or both. Thus, while *Sutra* marriage can be argued as a practical, "decent" and culturally relevant solution to many refugee women who are also single mothers, it cannot be viewed in isolation from other unjust conditions, such as fear from harassment or personal safety, that shape those women's decision to marry. Moreover, Mutaz al-Khatib, addresses some ethical issues surrounding the patriarchal interpretations of *Sutra* marriage in Muslim-majority societies that fail to engage meaningfully with issues surrounding conflict of interest, subliminal levels of exploitation and coercion, and limiting the purpose of marriage to pure lust and physical needs (al-Khatib 2018). Understanding the double precarity of those women should contribute to a better assessment in weighing the benefits (*manfaʿa*) and harm (*ḍarar*) of marrying refugee women. Which brings us to the next point.

- *Emphasizing knowledge about trauma, mental health and the double precarity status of many refugee women.* Many, if not most refugees, whether men, women or children, experience traumatic events such as injury, destroying of neighbourhood, residence and personal belongings, torture and persecution, inhumane living conditions, witnessing the death of others and close ones (Porter & Haslam 2005). For women refugees, gender-based violence (GBV) is a particular threat. The latter is not just limited to physical and sexual violence but includes psychological and emotional abuse as well (Young and Chan 2015). As a result, many refugee women suffer from mental health symptoms such as depression, anxiety, and posttraumatic stress disorder (Guruge et al. 2009; Young and Chan 2015). Putting that in mind, one cannot rule out the idea that despite suffering from an abusive relationship, or even just an unhappy marriage due to factors such as incompatibility, marrying based on what is available, romantic void or feeling of unfairness due to a first marriage or the secrecy of marriage, some refugee women will still choose or feel obliged to stay in that marriage (Ho and Pavlish 2011). Hence, it is important when issuing fatwas like fatwa (1) discussed above, to put notions such as trauma and double precarity into account when considering the best interest of the refugee women. Double precarity is the product of two elements: the woman's gendered uprootedness and the more than likely loss of her family and social support, as well as precarity resulting from the marriage itself. Many such marriages are often hidden from a first wife and even public spheres and in many cases, is not registered i.e. customary or *'urfī* marriage. The previous two criteria were present, at least at some point, in Maha, Nour and Marwa's stories. While Maha and Marwa didn't suffer major consequences from the precarious status of their marriages, other than complaints about not seeing their husbands enough, in Nour's case, it didn't make it any harder on her ex-husband to "try the new fruit in the market" and to eventually walk away leaving her emotionally violated. In Nour's story, however, the secrecy and the precarious status of the marriage extended the harm to the husband and his first family when Nour, who was full of vengeance and arguably still suffering from war trauma, eventually called the first wife and informed her about her husband's "betrayal." This puts us against the inevitable question of how much protection does protection marriage or *Sutra* marriage really offer to a refugee woman?
- *Recognizing the blurry line between the man's personal interest and his striving for religious oblation.* Recalling the issues discussed above regarding conflict of interest and subliminal levels of exploitation, the case of Nour demonstrates that the intention of *Sutra* is not always enough to secure

a "healing" solution to the refugee woman. In fact, more damage can be caused if the fatwa does not tackle the complex factors that inform the decision-making process of many men and women in current Muslim societies who are also highly influenced by modernity.[15] Here, I am more accurately referring to the Muslim world's shock as a repercussion of "European" modernity. Such shock has made the Muslim cultures' absorption of modernity to be "extremely complicated and problematic" (Tagharobi and Zarei 2015). One of the repercussions of modernity in some Muslim societies, particular to our Egyptian case study, is the idea of the nuclear family or the monogamous marriage that gathers a man, a woman and their decedents. The point of dragging monogamy and polygamy to this conversation is not meant to assess its rationale and ethics under contemporary conditions. Rather, this paper, as emphasized throughout, is meant to offer a deeper sociological understanding of the realities and the forces dictating contemporary Muslim societies for which fatwas are issued. A jurist's grasp of the implications of modernity and its impact on the emergence of a new sense of self amongst Muslim men and women should thus be factored in when assessing the modern world's social, particularly gendered, issues. More importantly, such implications should be considered in understanding and (re)defining the "ethical" and the relationship between the legal and the ethical in Islamic philosophy and jurisprudence.

8 Conclusion

Marriage as a tool to mitigate insecurity and precarity is not a novel practice to Syrian women, with Bosnians and Iraqis before them. Studies on Tsunami survivors (Hyndman 2007) and North-Korean female border crossers to China (Kim 2014), elaborate interesting aspects of marriage as a survival tool for forced migrants and migrants with a precarious status. Still, marriage between Arab men and Syrian refugee women was proven to be a problematic issue that has drawn a strong media and advocacy attention over the past few years. Often described as exploitation due to the precarious status of many of the women especially those in refugee camps, these marriages were labelled and compared to forced marriages, sex trafficking and child marriage.

15 While it is hard to define, the term "modernity" was coined to capture the changes occurring in Europe due to industrialization, urbanization and democratization. One major change is a revolution in the human experience due to "the development of a new sense of self, of subjectivity and individuality. This idea distinguishes the modern individual from the traditional one" (Haferkamp, and Smelser 1992).

This paper does not aim to understate gender-based violence and oppression to women all across the globe, Muslim cultures included. Nor is it concerned with passing moral judgements or ethical evaluation to the phenomenon and some of its repercussions, such as polygamy and the often-opaque marital rights. It should be noted here, however, that the jurisprudential culture and its ethical theories are not constant, nor do they spring from a void (Ramadan 2017, 8). As Ramadan puts it:

> the historical circumstances and internal debates within Muslim communities should not be overlooked. Relationships between political power, religious institutions, as well as internal conflicts between schools of thought and jurisprudence all had an impact on the way moral values were understood, organized and applied (ibid., 8).

Hence, the objective of this paper was concerned with identifying and dissecting social structures, hegemonic discourses and power relations that explain and shape both: gendered phenomena such as *Sutra* marriage as well as this jurisprudential culture in order to better inform the contemporary ethics of migration debates in a way that is inclusive and decolonized.

Along those lines, this paper is also a call to reflect on how the jurisprudential culture that influences the *ijtihād* process and sets the parameter for Islamic ethical theories often mirror hegemonic discourses and reinforce dynamics of social injustice. Thus, an equally important question that was left out of this paper is the dilemma of the-more-than-possible politicization of such moral parameters and the Islamic science of ethics. How could, for instance, nationalistic ideologies motivate the connection between certain legal norms and particular understandings of ethical principles? Marion Holms Katz's analysis of the notion of *Ḥayāʾ* (modesty) and how its cultivation became "a central trope of legal discussions of veiling in the modern period" is a case in point (Katz 2015, 26). While her argument was meant to clarify the evolution of the relationship between jurisprudence and ethics in Islamic sciences, her analysis draws attention to the problematic of how ethical parameters and moral theories can be utilized to reinforce political ideologies.

In addition, a concurrent objective of this case study is to contribute to the body of literature that aims to resist the misrepresented, simplistic and orientalised narratives that portray Muslim women, and refugee women in particular, as the passive victims and the Arab man as the oppressive pariah (see for instance, Alhayek 2014). I have utilized an anti-colonial lens to offer a deeper reading to the case of *Sutra* marriage in Egypt. While not without tension, I propose that using an anti-colonial language when assessing the phenomenon offers two benefits. First, it offers a critical language and a communication tool to respond to accusations from contemporary international humanitarian, refugee rights and feminist discourses and conceptions. Such conceptions often stigmatize similar conjugal arrangements under notions such as exploitation, sex trafficking and forced marriage. An anticolonial framework challenges the foundations of such rhetoric by questioning, as was argued above, the understanding of notions such as agency and victimhood.

Second, an anti-colonial feminist lens proposes a gendered approach to jurisprudence that is more in touch with the reality of marginalized groups. While one of the objectives of the paper was to demonstrate the difference between vulnerability and victimhood and the fact that the refugee woman may enjoy a substantial level of "relational autonomy" in the initial decision of getting married, relying solely on religious oblation and the man's "pure" intention from the marriage can be problematic to the trajectory or the end result of the marriage. A gendered approach to the fatwa then, should reinforce the role of the jurist beyond merely concluding the legal verdict to embracing a vision of "ethico-religious obligations" and include principles such as *Ulfa* (friendship, affection, and intimacy) (Katz 2015) to guide and rectify the society's intellectual and moral assessments of *when* and *how* to apply (or not to apply) *Sutra* marriage to refugee, as well as other, women. Moreover, the fatwa should offer provisions that effectively allow those women to exercise their marital rights. Recognition of patriarchal social forces, trauma and precarity, the exaggerated power in the hands of the man due to the double precarity of those refugee women along with the modernity shock are some elements that facilitate and inform this end.

Acknowledgements

This work would not have been possible without the funding of the Humanitarian Response Network of Canada (HRN) and the Logistical support of Syria Al Gad Relief Foundation that facilitated the interview appointments and location with the respondents. I would also like to thank the Center for Refugee Studies at York University and my supervisory committee, Professor Christopher Kyriakides, Professor Katherine Bischoping and Professor Jennifer Hyndman for their tireless commitment and support to my work.

Bibliography

AlHamoud, Ibrahim Bin Nasir. (2011). Huqooq al-Arāmīl wa al-Mutalaqāt (the rights of widows and divorcées). *Islam Today*, November 6.

Alhayek, Katty. (2014). Double Marginalization: The Invisibility of Syrian Refugee Women's Perspectives in Mainstream Online Activism and Global Media."*Feminist Media Studies*, 14(4): 696–700.

Al-Khatib, Mutaz. (2018). Zawjat al-Shahīd wa al-Zawāj ghayr al-Akhlāqī (the wife of the martyr and the immoral marriage). *Al-Jazeera blogs*, January 11. <https://blogs.aljazeera.net/blogs/2018/1/11/زوجة-الشهيد-والزواج-غير-الأخلاقي>.

Barkan, L. (2012). Criticism in Arab World Over Exploitation of Syrian Refugee Girls For Purposes Of Marriage. *The Middle East Media Research Institute*, November 12. Accessed May 25, 2018. <https://www.memri.org/reports/criticism-arab-world-over-exploitation-syrian-refugee-girls-purposes-marriage>.

Butler, Judith. (1990). Gender Trouble, Feminist Theory, and Psychoanalytic Discourse. In *Feminism/Postmodernism*, edited by Linda Nicholson, 324–340. New York: Routledge.

Castles, Stephen. (2002). Migration and Community Formation under Conditions of Globalization. *International Migration Review*, 36(4): 1143–1168.

Christman, John. (2004). Relational Autonomy, Liberal Individualism, and the Social Constitution of Selves. *Philosophical Studies*, 117(1): 143–164.

Dei, Geirge Sefa. (2012). Indigenous anti-colonial knowledge as "heritage knowledge" for promoting Black/African education in diasporic contexts. *Decolonization: Indigeneity, Education & Society*, 1(1): 102–119.

ECHO Factsheet—Egypt (2018), By European Commission's Directorate-General for European Civil Protection and Humanitarian Aid Operations, available at: <https://reliefweb.int/report/egypt/echo-factsheet-egypt-january-2018>.

Geha, Rani. (2012). Syrian Refugees Struggle in Egypt. *Al-Monitor*, November 21. Available at: <http://www.al-monitor.com/pulse/iw/politics/2012/11/the-plight-of-syrian-refugees-in-egypt.html>.

Guruge, Sepali, and Janice Humphreys. (2009). Barriers that affect abused immigrant women's access to and use of formal social supports. *Canadian Journal of Nursing Research*, 41(3): 64–84.

Haferkamp, Hans, and Neil J. Smelser, eds. (1992). *Social Change and Modernity*. Berkeley: University of California press. Available at: <http://publishing.cdlib.org/ucpressebooks/view?docId=ft6000078s&chunk.id=d0e1681>.

Hajdukowski-Ahmed, Maroussia, Nazilla *Khanlou* and Helene *Moussa*. (2008). *Not Born a Refugee Woman: Contesting identities, rethinking practices*. NY, USA: Berghahn Books.

Hassan, Khalid. (2015). Why Some Syrian Refugees See Marriage as the Only Option. *Al-Monitor*, December 8. Available at: <http://www.al-monitor.com/pulse/originals/2015/12/egypt-syria-refugees-women-marriage-aid.html#ixzz4LTGBszPg>.

Ho, Anita, and Carol Pavlish. (2011). Indivisibility of accountability and empowerment in tackling gender-based violence: Lessons from a refugee camp in Rwanda. *Journal of Refugee Studies* 24(1): 88–109.

Hyndman, Jennifer. (2007). The Securitization of Fear in Post-Tsunami Sri Lanka." *Annals of the Association of American Geographers*, 97(2): 361–372.

Katz, Marion Holmes. (2015). Ethics, Gender, and the Islamic Legal Project. *The Abdallah S. Kamel Lecture Series on Islamic Law and Civilization*. New Haven, Connecticut: Yale Law School.

Kim, Sung Kyung. (2014). "I am well-cooked food": survival strategies of North Korean female border-crossers and possibilities for empowerment. *Inter-Asia Cultural Studies* 15(4): 553–571.

Mahmood, Saba. (2001). Feminist theory, embodiment, and the docile agent: Some reflections on the Egyptian Islamic revival. *Cultural Anthropology* 16(2): 202–236.

Mir-Hosseini, Ziba. (2003). The construction of gender in Islamic legal thought and strategies for reform. *Hawwa* 1(1): 1–28.

Mohanty, Chandra Talpadi. (1984). Under Western eyes: Feminist scholarship and colonial discourses. *Boundary* 2(12/13): 333–358.

Natour, Rajaa. (2016). Neither Marriage Nor Protection for Syrian Women. *Linkedin*, February 27. Available at: <https://www.linkedin.com/pulse/neither-marriage-nor-protection-syrian-women-rajaa-natoure>.

Palestine Refugees: Locations and Numbers (2010), by IRIN. Available at: <http://www.irinnews.org/report/89571/middle-east-palestinian-refugee-numberswhere abouts>.

Porter, Matthew, and Nick Haslam. (2005). Predisplacement and postdisplacement factors associated with mental health of refugees and internally displaced persons: a meta-analysis. *Jama*, 294(5): 602–612.

Ramadan, Tariq. (2017). Islamic Ethics: Sources, Methodology and Application. In *Islamic Bioethics: Current Issues and Challenges*, edited by Alireza Bagheri and Khalid Alali. Series of Intercultural Dialogue in Bioethics, vol. 2: 1–21.

Sachedina, Abdulaziz. (1999). Woman, Half-the-Man? Crisis in Male Epistemology in Islamic Jurisprudence. In *Perspectives on Islamic Law, Justice and Society*, edited by R.S. Khare. New York, Rowman & Littlefield.

Spivak, Gayatry. (1988). Can the subaltern Speak. In *Can the Subaltern Speak?: Reflections on the History of an Idea*, edited by Rosalind C. Morris. Columbia, Columbia University Press, 21–78.

Tagharobi, Kaveh, and Ali Zarei. (2015). Accommodating an Unexpected Guest. *The Modernist World*, 439.

Young, Marta Y., and K. Jacky Chan. (2015). The Psychological Experience of Refugees: A Gender and Cultural Analysis. In Safdar, Saba, and Natasza Kosakowska-Berezecka. "Psychology of Gender Through the Lens of Culture: Theories and Applications. Springer International Publishing, 17–36.

CHAPTER 6

The Islamic Principle of *Kafala* as Applied to Migrant Workers: Traditional Continuity and Reform

Ray Jureidini and Said Fares Hassan

1 Introduction

The paper is an attempt to identify the continuities and discontinuities between the religious Islamic notion and practice of *kafala* (*kafāla*) and its contemporary application—with specific reference to the Gulf States where it has been most prominently legislated and practiced. While much research has been undertaken, mostly critical of the *kafala* as a system of oppression and exploitation of migrant labour in the GCC, there seems to be a consensus that there is no relationship at all between the traditional Islamic concept of *kafala* and its current application. In other words, it is argued that there is no evidence of a "genealogy" that links the Islamic jurisprudence of *kafala* to its contemporary forms (Franz 2011, 98).

In a recent paper on the origins of the *kafala* related to migrant labour in the GCC, the historian, AlShehabi (2019), provides documentary evidence showing how the British colonial rulers, first in Bahrain and later other GCC states from the 1920s, introduced what was for them a system of sponsorship and surety, but which was perfectly compatible with and adaptable to the principles of *kafala* in Islamic law and custom. It was, he argues, a "cheap" means of controlling foreigners and having local citizens take responsibility for them. Thus, there was no conscious decision on the part of the Muslim rulers of the region to apply the traditional form of *kafala* under new circumstances in the GCC that required massive numbers of foreign companies and workers. Rather, in this situation, the conflation of colonial rule and Islamic custom came together serendipitously. Notwithstanding this historical backdrop, we think it is worthwhile to attend to some of the nuances of the "old" *kafala* and the "new" *kafala* in order to see more precisely: 1) how it came about; 2) what are the similarities (apart from the name); 3) why the old *kafala* was modified into its present-day arrangements.

It is argued that the modern Islamic state, through the right of the leader (*waliy al-amr* and his *siyāsa sharʿiyya*), has the right, the power and authority to modify rules and regulations from traditional practices in accordance with the public interest (*maṣlaḥa*). This is a political dimension that has not been alluded to in previous accounts of the *kafala* as applied to contemporary management of migration workers in the Middle East. There is a considerable degree of criticism of the contemporary use of *kafala*. One author, for example, considers contemporary practice of *kafala* as an "insult to Islam." (Kakande 2015, 15). Others have equated *kafala* with "modern day slavery" (Chidiac 2014). It may be argued, however, that the contemporary problems of *kafala* are primarily because of the abuse of the principles rather than the principles themselves. In this sense, is there a continuity of a normative set of social arrangements, but that the exploitative potential has overtaken the ethical guidelines of trust, care, responsibility and obligations in relation to the presence and employment of foreigners? From the law and religious dicta through fatwas, we provide evidence of traditional ethical continuity, some traditional elements in the codified law, but non-compliance in contemporary practice—a perennial problem.

2 Similarities and Dissimilarities

> The term "*kafāla*" has a wide semantic scope in Arabic. Its root, kāf – fā' – lām (كفل), means to feed, support, vouch for or warrant; hence "*kafala*" refers to bail, guaranty, security or sponsorship (Wehr 1994, 976). According to Lane's nineteenth century Arabic dictionary, *kafala* meant "responsibility; answerableness; amenability; or suretyship; the conjoining of responsibility to another" (Lane 1872, 3001). Likewise, the *kafīl* is "one who is responsible, answerable, amendable, or a sponsor or surety" (ibid.). In the Islamic tradition, *Kafala* is a significant concept that has its social, moral and business dimensions. In Islamic family law "*kafala*" refers to a formal agreement to provide temporary support for an orphaned child until adulthood. Such support does not confer inheritance rights and is best understood as a form of legal guardianship rather than adoption. (Franz 2014, 97)

Businesswise, Muslim jurists extend the meaning of *kafala* to a business contract where someone formally guarantees somebody else in terms of delivering goods or carrying financial responsibilities (e.g., Ibn Rushd 1999, vol.1, 636-ff; Ibn 'Ābdīn 2003, vol.7, 553-ff). More generally, *kafala* was intended to provide a framework of social solidarity based on trust and cooperation among people in various realms of their interactions.

Kafala thus originally refers to a contract where a guarantor conjoins a guaranteed person (*makfūl*) and assumes liability for that person in various specified terms. *Kafala* is meant to provide an assurance of the fulfillment of an obligation of the guaranteed person. This can be to guarantee the payment of the guaranteed person's financial liability (*kafala bi-al-māl*) (as in a surety guaranteeing the repayment of a debt). It could also be to guarantee the presence of a certain person at a specified time and place (*kafala bi-al-nafs*) or the appearance of a certain person, as in the case of a lawsuit (*kafala bi-al-wajh*) (as in guaranteeing bail money). It could be a guarantee for the delivery of goods (*kafala bi-al-taslīm*) or a guarantee for the purchase of goods sold (*kafala bi-al-darak*). In short, the guarantor assumes responsibility for a certain liability due by the guaranteed that will include the *kafīl* as a representative of the guaranteed (*makfūl*) in front of the state and other government institutions and take responsibly for any breach of the law perpetrated by the guaranteed (see Bālī 2013, vol.1, 970ff; Ibn ʿĀbdīn 2003, vol. 7, Chapter on *Kafala*).

Thus, *kafala* contracts were used to protect the weak and vulnerable by instituting the patronage of a prominent local who provided whatever protection was required—a form of community responsibility for financial, legal or political representation (Franz 2014, 99). These forms or applications of *kafala* can still function in contemporary times. However, while the *Majella* (Ottoman codified *Sharīʿa* law) refers to *kafala* contracts of the various types mentioned above, there is no mention of *kafala* in the enactment or employment of labour (ibid.). Similarly, there is no mention of *kafala* contracts in analyses of Ottoman slavery arrangements (ibid.), although similar practices with non-Muslim foreign labour were evident in the port of Istanbul from the late sixteenth century (see Kanchana 2018, 8).

The earliest account of *kafala* in relation to labour in the Arabian Gulf seems to have been loose arrangements from the turn of the twentieth century to the 1940s (Longva 1997). Pearl divers, for example, were bound to a *kafīl* who owned the dhow boats that were used. This has been identified more as a "cultural legacy" (Hamza 2015: 94; Gardener 2010). As noted for Kuwait, there was no formal legal reference to *kafala* until the Aliens Residence Law in 1975, despite the requirements from the 1950s and 1960s that foreign businesses required a local Kuwaiti partner with 51 percent ownership and that migrants should be "vouched for by a respected citizen of Kuwait" (Longva 1997: 78).

As such, the similarity between the classical Islamic usage of *kafala* and the new form as applied to the management of foreign workers has been seen as a merely linguistic one that lends it a "veneer of legitimacy," i.e. the presence of a *kafīl* as guarantor (now sponsor) who would guarantee the legal residency of the foreigner who will abide by the rules of a contract and the laws of the country. As Franz observes,

> If the current use of the *kafala* system for migrant labour did descend from these earlier forms, it diverged dramatically in the context of nation states and neoliberal market forces and transformed into a system whereby non-nationals are bound to nationals for the purposes of work or business. (Franz 2014, 100)

The most highly critiqued issues of the contemporary *kafala* have indeed centered around the power, control and exploitation of the *kafīl* over foreign employees as well as business establishments. The criticisms have primarily been based on international human and labour rights law and conventions (International Labour Organization 2013a; Kapiszewski 2001).

On the other hand, investigating the technical usage and application of the classical Islamic *kafala* system, it is clear that an essential element of the classical system is that *kafala* is considered a contract without benefits on the part of the guarantor. That is, the service of the guarantor (*kafīl*) is meant to be free of charge.

> Nothing in the Ottoman or *fiqh* contexts referred to the use of such contracts for the purpose of rewarding the guarantor. Such a situation would in fact have constituted a legal breach since any payments made to the guarantor for providing *kafala* would have constituted *ribā* (usury), forbidden in Islam. (Foster 2001, 143)

It is in this sense that the new *kafala* may seem to violate a key traditional Islamic condition and may be seen more as a business-oriented system rather than one of trust and protection. A *kafīl* sponsors a worker and represents him/her on behalf of the state on the condition that this specific worker will sign a contract to work for him or for others in return for certain benefits. It is not a pure *kafala* system. It is a *kafala*-cum-*ijāra* (sponsorship-cum-hiring) system, and in this sense the *kafala-makfūl* relationship has been reversed where the *makfūl* guarantees the fulfillment of a labour contract with the *kafīl* who pays the *makfūl* for his/her labour, presumably making a profit from the labour. This new relationship is no longer *kafala*. The question remains, however, to what extent is this form of contract Islamically justified and reasoned?[1]

1 Although it is not pursued here, it should be noted that, while foreign companies require 51 per cent ownership by a national (individual or company), not all *kafīls*/sponsors of migrant

However, let us look more closely at the distinction between the principle and the practice. Although the original idea may have been for GCC citizens to take responsibility for the presence of foreigners, particularly professionals in the energy industries, the system quickly metamorphosed into one where the *kafīl* was not held responsible or accountable. For example, the *kafīl* is the one responsible for the obtaining of a work visa and residency permit. However, if the residency permit was not renewed, the employee becomes an illegal resident liable to arrest, detention and deportation, not the *kafīl*. Thus, the original idea of the *kafīl* taking responsibility for the *makfūl* does not resonate in the new form. As Franz notes, the *kafala* as adapted to migrant labour, "violates both the letter and spirit of the legal institution," where "something once associated with social protection has become more restrictive and punitive" (Franz 2014, 101).

As an example, it was the 1959 Kuwait Alien Residence Law and its several amendments (1963, 1965, 1968, and 1975) that made all migrant workers virtually dependent on their Kuwaiti employers for their entry visas, work, and residence. However, neither the content of the *kafala* nor the relationship between the *kafīl* and the migrant worker were clearly explained in the law (Alajmi 2007). Longva suggested it may have been because, "The [*kafala*] practice was well-anchored in Kuwaiti tradition and was, therefore, widely understood and taken for granted by the native population" (Longva 1997, 79). This suggests that the origins of the modern *kafala* was a more cultural, customary heritage rather than one based upon Islamic jurisprudence.

Current practice of the *kafala* system has been critiqued for its exploitation of migrant workers, to the extent of describing it as a slave system (Rodriguez 2014). It puts severe restrictions on labour mobility, and has prevented the development of a local labour market. *Kafīls* may withhold workers' payments while demanding longer hours and preventing access to legal rights by withholding workers' passports, contract substitution and the like (Jureidini 2014). *Kafīls* may also lease their *kafala* against payments. Workers may be forced to pay recruitment charges to the recruitment agency, thus burdening the workers with more expenses, feeding a system of bribery and corruption and binding them into a form of labour indebtedness and forced labour (Jureidini 2017a). There are many other forms of exploitation and malpractices of *kafala* (and where the *kafīl* profits) that are against the law and indeed frowned upon from an Islamic perspective.

---

workers in the Gulf States are nationals. They can also be non-nationals who have residency (*iqāma*). This means that a *kafīl*/sponsor can also be a non-Muslim. Further empirical research into the topic should take this into account.

In an answer to frequent questions on the Islamic legal framework of recruiting foreign workers through *kafala* in Saudi Arabia, the Permanent Committee of Scientific Research and Fatwas published a long research paper to provide legal reasoning for the legality of *kafala* and the parameters that should be considered in its application. The committee started its presentation by confirming that recruiting foreign workers is part of the state policy to care for the interests of its people. Consequently, the administration of labour recruitment is subject to the approval of the King, as the head of the state and the one in charge of the affairs of Muslims, i.e. the *waliy al-amr* (al-Lajna al-Dā'ima 1994, 39–60).

According to Islamic law, the *waliy al-amr* can issue laws to regulate people's lives (Taj, 1995, 33), including businesses in a way that protects the rights of contractors and the needs of the society, provided that these laws do not contradict a Qur'anic injunction or a Prophetic instruction. Given his powers, the *waliy al-amr* may exercise *ijtihād* and enact laws that command people to follow a certain set of regulations (and not others, even if those others are religiously permissible in themselves). People should abide by these regulations, or otherwise they will be of "the transgressors" (al-Lajna al-Dā'ima, 41). These regulations may provide rules of business such as work times, work places, work permits, job descriptions, etc. If such regulations exist, then people must follow them, otherwise they may be subject to certain penalties. This understanding of the rule of the *waliy al-amr* is formulated in the legal maxim, "*taṣarruf al-imām ʿalā al-raʿiyya manūṭ bi-al-maṣlaḥa*," i.e. the imam's power over his people is based on his effort to maintain their interests (al-Suyūṭī, 1983).

Based on these arguments, the *kafala*/sponsorship laws are considered part of this *siyāsa*. It is argued that the regulation of the process of *kafala* or hiring foreign workers is a task of the *waliy al-amr* or his representative. The regulation defines who should be recruited, conditions of their recruitment, rights and duties of both *kafīls* (sponsors / employers) and the *makfūls* (sponsored / employees). The main function of this regulation is to guarantee the interest of the work itself, the maintenance of security, the prevention of chaos and tension in the work environment. Once these regulations are set, both sides, employers and employees, should follow the contractual conditions and commit themselves to its conditions. In so doing, they follow the Qur'anic injunction, "O, you who believe, commit yourselves to your contracts"; and to the Prophetic directive, "Muslims must commit to their conditions, and whoever neglects them, he is from the transgressors." If they do not abide by them, then the *waliy al-amr* may discipline them in the way he thinks appropriate (al-Lajna al-Dā'ima, 41).

3 *Kafala*-cum-*Ijāra*

It has been argued that the *kafala* contract controls the movements of workers and subjects them to a set of draconian practices (e.g. keeping their passports, delaying their payments, forcing them to work more hours, etc.) that are against international labour law. To what extent, however, are these practices Islamic?

To discuss the laws of *kafala*, one needs to turn to the section on *ijāra* in Islamic law texts. The definition of *kafala* shows clearly the relationship between the new form of *kafala* and *ijāra*. *Kafala* refers to the permission given by the state to a certain individual/company to sponsor/hire non-natives to work for them through a contract to be signed and approved by both parties. This contract should state at least the names of the employer and the employee, the nature of the work, and the salary agreed upon. This contract is very similar to an *ijāra* contract in Islamic law. Jurists define *ijāra* as a contract to provide a lawful specific service to be performed in a specific span of time in a specific place for a specific wage/cost/benefit (al-Nahhām, 2011)—in short, "the trade of a particular service for a specific return" (Bālī 2013, 589).

Discussions of the *kafala* system in legal debates follow the same line of arguments in Islamic contracts in general and contracts of *ijāra* in particular in the sense that contract conditions are binding, business ethics have to be observed and elements of *gharar* (an element of contracts or exchange, usually in finance, associated with deception, risk and uncertainty—of dubious legitimacy) have to be eliminated. Reviewing *ijāra* sections in Islamic legal texts reveals that the *ijāra* contract requires precision, clarity, eligibility and approval. Missing one of these elements may invalidate the whole contract. Furthermore, the *kafala* system is more or less identical with the legal discussion of the *ajīr khāṣ* (private employee) (al-Nahhām 2011).

Generally, contracts are binding and sacred in Islamic law, provided they do not violate the principles of *Sharīʿa* and the public interest. The contractual relationship is not seen from within the exclusive realm of the contractors but also on the consideration that Allah oversees this relationship, not only as a guarantee of honoring the contract and maintaining contractual justice, but also as the Actual Disposer of Affairs (Shimizu 1989). A contract in Islam thus has a religious component within it, even if not stated explicitly in the contract. This has to do with two main points. First, contracts are based on the usufruct principle, namely, everything belongs to and is owned by Allah and man is only a trustee with usufruct rights (Doi 1984, 355). This means that the contracting parties should assume the presence of Allah as the Actual Contractor and that the subject matter of a contract has to be legally permissible. Second is the element of moral commitment that starts with the elements of intention and motive at the moment of undertaking the contract. Ibn al-Qayyim argues, "the motive behind the contract is an essential consideration and affects its validity" (Coulson 1984, 45). In other words, the individual conscience plays a significant role in the genuine accord of wills and mutual agreement among business partners. "The attitude of [Muslim] jurists endeavors to understand the total context or the real situation by examining the real intention of the individual. That is to say, it seeks for substance, and is not overly concerned with formalism…" (Shimizu 1989, 16).

In addition to the morality of the motive, moral commitment can also be observed through the principle of *taqwā*—literally, the fear of God and piety. The Qur'an says, "Men, We have created you from a male and a female and divided you into nations and tribes that you might get to know one another. The noblest of you in Allah's sight is *atqākum* (the one who fears Him most), Allah is wise and all-knowing" (Qur'an 49:13). In Islam, *taqwā* is the standard for the judgment of human actions. In action, *taqwā* means faithfulness or a desire to love all things universally in a social sense. This understanding is the more significant of the two connotations in considering the function of community, because the most precious relationships of human beings in a community are those founded on the basis of love or brotherhood. These relationships create a voluntary regard for others more than one's self, leading to unity and stability of a community. *Taqwā* always involves a sense of love and sympathy for others (Shimizu 1989, 43–44). In this sense, it creates a subconscious respect for compliance to certain principles that may be beyond the reach of formal enforcement.

In addition to the sacred, binding and moral nature of the contract, Islamic law stipulates that the contractors should not have conditions that may result in deceiving one of the contract parties, a kind of moral hazard. In technical terms, a contract should not have *gharar*, such as a practice or condition that may cause a profit for one party but a corresponding loss for another (Coulson 1984, 44). Thus, one of the reasons why *gharar* should be eliminated is that its absence is a precondition for confirming the equilibrium in a contract. Contracts are never legally bound until the real equilibrium (among the interests of contractors, the wellbeing of the community and the Will of the Divine) is ascertained. Thus, the *kafala* system can be Islamically reasoned and justified if it is framed in line with rules of contracts as established in Islamic law. If there is a breach of these rules, jurists will argue against these as malpractices.

As an example, in certain instances, employers have used the system to hire workers but exploit them by asking them to work for another employer, provided that the worker pays him either a percentage of his earnings or a set amount of money each month. In other instances, the employer hires workers with a certain wage, but once these workers arrive in the country, arrangements are made for them to work for another company with a higher wage, the *kafīl* taking the difference into his own pocket. In both cases, muftis from the Saudi General Committee for *Iftāʾ* and Research made the following comments: First, this form of contract contradicts the laws of the land as enacted by the *waliy al-amr* to preserve rights, to maintain security, and to prevent problems. Second, it includes earning money in return for the *kafala* that is, if not a *ḥarām*, at least a doubtful practice that Muslims are supposed to stay away from. Third, there is a form of *gharar* and ambiguity in the contract as sometimes the exact salary is unknown, the money for the sponsorship is unknown, and the employer will pay little money (visa, transportation, etc.) in return for a large sum of money to be paid in return (al-Lajna al-Dāʾima 1994, 56). Other fatwas also stressed the unlawfulness of the breach of contract in the *kafala* system, especially the case when a sponsor would ask his employee to work on his own and give him money in return for his sponsorship (al-ʿUthaymīn 1979, 214–5; al-Dawīsh, 377–8).

The argument of the illegality of this transaction is intriguing. Jurists argue that the *kafala* contract, if not involving direct work arrangement between the two parties, becomes a contract of *irfāq* and *tabarrauʿ*, that is, charity, goodness and compassion. Because of this, the *kafīl* should not ask for money. His services should be provided for free. If there has to be some money to be paid, then it can only be the costs the sponsor incurred to secure the needs of his "brother" (fatwa.islamweb.net, fatwa no. 137333). But even this is a problem because the labour law in Saudi Arabia forbids workers to be charged for recruitment costs and fees.[2] The visas obtained on a sponsorship principle are not commodities that one may trade in. They are just permits from the government to bring labourers to work for someone (fatwa.islamweb.net, fatwa no. 101777). Another reason is the element of deceit and cheating to the state, as the sponsor's action defies the purpose of the *kafala* system (islamqa.com, fatwa no. 101220).

A direct question from a *kafīl* regarding the taking of money from the *makfūl* was put to the Saudi General Committee for *Iftāʾ* and Research. It was in

2 "An employer shall incur the fees pertaining to recruitment of non-Saudi workers, the fees of the residence permit (*Iqāmah*) and work permit together with their renewal and the fines resulting from their delay, as well as the fees pertaining to change of profession, exit, re-entry visas and return tickets to the worker's home country at the end of the relation between the two parties." (Article 40, Saudi Labour Law, 2005); similarly, in the UAE (Article 18, UAE Labour Law No. 8, 1980) and Qatar (Article 33, Qatar Labour Law No. 14, 2004).

relation to employees who wanted to remain in the state even though he could no longer employ them:

> I am the sponsor of a number of Afghani workers and have no work for them at the present time. They, thus, engage in other work in the country and live in my house without paying rent. They keep the money they gain from work for themselves, whether it is a small or large amount. However, they pay me three thousand riyals for renewing their two-year residence permit and referring to the concerned authorities. I have asked them to return to their country, but they have entreated me not to withhold their *Rizq* (sustenance). Am I sinful for this? (Asadov 2015, 46)

The principle concern of the *fatwa* committee was that the *kafīl* should not receive any money just for extending their visas, for that is the *kafīl*'s responsibility.[3] Other similar inquiries met with fatwas strictly prohibiting the taking of money from the *makfūl*.

In addition to the fatwas, the practice of sponsors profiting from selling work visas to workers abroad and not providing employment has come to be known as "visa trading" or "free visas" (free of a job, not free of cost). Although widespread in the GCC over many decades (Fargues & Shah 2017), these practices are not condoned as a part of the *kafala* but are strictly illegal and perpetrators have been prosecuted, fined and blacklisted (see, for example, Sophia 2015; *Qatar News* 2014; *Gulf Times* 2018).

Interestingly, there is some similarity in the principle restrictions governing *kafala* as a means of fostering an orphan child.[4] Here, the *kafīl* also must not take money for rearing an orphan, but at the same time, the orphan is not to assume a blood identity with the family, particularly with regard to inheritance. Rules regarding marriage of fostered orphans also suggest the same form of distinction or separation. Kanchana notes that in *kafala* fostering,

> There is no change in the family name and the child does not get inheritance rights. The objective is to protect the original identity (including family relationship and religion) and the inherited property of the child. While *kafala* care could imply benefits such as access to the wider family

3 Interestingly, Asadov argued that the "highly moralistic approach" of the Saudi scholars issuing the *fatwa* was not helpful in reconciling the law with the reality; that the fatwa could have acknowledged that money could not be legitimately received for the visa extension, but for rent and thus "serve the interest of both" (Asadov 2015, 47).

4 "Many Muslim-majority countries do not recognize adoption and they instead facilitate a fostering arrangement, called *kafala*" (Kanchana 2018: 7).

> and the social networks, it also stresses the child's dependence on the adoptive parents' benevolence. (Kanchana 2018, 7)

The separation and dependence are similar to *kafala* in relation to foreign employees, where rights of citizenship are denied, but for different reasons (Dito 2014). As Lori (2012) notes, *kafala* has two key structural elements in the Gulf States. First, there is a government centralization where the sponsorship laws are administered through the Ministries of Interior that regulate entry work permits (visas) and residency, "without any outside intervention by the courts or other institutions." Second, citizen sponsorships of foreign individuals or corporations constitute "a built-in enforcement mechanism for temporary residency by holding citizens directly responsible for the residency violations of non-citizens." In this way, the "mechanisms for enforcing temporary residency are widely dispersed while authority over residency decisions remains highly concentrated" (Lori 2012, 12). And as Fargues notes, the demographic imbalance has meant that "decades of intense, but temporary, migration have resulted in citizens and non-nationals growing as two separate entities without a new, mixed, population emerging from their co-existence" (Fargues 2011, 280).

These fatwas and similar malpractices of the system show the disparity between the Islamic principles of *kafala* and exploitative practices and demonstrate the power relationship between the local citizens and foreign workforce. To treat these issues on the state level, many GCC states have been discussing the *kafala* system and introducing various amendments and reforms to their laws, hoping to create more equilibrium in the relationship between the businessman, the worker and the interests of the state.

One of the recent attempts in reforming the *kafala* system is in Qatar (see Jureidini 2017, 2014). By way of background, the original 1963 *kafala* legislation (Law 9, *Governing Aliens Entry and Residence in Qatar*) was drawn up with skilled professionals in mind, making it clear that foreigners can be granted an entry visa for work provided that they filled a technical expertise that Qatar requires. Second, that foreigners must have Qatari *kafīls* who are able to hire and *care for them*. Third, that the *kafīl* is required to sign a statement of the good conduct of the *makfūl* and make a commitment to present the employee to the Qatari authorities at the end of the contract and also commit to pay for their repatriation home. Reference to *kafala, kafīl* and *makfūl* were included right up to the 2009 legislation (Law 4, *Regulating the Entry and Exit of Expatriates in Qatar and their residence and Sponsorship*) with a more explicit requirement of an exit visa to be approved by the employer and which came under much criticism that it violated the right of freedom of movement (see for example: Human Rights Watch 2012; International Labour Organization 2013; Amnesty International 2013, 2016).

Despite the practices of preventing employees from leaving the country at will, the legislation requiring an exit visa was again mainly aimed at professionals and business people who may be in a position to defraud or leave the country with large debts that would not be repaid, perhaps the result of bitter experience. Article 19 states that the *kafīl* must "be qualified to bear the obligations of the sponsorship as imposed by law and employ the expatriate under its own supervision." Provisions were also made distinguishing between a *kafīl al-iqāma* (the residency sponsor) and *kafīl al-khurūj* (the exit sponsor, in case the residency sponsor was unavailable to sign off, or deceased). In either case, the *kafīl* is responsible for any debts of the *makfūl* and to "present a certificate from the authorized administrations that there is no claims or court decisions against him." Article 20 made clear that the residence or exit *kafīl* would only be responsible for the debts of the expatriate and no more. It states that the *kafīl* (in both of its categories as *kafīl al-iqāma* (sponsor of one's stay/visit to Qatar) and *kafīl al-khurūj* (sponsor of the *makfūl* in case of his departure) should not carry the responsibilities or be charged money more than what the *makfūl* owes. For example, if the *makfūl* has to pay 500 in debt, the *kafīl* is responsible for these 500 only, not more. In addition, there should not be any further conditions than those already due on the *makfūl*. For example, if the *makfūl* has to pay his debt in installments, it remains that way and the *kafīl* cannot be asked to pay it in a lump sum. The *kafīl's* responsibility for the debts of the foreigner was thus quite clear and consistent with the traditional *kafala* requirement. Of course in practice it was most unlikely that a *kafīl* would allow a situation where he would be required to pay the debts of a foreign *makfūl*. Indeed, it was precisely through the mechanism of the requirement of permission for an exit visa that allowed a sponsor to legally detain a foreigner when there was any form of dispute between them.

The most recent reform was Qatari law no. 21 in 2015 (*Regulating the Entry, Exit of Expatriates and their Residence*), which came into force in December 2016.[5] Reading this law closely, one can notice the following: First, there was a change in the level of language used. The term "*kafala*" and its derivatives have been eliminated from the whole document. They were replaced by the term *wāfid* (newcomer; in Arabic tradition, the "*wāfid*" has to be dealt with generously and honorably), rather than *makfūl*, which if not a positive term, is at least a neutral one that does not carry negative implications, other than that the

5 This is the latest amendment to the law regulating the entry, exit and residence of expatriates in Qatar, administered by the Ministry of Interior. The first was in 1963 (Governing Aliens Entry and Residence in Qatar) and amended in 1973, 1984, 1998, 2002, 2004 and 2009 (see Malaeb 2015).

person is not a citizen of the country. Also the *kafīl* (sponsor) is now called *al-musatqdim* (the one who summons the newcomer; sometimes translated as the recruiter, but this gets confused with recruitment agents so is less used). The "exit visa" was replaced with a "travel notice," but still requiring employer approval and the foreign employee can change employers at the completion of their contract. The *musatqdim* can make objections, but the onus is on them to provide valid reasons before grievance tribunals that have been established. Second, as before, the law is not only about low-skilled workers but it covers all non-nationals coming to Qatar, a matter that makes workers equal to other categories of non-nationals at least on the theoretical level. Third, there is no reference to any Islamic terms per se, a matter which recalls the role of the *waliy al-amr* in determining certain regulations as binding, even if these regulations are not referred to in the Qur'an and Sunnah. Fourth, the law establishes criteria for deportation, reconciliation and penalties, in an attempt to present a balanced position. To what extent the law is balanced or provides protection to the "newcomer" is a debatable matter, but the reform law and other commitments have satisfied the International Labour Organization that in November 2017 withdrew its complaint threatening a commission of inquiry.

More importantly for this discussion, the Qatar authorities have made clear that the *kafala* system has now been abolished in favour of a system that relies solely on the contractual relationship between the employer and employee (see International Labour Office 2017). Although it may be argued that a number of elements of control (and exploitation) over foreign workers have not been abolished, the conceptualization and emphasis on contractual relations is more explicitly *ijāra*, but articulated in secular terms.

4 Conclusion

The Islamic tradition of *kafala*, be it a *kafala* of an orphan, of a stranger, of a needy person, or for a business transaction, seems to be categorically different from the new forms of contemporary practices of *kafala* in the GCC working environment. Still, however, there are certain elements of continuity between the two systems of *kafala*, in the sense of the continuity of the guarantorship of the *kafīl* to the *makfūl*. Traditionally, *kafala* means to transfer the duties of the *makfūl* to the *kafīl*. Thus, if the *makfūl* has to pay money or to deliver a certain commodity, the *kafīl* stands in for the *makfūl* and becomes responsible for the delivery of the money, the commodity or the person. If the *makfūl* does not deliver, the *kafīl* carries the responsibility. The same concept of guarantorship remains in the new *kafala* form, though in a different mode. The *kafil* becomes responsible for the *makfūl* in terms of facilitating and regulating his/her life in the country. This *kafīl-makfūl* relationship is not a business-based contract (where the *kafīl* offers *kafala* in return for certain benefits). It is, on the contrary, a "contract" which is based on voluntary cooperation and social solidarity, where no benefit should be gained by the *kafil*. This principle has a great impact on the Islamic legal discussion of contemporary forms of *kafala*. Many *fatwas*, as those presented in this paper, show clearly that any request or expectation of compensation is not Islamically permissible.

This paper suggests that the new forms of *kafala*, if to be examined from an Islamic perspective, is perhaps better discussed not as a *kafala* per se, but as a *kafala*-cum-*ijāra* system. That is, a contract that combines these two systems of transactions and which is now articulated in a secular manner, as in the new Qatari legislation. Although this suggestion requires more discussion from the perspective of Islamic law, it is sufficient given the scope of this paper to argue that the *kafala* system is a new form of *ijāra* contract that attempts to maintain a customary tradition in the modern world of labour recruitment. To support this understanding, one can note that recent collections of *fatwas* always discuss questions on *kafala* under the chapters of *ijāra* (al-ʿUthaymīn, 1979; al-Dawīsh, nd).

Islamic law provides a theoretical framework that seeks to maintain the rights of all contracting parties in a way that keeps the balance among them, not only as work-partners, but also as human beings with moral commitments towards each other and toward God. Contracts may be the governing criteria in formal business discussions in the courtroom, in case of disputes, but intention and *taqwā* (i.e. real motives and conscience) are the ones to be accounted for before God.

In addition to the religious legal dimension in thinking about modern forms of *kafala*, the role of the state should be also underlined in this context. The state can interfere to regulate economic businesses in a way that should protect the rights of contractors and the needs of the society. Ibn Taymiyyah argues that "Indeed *waliy al-amr* (those in charge of the affairs of Muslims—governors or their appointed representatives) has the right to force certain workers in certain professions to meet people's needs … he would set for them the cost of their work, equivalent to a similar job…" (al-Salūs 2001, 64ff).

To what extent this religious-moral-legal foundation is practiced on the ground offers a different question. Exploitation, fraud and harm observed in the practice of modern forms of *kafala* go against the philosophy of Islamic contracts. It is therefore perhaps incumbent on critics of the contemporary application of *kafala* to invoke and address the nuances of those Islamic ethical principles that should still have resonance within contemporary economic arrangements in Muslim countries such as the Gulf States.

Bibliography

Alajmi, Abdullah Mohammad. 2007. *In the House, Around the House: An Ethnography of Hadar Hadrami Migration to Kuwait*. PhD Thesis. London School of Economics and Political Science.

AlShehabi, Omar Hesham. 2019. "Policing Labour in Empire: the modern origins of the Kafala sponsorship system in the Gulf Arab States." *British Journal of Middle East Studies*, DOI: 10.1080/13530194.2019.1580183.

Amnesty International. November 18, 2013. *The Dark Side of Migration: Spotlight on Qatar's Construction Sector Ahead of the World Cup*. London: Amnesty International.

Amnesty International. 2016. *The Ugly Side of a Beautiful Game*. London: Amnesty International.

Asadov, Ayaz. 2015. "Fatwa Making in the Context of Abnormal Justice: The Case of Migrant Workers in Saudi Arabia." In *Proceedings, Social Justice and Poverty in Muslim World*, International Ilem Summer School, Konya, Turkey, August 1–9, 2015: 43–54.

Bālī, Waḥīd ibn ʿAbd al-Salām. 2013. *Qawānīn al-Sharīʿa al-Islāmiyya al-latī Taḥkum bihā al-Dawla al-ʿUthmāniyya*. Shubra, Egypt: Dār al-Taqwā.

Chidiac, Omaya. 2014. *Migrant Construction and Domestic Workers in the Arab Gulf States: Modern-Day Slaves?* Master of Laws Thesis, Graduate Program in Law. York University Toronto, Ontario.

Coulson, Noel. 1984. *Commercial Law in the Gulf States*. London: Graham & Trotman.

al-Dawīsh, Aḥmad ibn ʿAbd al-Razzāq. *Fatāwā al-Lajna al-Dāʾima li-al-Buḥūth al-ʿIlmiyya wa-al-Iftāʾ*. Vol.14. Riyadh: Dār al-Muʾayyid.

Dito, Mohammed. 2014. "*Kafala*: Foundations of Migrant Exclusion in GCC Labour Markets." In *Transit States: Labour Migration and Citizenship in the Gulf*, edited by Abdulhadi Khalaf, Omar AlShebabi, Adam Hanieh. London: Pluto Press.

Doi, Abdulrahman. 1984. *Shariʿah: the Islamic Law*. London: Ta Ha Publishers.

Fargues, Philippe. 2011. "Immigration Without Inclusion: Non-Nationals in Nation-Building in the Gulf States." *Asian and Pacific Migration Journal* 20(3–4): 273–289.

Fargue, Philippe & Nasrah M. Shah, eds. 2017. *Skillful Survivals: Irregular Migration to the Gulf*. Gulf Research Center. Cambridge: Cambridge University Press.

Foster, Nicholas. 2001. "The Islamic Law of Guarantees." *Arab Law Quarterly*. 16(2): 133–57.

Franz, Elizabeth. 2011. *Exporting Subservience: Sri Lankan Women's Migration for Domestic Work in Jordan*. PhD diss., Department of Anthropology, London School of Economics.

Gardner, A, Pessoa, S. & L. Harkness. 2014. *Labor Migrants and Access to Justice in Contemporary Qatar.* Middle East Center, London School of Economics.

Gardner, Andrew M. 2010. *City of Strangers: Gulf Migration and the Indian Community in Bahrain*. Ithaca: Cornell University Press.

Gulf Times. 2018. "Three arrested for running fake companies, visa trade." March 20, 2018. <http://www.gulf-times.com/story/585889/Three-arrested-for-running-fake-companies-visa-tra#section_178>. Accessed May 27, 2018.

Hamza, Sara. 2015. "Migrant Labor in the Arabian Gulf: A Case Study of Dubai, UAE," *Pursuit—a Journal of Undergraduate Research at the University of Tennessee* 6(1), Article 10. Available at: <http://trace.tennessee.edu/pursuit/vol6/iss1/10/>. Accessed 27 May, 2018.

Human Rights Watch. 2012. *Building a Better World Cup*. New York: Human Rights Watch.

Ibn ʿAbdīn, Muḥammad Amīn. 2003. *Rad al-Muḥtār ʿalā al-Durr al-Mukhtār Sharḥ Tanwīr al-Abṣār*, edited by ʿAdil ʿAbd al-Mawjūd and ʿAlī Muʿawwaḍ. Riyadh: Dār ʿĀlam al-Kutub.

International Labour Office. 2017. *Complaint concerning non-observance by Qatar of the Forced Labour Convention, 1930 (No. 29), and the Labour Inspection Convention, 1947 (No. 81), made by delegates to the 103rd Session (2014) of the International Labour Conference under article 26 of the ILO Constitution*. 329th Session of the Governing Body, Geneva, 9–24 March 2017.

International Labour Organization. 2013. *Tricked and Trapped: Human Trafficking in the Middle East*. Geneva: International Labour Organization.

International Labour Organization. 2013a. *The Living and Working Conditions of Migrant Workers in the Gulf Cooperation Council Countries*. Geneva: International Labour Organization.

Jureidini, Ray. 2014. *Migrant Labour Recruitment to Qatar: Report for Qatar Foundation Migrant Worker Welfare Initiative*. Qatar, Doha: Bloomsbury/Qatar Foundation.

Jureidini, Ray. 2017. "Islamic Ethics and Migrant Labor in Qatar." In *Labor in an Islamic Setting: Theory and Practice*, edited by Toseef Azid and Necmettin Kızılkaya. London: Routledge.

Jureidini, Ray. 2017a. "Transnational Culture of Corruption in Migrant Labor Recruitment." In *Migration Research Leaders' Syndicate: Ideas to Inform International Cooperation on Safe, Orderly and Regular Migration*. Geneva: IOM.

Kakande, Yasin. 2015. *Slave states: the practice of kafala in the Gulf Arab Region*. UK: Zero Books.

Kamrava, Mehran and Zahra Babar. 2012. "Situating Labor Migration in the Persian Gulf." In *Migrant Labor in the Persian Gulf*, edited by Mehran Kamrava and Zahra Babar. New York: Columbia University Press, 1–20.

Kanchana, Radhika. 2018. "Is it the *Kafala* Tradition to Blame for the Exploitative Work Conditions in the Arab-Gulf countries?" In *South Asian Migration in the Gulf: Causes and Consequences*, edited by Mehdi Chowdhury and S. Irudaya Rajan. London: Palgrave Macmillan.

Kapiszewski, Andrzej. 2001. *Nationals and expatriates: Population and Labour Dilemmas of the Gulf Cooperation Council States*. UK: Garnet Publishing Limited.

al-Lajnah al-Dāʾima li-al-Buḥūth al-ʿIlmiyya wa-al-Ifāʿ. 1994. "Istiqdām al-ʿAmāla al-Ajnabiyya wama Yataʿallaq bihā min Aḥkām. *Majallat al-Buḥuth al-Islamıyya* 41. KSA: Al-Riʾāsa al-ʿĀmma li-al-Buḥūth al-ʿIlmiyya wa-al-Iftāʾ, 39–60.

Longva, Anh Nga. 1997. *Walls Built on Sand: Migration, Exclusion and Society in Kuwait*, Oxford: Westview Press.

Lori, Noora. 2012. *Temporary Workers or Permanent Migrants? The Kafala System and Contestations over Residency in the Arab Gulf States*. Paris, Institut Français des Relations Internationales (IFRI), Center for Migrations and Citizenship.

Malaeb, Hanan. 2015. "*Kafala* System and Human Rights: Time for a Decision." *Arab Law Quarterly*, Volume 29, Issue 4: 307–342.

al-Nahhām, Ṣāliḥ. May 2011. "Anwāʿ al-ijāra." *Majallat al-Waʿi al-Islāmi* 550.

Qatar News. 2014. "Ministry punish 51 companies for illegal visa trade." 5 September 2014. <http://www.qatarliving.com/forum/news/posts/ministry-punish-51-companies-illegal-visa-trade>. Accessed 27 May, 2018.

Rodriguez, Andres. 2018. "The *Kafala* System in the GCC." *The Gazelle*, May 15, 2014. <https://www.thegazelle.org/issue/33/features/kefala-system>.

Shimizu, Hideyuki. 1989. *The Philosophy of Islamic Law of Contract, A Comparative Study of Contractual Justice*. IMES working paper 15. Japan: IMES, International University of Japan.

Sophia, Mary. 2015. "Saudi Arabia Clamps Down On Visa Trading." *Gulf Business*. 18 February 2015. <http://gulfbusiness.com/saudi-arabia-clamps-down-on-visa-trading/>. Accessed 8 May, 2018.

al-Sālūs, ʿAlī Aḥmad. 2002. *Mawsūʿat al-Qaḍāyā al-Fiqhiyya al-Muʿāṣira wa-al-Iqtiṣād al-Islāmī*. Bilbīs, Cairo: Maktabat Dār al-Qurʾān.

al-Suyūṭī, ʿAbd al-Raḥmān ibn Abī Bakr ibn Muḥammad. 1983. *Al-Ashbāh wa-al-Naẓāʾir fī al-Furūʿ al-Fiqhiyya*. Beirut: Dar Al-Kotob Al-Ilmiyah.

Tāj, ʿAbd al-Raḥmān. 1995. *Al-Siyāsa al-Sharʿiyya wa-al-Fiqh al-Islāmi*. Al-Azhar Magazine gift, Ramadan issue, 1415 AH. Cairo: al-Azhar Printing House.

al-ʿUthaymīn, Muḥammad ibn Ṣāliḥ. 1979. *Fatāwa Nūr ʿalā al-Darb*. Vol. 9. Riyadh: Muʾassasat al-Shaykh Muḥammad ibn Ṣāliḥ Al-ʿUthaymīn al-Khayriyya.

Vora, Neha. 2013. *Impossible Citizens: Dubai's Indian Diaspora*. Durham: Duke University Press.

Wehr, Hans. 1994. *A Dictionary of Modern Written Arabic*, edited by J. Milton Cowan, 4th edition, Ithaca: Spoken Languages Services.

Online Fatwas <http://fatwa.islamweb.net/fatwa/index.php?page=showfatwa&Option=FatwaId&Id=137333>. <http://fatwa.islamweb.net/fatwa/index.php?page=showfatwa&Option=FatwaId&lang=A&Id=101777. <https://islamqa.info/ar/101220/>.

CHAPTER 7

Normativity of Migration Studies Ethics and Epistemic Community

Sari Hanafi

> Human rights must by definition be universal because they are the rights of every human being, but I also see their universality as possible only through an overlapping cross-cultural consensus, and not by universalizing relativist liberal values.
>
> AN-NAʿIM 2013

∵

1 Introduction

Much scholarship highlights the importance of using indigenous paradigms for social science and of stripping social science from some hegemonic trends influenced by "Western materialistic and colonial ethos." While several schools of thought have pushed in this direction, this approach has some excesses, including positing antagonistic binary categories (tradition/modernity, East/West, immanent nature/transcendent supernatural, reason/faith, rational/irrational, English language/vernacular language, universalism/contextualism, etc.). In previous work, I have criticized the outcome of the Islamization of social science (Hanafi 2016a) and its use of post-colonialism as the only perspective (Hanafi 2016b). In this article, I argue about the conceits of such trends harbored within the intellectual, spiritual, and political configurations of today's debate about social science and ethics.

In the concept paper for the seminar "Migration and Islamic Ethics: Issues of Residence, Naturalisation and Citizenship," organized by the Center for Islamic Legislation and Ethics, the organizers point out the following: "Since the postcolonial era, much of the contemporary literature on the compatibility of Islamic values and "modernization" processes, such as globalization, democracy and citizenship have focused upon Muslims residing in Europe and the US. *The compatibility is often studied under a secularist framework, implying*

© SARI HANAFI, 2020 | DOI:10.1163/9789004417342_008

that many aspects of modernization are incompatible with religious frameworks" (emphasis added). I do not think talking about compatibility under secularist framework helps us to understand the difference between current knowledge production in migration studies and what would be a social science of migration informed by Islamic ethics. In addition, this is very different from the series of questions that were raised in the concept paper, such as, "What are the basic criteria upon which an individual can be considered a "citizen" of a certain country from an Islamic ethical perspective? How similar/different are these criteria from the contemporary legal frameworks adopted by Western countries? Which frameworks seem closer to the Islamic ethical perspective" These questions are well formulated, as they are not juxtaposed in antagonistic polar opposites.

In this article, I will raise three questions to echo this debate: first, can one talk about an epistemic social science community that possesses certain normative stances? If yes, what would these stances be? Would binary categories generated by the two above-mentioned perspectives inform us about the way social science should head to reach a context where Muslims live in the world? I chose the topic of migration as a particularly salient topic in the twenty-first century, which is rife with major waves of forced and voluntary migration, racism, Islamophobia and ethnic diversity. I conducted a content analysis of 74 recent academic articles: 24 articles in English, selected from the library database of the American University of Beirut and 26 in Arabic, selected from Al Manhal database, and 24 in French, mainly from the French journal *Revue Européenne des Migrations Internationales*. I chose two keywords: "migration" and "religion," to locate how religion is viewed in migration studies, and how Islam in Western society becomes an immigrant religion. However, for the articles in Arabic and French, I was obliged to drop the word religion to yield and select more recent articles. It is not assumed that academic journals are singularly important, but they do impact public and policy debates on migration.

In the following section, I will start by defining two moments in social science: the global/universalistic moment and the normative moment. Then I will explain the empirical sample and its "sociological markers" which include some quantitative measures of variables such as discipline, language and institutional affiliation. Finally, I will show the outcome of my content analysis.

1.1 *Two Moments in Social Science*

I distinguish between the global/universalistic moment and the local/normative moment in knowledge production of the social sciences. First, within the global/universalistic moment, this Aristotelian moment of *Reason* insists that social science is like any science and hence needs techniques of conducting research. This requires a nomothetic approach to produce data that will allow for comparability with studies in other contexts. This comparability is the equivalent of laboratory experimentation in the "hard" sciences. The second moment is the local/normative moment where the notion of consciousness, in the words of Hawari Al-Adi (2014), became important. The subjectivity of actors and the influence of culture/religion became compelling, requiring a more idiographic approach that seeks to fully understand the causes of social events, while taking into account the local culture. Of course, normativity can also come from the global and we can draw a more complex matrix that will not be tackled here. For some time, there has been a positivist debate about the social research that hides its normative moment of consciousness. However, since the 1960s it was developed more openly. For instance, the President of the International Sociological Association, Georges Friedmann (1961) insisted on the normative moment, suggesting that true sociologists share fundamental values, and the new sociologist has become "the moralist of industrial society." As we will see in the analysis below, social scientists, at least in migration studies, combine a Weberian ethic of conviction (defined here as liberal, multiculturalist and with a neo-enlightenment framework) and an ethic of responsibility.

2 Sociological Markers of the Articles under Review

This section introduces some of the main characteristics of the sample articles by quantifying the sociological markers of each of them. While 74 articles were submitted to content analysis, only 46 (in Arabic and English) were included in the statistical analysis (French articles were excluded as their analysis was added later). More than the half of the articles are in Arabic and published in journals located inside the Arab region (see Tables 7.1 and 7.2). All but 4 articles are single-authored. Eighty five per cent of them are written by academic faculty, while the remaining are professional researchers (Table 7.3). The authors are mainly sociologists and political scientists, but some are from other disciplines (Table 7.4). More than half the authors are affiliated to institutions located in the Arab World, especially in Algeria and Morocco. The US and Germany are the most important two Western countries (Table 7.5). Most of the articles were published in the last 5 years (Table 7.6).

Most of the articles are largely desktop critiques of existing literature, while a quarter are based on fieldwork, using mainly qualitative methods (except for articles using secondary data, mainly those in Arabic) (Table 7.10). A few are essays without references (Table 7.7). In terms of geographical scope of the article, more than half are case studies about one country, while the rest are dealing either with particular regions or international (Table 7.8.).

Both Arabic and English articles in the sample deal with the different modes of incorporation of migrants. The English articles focus on religion as practice and institutions in host societies, the public perception of migrants and political problems in the host countries. As Martikainen (2014, 78) noted regarding the literature in English language: "In the 2000s, the input of political science in the study of Muslim minorities has become stronger and in this context state–church/religion relations have been seen as significant in explaining differences between immigrant receiving countries and how they handle their immigrant-origin Muslim minorities." The Arabic articles focus more on the causes of migration, policy, refugees and security. More than half of the articles dealing with religion have dealt with Islam as a religion either alone or comparatively with other religions (Table 7.9).

3 Content Analysis of Themes

The analysis will not address the quality of the scholarship, neither in terms of the methodologies that have been deployed, nor on the validity or reliability of data, nor be concerned with the manner in which they provided descriptions of public opinions, the benefits of migrants for sending countries, or their ethnographic accounts. The interest is more about the normative statements and arguments produced by this scholarship, whether as topic choice, starting hypotheses or finalizing conclusions. This is why the analysis shows more topics related to migrants' host societies than to their origin societies.

Generally speaking, most of the articles in my sample combine two Weberian ethics: the ethic of conviction and the ethic of responsibility. Weber explains these two political ethics in his essay on politics as a vocation (Weber 2008). The first, as a free agent, the individual should be able to choose autonomously not only the means for an action, but also the end: "this concept of personality finds its 'essence' in the constancy of its inner relation to certain ultimate 'values' and 'meanings' of life" (Starr 1999, 410). The ethic of conviction thus drives value-rational action, which is defined by Weber as being "determined by a conscious belief in the value for its own sake of some ethical, aesthetic, religious, or other form of behavior, independently of its prospects for success" (ibid.).

While the ethic of conviction "recognizes a given hierarchy of values as the context for a moral endeavor, the ethic of responsibility acknowledges value obligations, but assumes the absence of any given hierarchy of values and the inevitability of value conflict as the context for a moral endeavor" (Starr 1999, 407). This means that the ethic of responsibility focuses on the possible consequences in the application of certain values. Having said that, "an ethic of conviction and an ethic of responsibility are not absolute contrasts but rather supplements, which only in unison constitute a genuine man—a man who can have the calling for politics" (Starr 1999, 408).

The below analysis of the articles concerning migration will inform us as to how researchers have negotiated both their ethic of conviction and responsibility while not necessarily being in conflict with Islamic ethics. By that I mean they do not reject revelation, nor do they make mention of it. I argue here that a great number of researchers in social science who deal with migration issues constitute an *epistemic community* that negotiates with and constantly combines both two ethics. We will see that since the 1990s, there has been a qualitative and quantitative leap in studies concerning immigrants' religion, acknowledging their colonial past and their religious diversity.

The sample of articles shows that they espouse the major long-standing normative claims of liberalism, multiculturalism and the neo-enlightenment. Liberalism is understood as neutrality in the public sphere, the universal application of human rights, the requirement to treat all subjects equally and the prioritization of economic and political liberty (Hansen 2011). Multiculturalism here means the politics of recognition and acknowledgement of cultural specificity and communitarian life (as distinct from assimilation). As for the neo-enlightenment, it is a continuation of the enlightenment as an expansion of its original project of secular-liberal, pluralist, democratic, egalitarian, inclusive, rationalist and humanitarian society. It is more a way of life rather than a political movement (Zafirovski 2010), and a culture where the production of performative, problem-solving ethical orientations supersedes the application of overarching moralities coming from on high (Osborne 2003).

This sample of articles in migration studies demonstrates, as well as combines, the above ethics with the ethics of responsibility that has resulted in favoring migrant-admission policies, especially for refugees in host societies. They call for further integration into host societies and call upon migrants to exert more effort into the integration process.

Paradigmatically, we have witnessed a clear move from the republican paradigm that "forces" the migrant to be assimilated and even integrated to another paradigm that acknowledges the migrants' lived experiences, their diversity, and the role of religion in their day-to-day life. Below I will select from the sample of the 74 articles some quotes that show the normative stand of the scholars. From these articles, three synthesis ones will be highlighted: 1. Peggy Levitt's (2003) "'You Know, Abraham Was the First Immigrant': Religion and

Transnational Migration"; 2. Sophie Bava's (2011) "Migration-Religion Studies in France: Evolving Toward a Religious Anthropology of Movement," and 3. Piché's (2013) "Les théories migratoires contemporaines au prisme des textes fondateurs."

3.1 *Acknowledging the Role of Transitional Religion*

First, it is interesting to note the relative absence of the theme of religion in the French social science literature while there is more in Arabic and much more in English articles. While Chaaban Sakib (2013) was interested in giving us an historical account of how Islam in Africa is a major and crucial factor that shaped Arab-African relations, Peggy Levitt (2003) in her survey of studies published about religion and transnational migration was more interested in the contemporary religion in the diaspora that grew out of diaspora studies in general, as well as in the examination of religion's role in heightened globalization. She argues that there were debates "whether religion functions as a discrete, homogenizing force in its own right or if it is an arena within which individuals assert particularistic, localized identities in the face of globalization" (Levitt 2003, 850). Also other researchers document "the macro-level connections between global religious actors that cross national boundaries... Research on the religious practices of transnational migrants is connected to the literature on global and diasporic religion because transnational migration households, congregations and communities are sites where diasporic, global and transnational religions are created" (Levitt 2003, 857).

The role that religion plays in enabling transnational membership began to be accounted for in early 1990s: "Recent work on global religions brings to light the ways in which [migrants] create international connections that engender universal identities. Because, ... religion is a global societal system as transnational in its operation, as the economy or the nation-state, it is no surprise that migrants use religious institutions to live their transnational lives" (Levitt 2003, 861).

These transnational lives provide the possibility of plurality beyond the community: "Religion and, in particular, religious movements operating in broad geographic contexts, engage in increasingly homogenized forms of worship and organization creating global communities that locals then join. *Followers can choose from an array of membership options which reach far beyond their communities and cultures and transform local religious life*" (Levitt 2003, 862).

Research shows that there is a diversity of lived religious experiences that have their impact not only in the host society but also the society of origin:

> The hybridized or creolized religious beliefs and practices that the migration experience gives rise to emerge where local and global religious influences converge. Global religious institutions shape the transnational migration experience at the same time that migrants chip away at and recreate global religions by making them local and then starting the process anew. Transnational migrants bring particular incarnations of global religion with them, create new forms by combining what they bring with what they encounter, and then reintroduce these ideas, practices, identities, and social capital or what I call social remittances—back to their sending communities. (Levitt 2003, 851)

Some scholars highlight the increase of the impact of religion and religiosity: "there has been an increase not just in practitioners of Islam in Europe, but overall religiosity due to migration" (Martikainen 2014, 79). In the same vein, though with more normative statements about accepting Islam in Europe, Valerie A. Lewis and Ridhi Kashyap argue,

> it is important not to view high levels of religiosity as an anomalous outcome, but as a potential indication of multiple pathways to immigrant adaptation within British society. Because the "actively practicing" Muslim community is diverse in both ethnic and socioeconomic backgrounds, institutional supports which afford equal religious opportunity (for example, easing restrictions on setting up places of worship and community centers) may enable plural forms of religion catering to this diversity to take shape. In the long run, the development of local religious infrastructure, training in government settings that respect religious diversity, and legal changes that put Islam on more equal footing with the state-sanctioned Anglian Church, will nurture a British Islam in healthy public discourse and reduce public hostility against Muslims. (Lewis and Kashyap 2013, 64)

In this same vein, Alexandros Sakellariou criticizes Greek authority for not allowing the construction of mosques in Greece:

> This anti-Islamic political discourse has practical ramifications for Muslim communities in Greece from the moment it influences policy formation: they still enjoy less freedom to practice their religion than those of other faiths, clearly reflected in the lack of a proper place to worship and a cemetery to bury their dead. While they are considered a threat to national identity and to Greek society in general, [...] Such

> anti-Islamic rhetoric has had a profound impact on the Greek Muslim community, precluding them from worshipping in any normal fashion, and making the public resistant to the construction of new mosques. (Sakellariou 2017, 514)

Some scholars report that high religiosity is also a source of civil and political engagement:

> Different dimensions of religiosity affect immigrant attitudes in a number of ways. It was public religiosity such as mosque attendance, rather than internalized religious beliefs, which had the greatest impact on my respondents' integration outcomes. Thus, we need to differentiate between the exoteric (ritualistic/public) and esoteric (spiritual/internalized) domains of religion to accurately evaluate its impact on social and political phenomena. […] The self-narratives of my informants suggested that Muslim immigrant women in Southern California are engaged in two interrelated integration strategies. On the one hand, they are engaged in a selective integration process whereby they become involved in the civic and political institutions and processes of the US, but psychologically and culturally remain distanced from the wider US society. Muslim immigrant women rely on the resources and values of their religious community and the teachings of religious institutions to determine which domains of American society to selectively integrate into and at what level. (Ozyurt 2013, 1617)

Other researchers see high religiosity as a burden (13 articles), not in a normative way, but simply describing public opinion as suspicious of migrants' religiosity or as may lead to difficulty for integration: "Religion can be a highly insulating force, driving a wedge in nations and making migrant assimilation difficult" (Golomski 2016, 451).

3.2 *Institutionalization of Migrants' Religion*

Theorists of post-secularism, Jürgen Habermas, William Connolly and José Casanova, most notably, among others, pointed out a new presence of religion in the public sphere. Martikainen (2014) argues that Casanova relates the emergence of public religion—or "deprivatization"—to "the fact that religious traditions throughout the world are refusing to accept the marginal and privatized role which theories of modernity as well as theories of secularization had reserved for them" (Casanova 1994, 5).

For Habermas, the moral intuitions of faith should be part of public discourse and be allowed to contribute to the common good. For him, the significance of public religion is in developments towards a new, "post-secular" society. Post-secularity has three characteristics: the relativization of European secularism; religious pluralization, whereby churches and other religious organizations increasingly create their own "communities of interpretation" in the public arena; and finally a realization of the permanence of a new, originally Immigrant Other, whose values are traditional and collectivist and strongly associated with religion. Post-secularity, argues Habermas, implies that society remains organized by secular legal institutions and law, which nevertheless are obliged to enable religion to maintain "a public influence and relevance" (Habermas 2008). These new notions within post-secularism will recently have impact on migration scholarship, even if post-secularism, according to Adriana Pabst (2012) is still within the framework of secularism.

Within this framework, Foner and Alba argue that religion as a belief system, institution, and community has played a major role for both first and second generation immigrants and served as a bridge to inclusion in their new society in the US, but not in Europe (Foner and Alba 2008). This position was challenged by Martikainen's (2014) work in Finland showing that Muslim organizations are increasingly seen as locations of active citizenship and as arenas of social integration. In contrast, Bassam Tibi (2010) provides an ethically responsible warning by requesting both Islamic institutions in Germany and the official German authority to work together to overcome a perceived "ethnicity of fear': "This study presented a positive alternative to the negative scenario, namely the promotion of a European Islam as a variety of a civil Islam such as the one that exists in Indonesia. This vision could become reality, if both parties were committed to it. The notion "an ethnicity of fear" has nothing to do with panicking. It is an ethically responsible warning" (Tibi 2010, 150). He also criticizes the German dual system that kept *Jus sanguinis* and the new law of nationality (Tibi 2010). In fact, the issue of who bears responsibility is an important topic that has been dealt with by some scholars. For example, Abdel Wahid Akmeer (2014), while criticizing European policy toward Muslims, insists on a role for Islamic institutions in Europe in organizing the community and facilitating their integration in the host society.

Religious institutions play a role in communitarian solidarity: "Empirical studies have also shown that believers not only possessed a greater ability to emigrate, but a greater desire to do so as well. As the "church of migrants" becomes increasingly just that, the infrastructure of the church itself has expanded abroad, accommodating the needs and wishes of its migrant congregation" (Strielkowski, Bilan, and Demkiv 2016, 2). Peggy Levitt argues beyond the role of institutions by highlighting the contribution of the Birmingham School. This school "explores identity construction and the role of consciousness and subcultures in encouraging collective solidarity at the social margins" (Levitt 2003, 854). One may argue here that the reference to religion and culture is very important in explaining how the two enhance the sense of solidarity in migrant communities, as it was in the Islamic history between migrants (*al-muhājirūn*), but also between them and the hosting community in Medina, later known as the helpers (*al-anṣār*).

4 Post-Coloniality

Some scholars highlight the continuing legacy of empire that has also strongly influenced diaspora studies:

> These explore how discursive practices and identities are constructed and imagined during the colonial, national and post-colonial periods. While this work generally tells us a lot about the transformation of religious life in the immigrant context, it has less to say about the ways in which migration continues to transform sending-country life. It tends to treat migrant and non-migrant religious life as discrete entities rather than as occurring within the same transnational social field, and influencing each other. (Levitt 2003, 854)

Other scholars point out the reason religion has been used by colonial authorities: "While religion often can be used by colonial authorities to control migrants, they also can find these ideologies difficult to manage and manipulate, at times causing serious issues" (Hansen 2011, 881).

Methodologically, many articles in my sample consider the migrant voice in their research and acknowledge the context of the colonial past. In his study of Islam and the North African Second Generation in France, Jean Beaman (2015, 45) confronts the mainstream idea that French Muslims are an obstacle to integration or in some way not compatible with the ideals of a secular French Republic. He conducted an ethnography of 45 Maghrebi immigrants to France. His questions centered on their religious practices, their understanding of their degree of marginalization, and how they view the two as connected, or not. The respondents viewed their religiosity not as in conflict with their French identity, but, rather, as supportive of it. One of the answers supplied Beaman with the title for his article, viewing themselves "As French as Anyone Else."

4.1 *Marginalization and Alienation in Host Society*

There is a major gap between social science production in migration policy and the attitude of the European majority toward migrants. Scholars often develop normative conclusions about the problems that migrants have in host societies and the alienation that migrants feel. Sayad's (1999) concept of "double absent" became very paradigmatical, even though Sayad did not consider the relevance of the question of religion in the context of migration (Bava 2011).

In a country such as France, migration studies moved from a republican stance, encouraging of assimilation, to a more complete acknowledgement of multiculturalism:

> During this period—the late 1980s—which witnessed the beginnings of academic inquiry into multicultural society, sociologists and political scientists took an interest in the religion of the "immigrant" Other. These were the first studies of Islam in suburban France in hostels and prayer rooms; furthermore, they comprised the assumption that immigrants needed to be able to practice their religion in decent conditions and to experience their cultures fully within French society. [However], they did not analyze immigrants as full-fledged protagonists of their religion, nor did they observe the diversity of religious options available because of migration or simply on the transnational religious market. One might consider that sociologists made too strong an assumption that migration was permanent and, therefore, saw religion as one of many transplanted values that would (or must) adapt to the French secular model. (Bava 2011, 499)

Bava goes on in describing a paradigm shift:

> Many studies already initiated by anthropologists by the end of the 1990s have opened the way to learning about Islam as it is experienced (the conditions in which *halal* meat is produced, how al-ʿEid al-Kabīr festival is organized in French urban space [...], the meaning believers invest in their religious practices [...], and the links between economic networks and religion [...]. What motivates these researchers is no longer an approach to integration, but the objective of actual knowledge of migrants' Islam by exploring elements of continuity between the migrants' countries of origin and those to which they migrate." (Bava 2011, 499)

In Germany, debate has revolved around the violence against migrant communities. Schrempf criticizes the recent wave of hate crimes, and calls for more contact between migrant and host communities in order to effectively combat xenophobia (Schrempf 2001).

Other Arab authors discuss secret/illegal migration, which is driven by unbearable economic conditions, the apparent economic and social ease of those who migrated, the revenues of illegal migration, the trust in illegal migration networks, and most importantly the restrictions on legal migration. ʿAbd al-Qādir Muḥammad Wild-Dādā provides an example of the French government's consideration of migrants as the scapegoat of its internal problems, like unemployment, crime, drugs and even terrorism, while neglecting to credit the economic contributions of migrants. He discusses the dangerous public discourse of intolerance, discrimination, terrorism, and racism, which entail more restrictions on legal migration. However, he did not study the association of religion with these discourses or with terrorism. He proposes several solutions, including dealing with migrants not as a commodity needed for the economy, or as a source of trouble and as victims of crime networks, but as a source of economic growth. He went so far as to call for the erasure of borders (al-Dāh 2013).

Another Arab author, Hala al-Hifnāwī, considers that the failure of integration of the Muslim minority of Europe is one of the factors driving extremism, though there are several other factors (unemployment, economic and political marginalization, the absence of moderate religious education, the support of European countries of Israel and the United States war in Iraq). The solution, according to the author, is to pursue integration policies that balance the Muslim identity of migrants, and the European identity of the host population, and to stop the discriminatory practices in Europe against Muslims. The author suggests that any imbalance between the different identities leads to extremism. That is why she suggests policies that take into consideration the balancing of identities of Muslim minorities in Europe (al-Hafnawi 2015, 4).

In a review of the Hashem Fayad's book *The Immigration of Labor from Maghreb to Europe: Netherlands as a Model* by, Abdelkader Latrach (2015) notes that there has been an increase in research interest in the Arab World on international immigration. According to him, the rise in international migration is due to the expansion of migratory patterns across the world, and the emergence of new societal, demographic, cultural, legislative and economic problems in the receiving countries as well as the sending countries. The author assesses the field, shedding light on what constitutes an immigration study: an historical context of the emergence of international migrations, an analysis of its effects on the reality of the receiving countries, their population, social, cultural and security dimensions, the study of the relationship between migrations, and the development of brain drain. Latrach highlights the importance of the analysis of the historical context of the phenomenon and the demographic aspect of migration, yet he criticizes the book, stating that the colonial history does not solely dictate the direction of immigration, but the phenomenon of the globalization of international immigration flows, the strategies of groups and individuals, and institutional differences also play a major role in the formation of those directions. The book also considered the integration of Moroccans into Dutch society as weak, but this is not due to the multiplicity of organizations of Moroccans, but to the lack of diversity in their areas and the absence of initiatives to open up to Dutch culture and to bring Moroccan culture closer to Dutch culture. In addition, integration is also related to the vision of the other, be it in educational programs, media, political party programs or social policies, or political discourse related to issues of security and identity. Here we see both the author of the review and the book consider that the Moroccan institutions (community centers abroad and the administration in charge of dealing with emigrants) are mainly responsible for the lack of integration. Also, the book considers that one of the central issues raised by international migrations is the rise of racism. This racism is due to growing hostile attitudes towards immigrants in general and Arab and Muslim immigrants in particular, and has led to the emergence of a declared "Islamophobia." This situation coincides with the contraction of employment opportunities in the European labour markets and the decline in social policies, which leads to the raising of political slogans hostile to Arab immigrants based on the difficulty of integration of Arabs and Muslims in European societies—thus creating the problem of the integration of immigrants one of the priorities of governments in many European countries. Finally, the review article discusses the positive role of immigrants on the sending country. The author discusses how some aspects of religiosity make difficult the integration and increases racism in the Netherlands (Latrach 2015).

Another author, Mohamad Saidi was interested in the question of the integration of young Belgians of Moroccan origin into Belgian society after the attacks in Paris. According to this author, these young people have failed academically, are unemployed, and many live as part of fractured groups isolated from both their parents' culture and the wider society around them. They suffer from issues of social stigma, social exclusion, religious extremism, identity rupture, and academic failure. The article's main argument is that the phenomenon of poverty, marginalization, policies of exclusion and discrimination, and even the dominant Islamic religious culture there (which tends in some respects to extremism and the rejection of the other), are not sufficient to explain the rebellious tendencies and non-integration that drive them to religious extremism. They suffer from an identity based confusion and an insecurity which leads them to create fragile social and societal affiliations, thus leaving them unable to satisfy their feelings of insecurity and dissatisfaction, and therefore also unable to belong to the Belgian society. The greater the sense of identity confusion caused by self-isolation or social exclusion, the less plausible is the development of values of pluralism, coexistence and the integration of these young people into Belgian society (Saadi 2017).

In my sample, few Arab scholars were interested in the situation of migrants/ refugees in the Arab world. ʿĀshūr Raḥūma wrote about refugees in South Darfour who suffer major human rights violations due to governmental and organizational failures to accommodate their basic human rights (Raḥūma 2016). Nabīl al-Sahlī made similar statements about the reason why Lebanese authorities treated the Palestinians from Syria poorly (al-Sahlī 2014). In the same vein, in his article "South-South Migration and Security Risks: Political Islam and Violent Extremism in the Shadow of Globalisation in Bangladesh" Hasan Mubashar argues how migration to Saudi Arabia by many Bangladeshis led to the creation of ISIS in Bangladesh, but he also argues against a mere security solution, and calls for "a long soft campaign to counter propaganda of Islamists who undermine state and peace. The government also needs to scale up countering messages for violent extremism coming through the Internet and social media" (Mubashar 2017, 312).

Other scholars call for investing in Islamic rules and regulations, as they constitute "a valuable source for protection of the rights of refugees, migrants and asylum seekers. In addition to contractual responsibilities, they could serve as a faith-based guarantor of the rights of refugees, particularly women and children. Further exploration of respected Islamic sources could result in new mechanisms in this regard" (Rahaei 2009, 4).

4.2 *Against Security and Selectivity Paradigms*

Although the theme of radicalization in Europe and North American was present in many articles (12 articles), many scholars argued against the securitization of migration. Falco criticized some extreme statistical studies that argue against receiving refugees and migrants from Islamic countries and point out that more "radical" individuals in the Muslim community are less likely to migrate than the more moderate (Falco and Rotondi 2016). Other scholars argue that closed borders will not end the illegal migration and criticize the reason why the European Union deals with illegal migration as a security problem and links it to terrorism and crime. This emphasis, according to him, should shift from the problem of helping the southern Middle East in solving economic, political, and social problems (Farijeh and Farijeh 2018; Haroush 2015).

For some, there is no need for help from Europe; changes are already occurring locally: "the Arab Spring revolutions have succeeded in bringing political change. This change can open the door to political freedom and economic prosperity that can put an end to Arab migration, especially among young people" (Abdul-Rahman 2013, 245).

All migration policies of the twentieth century are based on a postulate considered immutable: immigration is a privilege and not a right (Piché 2013). Many scholars have challenged that and the selectivity introduced by the liberalism and logic of a globalized labour market (e.g. Kabbanji 2011). With the increased number of asylum seekers, many scholars argue for burden sharing between all countries. Four prominent French scholars in a report delivered to Directorate General for International Cooperation and Development of the French Ministry of Foreign and European Affairs call for multilateralism (Badie et al. 2008). Generally speaking, the journal of *Revue Européenne des Migrations Internationales* has adopted a human rights approach against the security and selectivity paradigms. Many articles in this journal have provided excellent fieldworks about the frontier zones that become places of police repression against refugees who wait a long time to be granted refuge (e.g. Agier 2014). A special issue of this journal was about migrant minors. For instance, Jacqueline Bhabha argues,

> Whether they are asylum seekers, independent migrants, trafficked youth or children smuggled for family reunion purposes, or whether their status is unclear (between categories or within several), all young migrants need protection and assistance of one sort or another—safe accommodation, and protection from exploitation, from the risks of criminalization, from deprivation of food and medical care at a minimum. (Bhabha 2014, 37)

It is noteworthy that this journal is published by the Migrinter, a research laboratory specialized in international migration, hosted by the Maison des Sciences de l'Homme et de la Société de Poitiers (France). Adopting the "migration project" as a paradigm that privileges to present migrant voices and their points of view, this research center was for a long time consulting with the Ministry of Social Affairs (the French institution which deals with the questions of migration and naturalisation) and the Institute of High Studies of Defense. Its researchers have kept their critical edge while conducting some policy studies. At the European level, the recent EU report *Research on*

Migration: Facing Realities and Maximising Opportunities (King and Lulle 2016) displays a summary of the findings of six projects funded by EU. All push for more integration of migrants and refugees in European space, with more pluralism and increased admissions.

5 Academics as Activists

Some members of this epistemic community have become active in volunteering to help refugees learn languages and apply to universities. Holmes and Castaneda point out that anthropologists and Syrian refugees in Germany have begun ethnographic experiments on verbal and musical dialogue, weekly socializing in a neighborhood café, dialogical courses in the department of anthropology involving Syrian refugees and university students, activism to push the university to admit Syrian refugees, and collaborative writing and publishing to participate in the war of position more actively together. In addition, many of the faculty and students volunteer regularly in housing, health care, registration, and other services for refugees. These efforts have complemented other forms of horizontal political solidarity that have emerged (Holmes and Castaneda 2016). The conference that was organized at the American University of Beirut in November 2017 witnessed many initiatives conducted by the faculty in receiving refugees. Indeed, there is a long tradition of connection between academics and religious scholars who championed the cause of immigrants. One example would be clergymen Father Jacques Ghys of the missionary order of the White Fathers who established an academic journal in early 1950s *Hommes et Migrations* ("Men and Migration") and who created Amana (Assistance Morale Aux Nord-Africains), an association for aid and mutual assistance for North Africans with a focus on literacy training.

5.1 *The Counter-Paradigm*

So far, I have argued that there is a sort of mainstream epistemic community that combines the ethic of conviction with responsibility and that normatively supports acknowledging the migrants' causes. However, some exceptions can be found. Some conservative scholars who call for no innovation in the *fiqh* related to economic matters when migrants are in non-Muslim majority countries (Bardaweel 2016). For example, some Lebanese scholars (and politicians) have used the fear of permanent Palestinian settlements as a scarecrow, while declaring both their support for Palestine, and opposition to imperialism and Zionism. In the language of the Lebanese novelist Elias Khoury "they love Palestine and hate the Palestinians." It is as if they were telling us that the liberation of Palestine was possible only through the further debilitation and humiliation of the Palestinian refugees.

6 Conclusion

When migration studies scholars are normative, they combine the Weberian ethics of conviction and of responsibility in order to make sound social/political judgments. This combination leads to a refusal of positions that are too permissive in the sense that any means are justifiable to secure particular ends (for example, refuting overemphasis on the security approach in relation to migration). This combination often puts social scientists in a dilemma that sometimes encodes paradoxes: protecting local employment v/s open borders for refugees/migrants; multiculturalism v/s some migrant cultural habits that contradict some basic principles of human rights. This cannot be discussed by simply invoking famous dichotomies of scholars of Islamization of social science or post-colonial studies (community v/s individual, tradition v/s. modernity, revelation v/s reason, history v/s present time, central v/s periphery, etc.). This is only possible by bringing in some complexity, nuance, precision and caution and by constructing a more appropriate framework for understanding the mix of micro and macro that characterizes the global situation today.

Coming back to what I posit in the introduction, I distinguished between the global/universalistic moment and normative moment in social science. I argue here that for religious science it has similarly two moments which requires its own technics of interpreting revealed text and religious tradition. While I expect mainly a *separation* of methods for the first moment, I don't for the local/normative moment. I expect collaboration between social science and religious ethics as each can be informed by the other. Social scientists combine ethics of conviction (defined here as liberal, multiculturalist and with neo-enlightenment framework) and ethics of responsibility, while Islamic ethicists would provide what would be a primordial constant in Islam that should be taken into account in this normative moment. These different ethics will enter into tension that should be resolved through dialog, mutual learning and beyond a mere legalism or rationalism. Here the connection between social scientists and religious scholars are very important. Both should be allied to developing a thought that takes into account the benefit of their society and balances determinism and utopia. Social scientists need to learn about people's traditions in order to understand their spirituality, emotion and habitus, and religious scholars need to understand how people perceive what is good and bad in everyday life and their *ʿurf* (customs) in order to establish *fiqh al-wāqiʿ* (social and political jurisprudence that changes in accordance with the external reality).[1] In this regard, Abbas Barzegar provides in this volume an excellent example how Muslim humanitarianism that was developed through "synthesis between living traditions of *aklhāq*, *adab*, and *fiqh* in Islamic terms as well as a type of 'practical theology' in Western terms." He argues:

> Muslim humanitarianism can inform emerging Islamic legal and ethical approaches to civic engagement, democratic culture, and global citizenship by virtue of the fact that existing custom (*ʿurf*) of Muslims in these spaces has now come to prioritize humanistic principles that transcend national, ethnic, sectarian, and ideological agendas. At the same time, these practices are thoroughly fused with the larger aims and objectives (*maqasid*) of Islam and the Shariʿa and thereby have become part of the customary understanding of Islamic truth by millions of Muslims around the world.

As discussed above, our results show that, in my sample, scholars support the claim of migrants for keeping the specificity of their religious differences and acknowledging their biographies and histories and pace of integration. Instead of being praised, however, there has been a trend of Don Quixote phantasmagoric battles with these scholars, taxed by many postcolonial and knowledge Islamization scholars for being inattentive to the lived experience of Muslims, including their spiritual life and their colonial past. Having said that, it is time also for social science, mainly, but not only, in the West, to put more effort into accounting for the voice of the migrant community and to read and to cite from the research produced in the South and in local languages.

I argue here, at least in regard to migration studies, that the requested new paradigms are there. The real discussion would be how to reconcile the competing values of liberalism, multiculturalism and neo-enlightenment with local culture and religious ethics. This cross-fertilization between both sets makes migration studies robust. Basically, yet with many exceptions, the literature calling for the Islamization of social knowledge does not deliver many tools for connecting social science with Islamic ethics. While focusing so much on the primary assumptions concerning secularist, materialistic or utilitarian biases, they forgot that the main mission of social science is being critical, i.e.

1 In the text of Qaradawi who coins the concept of fiqh al-wāqiʿ, this concept is defined as an approach "based on a scientific and objective study of the nature [of a phenomenon], a study that reveals all its dimensions and elements, [clarifies] their advantages and disadvantages, and [highlights] the relevant influencing factors" (Al-Qaradawi 1999, p. 23).

it has the capacity to question the current social and political powers from any intentional and unintentional bad consequences. One may look at the trajectory of migration studies, as it went from encouraging assimilation to acknowledging diversity and lived-experience, instead of trying to untie social scientists' shoelaces every minute, hoping for them to trip. The engagement with social science should be by providing a critique, rather than a criticism. This means that instead of trying to challenge its production based on a set of independently defined values and categories, one is to proceed immanently to different migration theories, from within their own terms and categories in order to show how they relate to one another, and whether they are mutually consistent. Good critique should be empirical and not based on conspiracy theories. In the time of post-truth discourses, especially in social media, critical sciences have been dismissed as ideological, useless and therefore unworthy of public funding (Piovani 2017). Now should be the time for consolidation, rather than dividing academics between universalists vs contextualists. In the direction of consolidation, one may find common ground with contemporary reformists such as Ali Shariati, Abdolkarim Soroush, and Abdullahi Ahmed An-Naʿim who called for Islamic liberalism (Mir 2017).

Appendix

TABLE 7.1 Number and percentage of articles by language

	N	%
Arabic	26	56.5
English	20	43.5
Total	46	100.0

TABLE 7.2 Geographical regions of the journals

		N	%
Valid	Arab World	26	59.1
	Abroad	18	40.9
	Total	44	100.0
Missing	System	2	
Total		46	

TABLE 7.3 Types of institutional affiliation

		N	%
Valid	University	35	85.4
	Research center	6	14.6
	Total	41	100.0
Missing	Total	5	
Total		46	

TABLE 7.4 The discipline of the first author

		N	%
Valid	Sociology	13	30.2
	Anthropology	3	7.0
	History	2	4.7
	Communication/Media	1	2.3
	Political Sciences/IR	12	27.9
	Literature	3	7.0
	Other	9	20.9
	Total	43	100.0
Missing	System	3	
Total		46	

TABLE 7.5 Country of the affiliated institutions

		N	%
	United States	7	17
	Algeria	6	14
	Morocco	5	12
	Germany	3	7
	Canada	2	5
	Libya	2	5
	Palestine	2	5
	Switzerland	2	5
	The United Arab Emirates	2	5
	Bahrain	1	2

TABLE 7.5 Types of institutional affiliation (cont.)

		N	%
	Bangladesh	1	2
	Egypt	1	2
	France	1	2
	Greece	1	2
	Italy	1	2
	Lebanon	1	2
	Mauritania	1	2
	Poland	1	2
	Sudan	1	2
	Tunisia	1	2
	Total	42	100
Missing		4	8.7

TABLE 7.6 Year of publication

Year	N	%
2017	6	13
2016	10	22
2015	10	22
2014	5	11
2013	8	17
2012	3	7
2011	2	4
2010	1	2
2003	1	2
Total	46	100

TABLE 7.7 Types of articles

		N	%
	Fieldwork	11	26.8
	Critical of existing Literature	24	58.5
	Essay	6	14.6
	Total	41	100.0
	Missing	5	
Total		46	

TABLE 7.8 Geographical scope of the articles

	N	%
Local	21	54
Regional	7	18
International	9	23
Comparative	2	5
Total	39	100
Missing	7	
Total	46	

TABLE 7.9 Frequency of keywords by language

	Language		
	Arabic	English	Total
Voluntary migration	0	7	7
Remittances	0	1	1
Sexuality	0	1	1
Refugees	6	1	7
Human trafficking	3	0	3
War and ethnic/ international conflict	2	1	3
Refugee camps	1	0	1
Crime	1	0	1
Social conflict	2	2	4
Border	3	0	3
Perception	0	4	4
Internal migration	2	1	3
Impact of host society	0	2	2
Security	5	2	7
Impact of place of origin	2	3	5
Family	0	1	1
Policy	7	1	8
Gender	2	0	2
Causes of migration	12	2	14
Labour market	2	0	2
Demography	0	3	3
Cultural effect	1	3	4
Mode of incorporation	5	4	9

TABLE 7.9 Frequency of keywords by language (cont.)

	Language		
	Arabic	English	Total
Political problems	1	4	5
Psychological problems	0	2	2
Ethnicity	0	2	2
Racism	0	1	1
Religion	4	6	10
Total	23	18	41

PERCENTAGES AND TOTALS ARE BASED ON RESPONDENTS.

TABLE 7.10 Methods used (multiple responses)

	N	Percent
Using existing data	17	33.30%
Content analysis	10	19.60%
Multiple methods	7	13.70%
In-depth interview	6	11.80%
Survey	5	9.80%
Ethnography	3	5.90%
Observation	2	3.90%
Focus groups	1	2.00%
Total	51	100.00%

Acknowledgements

I would like to thank Alaa Khaled and Michael Avanzato for their help in analyzing the articles of the sample and Azzam Tomeh for his comments.

Bibliography

Abdul-Rahman, Iyyas. 2013. "Migration from the Arab region after the "Arab Spring" and the Global Economic Crisis (al-hijra min mantiqa al-arabiyya baad al-rabi' al-arabi wa al-azma al-iqtisadiyya al-alamiyya)." *'Umrān lil-'Ulūm al-Ijtimā'īyah wa-al-Insānīyah* 3(1): 243–48.

Adi, Hawari al-. 2014. *Cognitive Gaps in the Arab Social Science*. Future of the Sociology in the Arab World. Beirut: Center for Arab Unity Studies.

Agier, Michel. 2014. “Parcours Dans Un Paysage Flottant de Frontières.” *Revue Europeenne Des Migrations Internationales* 30(2): 13–23.

Al-Qaradawi, Yusuf. 1999. *The Lawful and the Prohibited in Islam*. Indianapolis, IN, USA: American Trust Publications.

An-Naʿim, Abdullahi Ahmed. 2013. “Editorial Note: From the Neocolonial “Transitional” to Indigenous Formations of Justice.” *International Journal of Transitional Justice* 7(2): 197–204. doi: <https://doi.org/10.1093/ijtj/ijt012>.

Badie, Bertrand, Rony Brauman, Emmanuel Decaux, Guillaume Devin, and Catherine Wihtol de Wenden. 2008. “Pour Un Autre Regard Sur Les Migrations: Construire Une Gouvernance Mondiale.” Paris: Direction générale de la coopération internationale et du développement du ministère des Affaires étrangères et européennes. <https://www.diplomatie.gouv.fr/IMG/pdf/Etude_gouvernance_globale_migrations.pdf>.

Bardaweel, Shawqi. 2016. “The Ijtihad of the Conscious Integration of Migrants Concerning Financial and Economic Transactions (nawazel al-indimaj al-waaʿI lli-muhajireen fima yataʿalaq bial-muʿamalat al-maliyya wa al-iqtisadiyya).” *Majallat al-Dirāsāt al-Tārīkhīyah wa al-Ijtimāʿīyah* 9: 120–29.

Bava, Sophie. 2011. “Migration-Religion Studies in France: Evolving Toward a Religious Anthropology of Movement.” *Annual Review of Anthropology* 40(1): 493–507. <https://doi.org/10.1146/annurev-anthro-081309-145827>.

Beaman, Jean. 2015. “As French as Anyone Else: Islam and the North African Second Generation in France.” *International Migration Review* 1(50): 41–69.

Bhabha, Jacqueline. 2014. “Moving Children: Lacunae in Contemporary Human Rights Protections for Migrant Children and Adolescents.” *Revue Européenne Des Migrations Internationales* 30(1): 35–57. <https://doi.org/10.4000/remi.6747>.

Falco, Chiara, and Valentina Rotondi. 2016. “The Less Extreme, the More You Leave: Radical Islam and Willingness to Migrate.” *World Development* 88 (December): 122–33. doi: <https://doi.org/10.1016/j.worlddev.2016.07.017>.

Farijeh, Ahmad, and Lidmiyya Farijeh. 2018. “The Current Mechanisms By the European Union to Face the Illegal Immigration (al-Aliyyat al-moʿtamada min qibal al-itihad al-urubi limuwajahit al-hijra gheir al-sharʿiyya).” *Revue Mofakir*, no. 12: 1–24. doi: <https://doi.org/10.12816/0021858>.

Golomski, Casey. 2016. “Religion and Migration: Cases for a Global Material Ethics.” *African Studies* 75(3): 449–62. doi: <https://doi.org/10.1080/00020184.2016.1193379>.

Hafnawi, Hala al-. 2015. “Born in Europe: The Third Generation of Muslim Immigrants (Wolida Fi Uroba: Al-Jil Al-Thalith Mina Al-Muhajirine All-Muslimine).” *Itijahat Al-Ahdath* 7: 1–4.

Hanafi, Sari. 2016a. “Islamization and Indigenization of the Social Sciences: A Critical Appraisal (Islameh Wa Ta’sil Al-Ulum Al-Ijtimaiyya: Dirasat Fi Baad Al-Ishkaliyyat).” *Al-Mustaqbl Al-Arabi* 451: 45–64.

Hanafi, Sari. 2016b. "Global Knowledge Production in the Social Sciences: A Critical Assessment." *Sociologies in Dialogue* 2 (August): 16.

Hansen, Randall. 2011. "The Two Faces of Liberalism: Islam in Contemporary Europe." *Journal of Ethnic and Migration Studies* 37(6): 881–97.

Haroush, Nour al-Dine. 2015. "Academic Attention to the Phenomenon of Illegal Immigration: An Analytical Study Through Some of the Algerian University Letters (Al-Ihtimam Al-Acadimi Lizahirat Al-Hijra Gheir Al-Shariyya: Dirassa Tahliliyya Min Khilal Ba'id Al-Rasa'il Al-Jami'iyya)." *Majalit Kuliyyet Al-Iqtisad Wa Ulum Al-Siyyasiyyah* 16(2): 151–72.

Holmes, Seth, and Heide Castaneda. 2016. "Representing the "European Refugee Crisis" in Germany and beyond: Deservingness and Difference, Life and Death." *American Ethnologist* 43(1): 12–24.

Kabbanji, Lama. 2011. "Vers une reconfiguration de l'agenda politique migratoire en Afrique de l'Ouest." *Études internationales* 42(1): 47–71. <https://doi.org/10.7202/045877ar>.

King, Russell, and Aija Lulle. 2016. *Research on Migration: Facing Realities and Maximising Opportunities. A Policy Review*. Brussels: Directorate-General for Research and Innovation Open and inclusive Societies.

Latrach, Abdelkader. 2015. "Emigration of Maghreb People: Holland as a Case Studies (Al-Hijra Al-Magharibiyya Al-Kharijiyya: Holanda Namuzajan)." *Umrān Lil-ʿUlūm Al-Ijtimāʿīyah Wa-Al-Insānīyah* 3(12): 173–80.

Levitt, Peggy. 2003. "'You Know, Abraham Was Really the First Immigrant': Religion and Transnational Migration." *The International Migration Review* 37(3): 847–73.

Lewis, Valerie, and Ridhi Kashyap. 2013. "Piety in a Secular Society: Migration, Religiosity, and Islam in Britain." *International Migration* 51(3): 57–66.

Martikainen, Tuomas. 2014. "Muslim Immigrants, Public Religion and Developments towards a Post-Secular Finnish Welfare State." *The Nordic Welfare State* 8(1): 78–105.

Mir, Suheel Rasool. 2017. "Ali Shariati, Forgotten Sociologist of Islam." *Global Dialog: International Sociological Association Newsletter*, 2017.

Mubashar, Hasan. 2017. "South–South Migration and Security Risks: Political Islam and Violent Extremism in the Shadow of Globalisation in Bangladesh." *India Quarterly* 73(3): 312–26.

Osborne, Thomas. 2003. "What Is Neo-Enlightenment? Human Rights Culture and Juridical Reason." *Journal of Human Rights* 2(4): 523–30.

Ozyurt, Saba Senses. 2013. "The Selective Integration of Muslim Immigrant Women in the United States: Explaining Islam's Paradoxical Impact." *Journal of Ethnic and Migration Studies* 39(10): 1617–37. doi: <https://doi.org/10.1080/1369183X.2013.833691>.

Pabst, Adrian. 2012. "The Secularism of Post-Secularity: Religion, Realism, and the Revival of Grand Theory in IR." *Review of International Studies* 38(5): 995–1017.

Piché, Victor. 2013. "Les théories migratoires contemporaines au prisme des textes fondateurs, Las teorías migratorias contemporáneas vistas a través el prisma de los textos fundadores." *Population* 68(1): 153–78. doi: <https://doi.org/10.3917/popu.1301.0153>.

Rahaei, Saeid. 2009. "The Rights of Refugee Women and Children in Islam." *Forced Migration Review* 1: 4–4.

Raḥūma, ʿĀshūr. 2016. "The Phenomenon of Migration in Darfur Province (Zaheret al-hijra fi Iqlim al-Darfour)." *al-Majallah al-ʿArabīyah lil-ʿUlūm al-Ijtimāʿīyah* 117(3860): 1–28.

Saadi, Mohamad. 2017. "Lost and Fractured Identities : The Third Generation Immigrant in Belgium: A Case Study of the Borgerhout Neighborhood in Antwerp." *ʿUmrān lil-ʿUlūm al-Ijtimāʿīyah wa-al-Insānīyah* 15: 27–53.

Sahlī, Nabīl al-. 2014. "The Palestinians of Syria and the Tragedy of Refuge and Forced Displacement (al-falastiniyyon fi suria wa trajidia al-lojou' wa nouzouh al-qasri)." *Majallat al-Dirāsāt al-Filastīnīyah* 25(97): 139–49.

Sakellariou, Alexandros. 2017. "Fear of Islam in Greece: Migration, Terrorism, and "Ghosts" from the Past." *Nationalities Papers* 45(4): 511–23. doi: <https://doi.org/10.1080/00905992.2017.1294561>.

Sakib, Chaaban Dakhil Saed Amer Bin. 2013. "The Arabic and Islamic Immigration and Its Influence on the African Coasts (Al-Hijrat Al-Arabiyya Wa Islamiyya Wa Atharuha Fi Al-Sawahel Al-Ifriqiyya)." *Al-Majallah Al-ʿArabīyah Lil-ʿUlūm Al-Ijtimāʿīyah* 2(3): 305–26.

Sayad, A. 1999. *La Double Absence. Des Illusions de l'émigré Aux Souffrances de L'immigré.* Paris: Ed. du Seuil.

Schrempf, Mona. 2001. "Migration–Religion–Integration: Buddhistische Vietnamesen Und Hinduistiche Tamilen in Deutschland. By Martin Baumann." *Journal of Global Buddhism* 2(0): 119–22.

Starr, Bradley E. 1999. "The Structure of Max Weber's Ethic of Responsibility." *Journal of Religious Ethics* 27(3): 407–434.

Strielkowski, Wadim, Yuriy Bilan, and Oleh Demkiv. 2016. "Religion and International Migration: A Case Study of Ukraine." *Religions* 7(6): 64. doi: <https://doi.org/10.3390/rel7060064>.

Tibi, Bassam. 2010. "Ethnicity of Fear? Islamic Migration and the Ethnicization of Islam in Europe." *Studies in Ethnicity and Nationalism* 10(1): 126–157.

Weber, Max. 2008. "Politics as Vocation." In *Max Weber's Complete Writings on Academic and Political Vocations*, edited by J. Dreijmanis. New York: Algora Publishing.

Zafirovski, Milan. 2010. *The Enlightenment and Its Effects on Modern Society*. Springer Science & Business Media.

CHAPTER 8

How do Muslim States Treat their "Outsiders"?: Is Islamic Practice of Naturalisation Synonymous with *Jus Sanguinis*?

Radhika Kanchana

1 Naturalisation Practice in Muslim States Today

Aḥmad al-Ṭayyib, the Grand Imam of the renowned Al-Azhar Sunni Arab institution of learning in Egypt, made four points at the Islamic-Christian conference in Cairo (28 Feb–1 Mar 2017). This came to be called the *Al-Azhar Declaration,* which asserted that Islam is compatible with religious pluralism. He upheld the principle of equality of rights and duties for both Muslims and non-Muslims within a "national constitutional state." He insisted that the concept of "citizenship" was part of the foundations of Islam, citing reference to the Prophet's Constitution of Medina in the first Muslim society.

The *Al-Azhar Declaration* challenges the prevailing popular perception that Muslim countries are relatively closed societies, especially in relation to non-Muslims in their territory. Islam's principles supposedly do not live easily with contemporary international law and norms that demand, for example, more secular and egalitarian values and institutions. The present paper concerns the treatment of "the other" by focusing on the practice of naturalisation in states with majority Muslim population or states that define themselves as Islamic. How states deal with foreigners who eventually become residents is an important question in the discussion on ethics relating to migration. This preliminary research is part of a broader project to empirically explore the subject. It concerns the practice of Muslim states on naturalisation since the mid-twentieth century, to see whether the *Jus sanguinis* citizenship principle is generally a "by default" occurrence, or if they show other nuanced arrangements in law and policy.

The focus is on *Jus sanguinis* to ascertain the potential access of foreigners, especially non-Muslim, to acquire citizenship and ensuing rights in Muslim countries. Individuals are granted citizenship of a nation either *Jus soli* (those that are born there and automatically acquire the status), or *Jus sanguinis where one or both parents are citizens.* Alternatively, they can acquire citizenship by a deliberate process—through naturalisation. Naturalisation is a key mechanism by which a state either facilitates or blocks the incorporation of new candidates for citizenship. Thus, the content of the national provisions to grant access to naturalisation is important. A society's degree of access to citizenship shows its level of inclusiveness or exclusiveness. *Jus soli* and *Jus sanguinis* are the two dominant regimes that inform states' choice in granting citizenship. *Jus soli* ascribes citizenship automatically to everyone born on the territory: the USA is a primary example of a liberal *Jus soli*. *Jus sanguinis* ascribes citizenship automatically to individuals born to parent/s that are citizens of the state. It is also known as the citizenship "by descent," meaning via blood or ethnic affiliation. Many states follow a combination of the two, roughly termed as *Jus domicile*. *Jus sanguinis* becomes particularly relevant when the naturalisation criteria over-emphasize this principle for the allocation of citizenship. In effect, this restricts state membership with the stress on ties before birth.

I approach naturalisation and the access to citizenship in this paper as the progressive process for an individual to belong and to consolidate rights in the local society where he/she resides, irrespective of prior or current affiliations. The concept of citizenship, broadly constituting three key dimensions namely legal status, participation and membership of an individual in a political community, is itself far from frozen. It is evolving—in its definition, the specific rights and duties it entails and the regulating institutions. States with majority Muslim populations or that follow Islamic law similarly experience new articulations of citizenship. For instance, Kiwan observes that the Arab uprisings from 2011 demonstrate reformulations of citizenship identities (2005, 311): "Emerging constructions of citizenship across the Arab world are being 'reimagined' in relation to intersecting identities of ethnicity, religion and nationality, as well as age, gender, and socio-economic status." She refers here to the disaffected youth, the women, the Islamists stepping in to close the gap left by the non-performing regimes, and the refugees.

More scholarship exists on Muslims' integration or as minorities in the mainly Christian and Western democracies. Much less scholarship has been forthcoming in the converse case regarding non-Muslims in Muslim states from the perspective of Islamic law and empirical studies. Contemporary Muslim states generally follow the *Jus sanguinis* principle for citizenship. While "democratic citizenship" in the dominant parlance allegedly does not find an easy resonance in Islam, Islamic law has traditionally allocated a secondary status of *dhimmi* to the non-Muslim, most evident in the *millet system* of the Ottoman period. The objective here is to investigate how "open" is the gate of citizenship to the outsider in contemporary Muslim states, from the background of Islamic doctrine, existing international norms and contemporary practice.

The paper looks at the naturalisation provisions of 18 Muslim states with attention to their historical and socio-political factors. It first observes the general trend of the naturalisation provision to foreigners in a cross-section of Muslim states and then in the six Arab-Gulf states in closer detail (Oman, Saudi Arabia, the UAE, Qatar, Bahrain and Kuwait), drawing from my dissertation research (Kanchana 2016).

2 Membership of the Other in an Islamic Society

Muwāṭana is the nearest term in Islamic texts that best resonates with the concept of citizenship, in the sense of "democratic citizenship" as we widely understand it (Parolin 2009). Whereas, *Jinsiyya*, something like a nationality certificate (Davis 1995) and *Wataniyya*, or nationalism in the Western sense, i.e., attachment to a territorialized sovereign nation-state (Longva 1995: 214) are two other terms with similar connotation that often cause confusion. Thus, *muwāṭin* is a citizen in the legal sense. There is allegedly a discord with this concept in Islam. For example, Fetni (in Ciprut 2008) argues that "citizenship" does not exist in "traditional" Islam, as a relationship between the individual and the state. She instead proposes the notion of "Islamic citizenship" resembling a club, where membership is through the faith because the idea of "individual" does not exist in the "umma" or the collective ethos: "Islam is a *din wa dawla*'. That is, religion and state go together in the goal to better propagate Islam or the message of peace and warning. Therefore, "membership" is exclusive to the faith-community, making non-Muslims the outsiders by default.

However, Islam concedes protection and rights to non-Muslims based on their residence status in an Islamic territory. Early Islamic dogma famously recognized and accepted, although in a somewhat qualified manner, religious pluralism in Islamic societies by giving Jews and Christians freedom to practice their religion. Islam also provided for crossing ethnic lines. For instance, Arabs, Kurds, Berbers and Turks who were fused together within a global and universal Islamic community (*umma*), have acted as its political leaders in the past (Shatzmiller 2005: 285).

Islam in the written text officially relegates non-Muslims living in *dār al-Islām* (or lands under the Islamic rule) to the status of *dhimmi*. Under the Islamic law, or the *Sharīʿa*, which directs the social behaviour of individuals in an Islamic society, the *Qāḍis* or judges granted this alternative *dhimmi* status. The status applies only to the *ahl al-kitāb* ("People of the Book") who also followed religions with divinely revealed scriptures—in other words, with monotheistic beliefs like the Jews, the Ṣabi'ans of Harran and the Christians (the *kitābis*). The non-Muslim could remain within their own religious community both physically and under their own laws and regulations. The *dhimmi* (under the "protected" status) and the *musta'min* (allowed to conduct business) were foreigners in an intermediate category, between a believer and a non-believer. The *millet system* in the Ottoman period during the late Middle Ages was a clear example, which legally defined and protected religious minorities within the empire:

> In exchange for official tolerance and legal recognition under the law, all male, free, and sane *dhimmis* were required to pay a poll tax (*jizya*) and those who were land- and property-owners were also obligated to pay the tax known as *kharāj*. (Martin in Shatzmiller 2005: 5)

Religious pluralism thus existed in the normative sense in Islamic societies and elsewhere, like the pre-colonial Muslim-ruled states in India. In social reality, the *dhimmis* under the Ottomans appear to have enjoyed fair treatment if they did not contest the preponderance of the Muslims. "*Dhimmis* were granted independence in the practice and maintenance of their own religious and social affairs so long as they did not impinge upon Muslims" (Martin in Shatzmiller 2005: 5). In this sense, they were second-class citizens. Hourani (1947) noted that nationality was a less important marker than religion, language and ethnicity in his identification of thirty-one minority groups in the Middle East.

However, tradition or religious text alone did not influence all the Muslim states in an identical fashion, even in specific domains like legal practice. The Pew report (2013) observed that modern-day states, which favoured applying the *Shari'a* especially to family law ("for human relations of a private and familial nature," such as marriage and inheritance) appear in this order: South East Asia, South Asia, the MENA and Central Asia. Fetni (in Ciprut 2008) also highlights the diversity of other examples. For example, Turkey separated with the *Shari'a* for its national law; the Gulf States as "the new nations in the Arabian Peninsula allowed *Shari'a* law to remain practically intact'; and most states in the larger trend adopted a combination of the Western legal system and the *Shari'a*. Therefore, multiple factors are needed to explain the varied trajectory of the Muslim states concerning citizenship allocation practice; these can include indigenous legal and political cultures, postcolonial contexts, experiences under communist rule and secularisation (such as in Central Asia and Eastern Europe). The Ottoman law of 1869 was the first nationality law that set the precedent concerning citizenship, allegedly inspired from the French law of 1851[1] (Parolin, 78).

3 Prominent Evidence of *Jus Sanguinis* in Muslim States: But Diversity in Context and Application

In 2017 Kuwait mounted a massive campaign to capture foreigners who had forged citizenship documents. In one case, a Syrian had fraudulently acquired Kuwaiti citizenship 22 years earlier, had enjoyed a job in the public sector and established family with a Kuwaiti wife (*Gulfnews*: September 19, 2017). Typically, foreigners gave money or entered into an agreement with a Kuwaiti national to obtain forged documents claiming to be a son or member of his family. This enabled him "to obtain a birth certificate, then a national identity card and finally a passport. The Interior Ministry revoked the citizenship of those proven guilty and in some cases also revoked the citizenship of their children. In 2016, the Criminal Court sentenced another Syrian to 15 years in jail, to be followed by deportation and a fine equal to the salaries he received in government job. The Kuwaiti accomplice got 5 years in jail (ibid.).

The several cases of citizenship acquisition through forgery involving nationals in Kuwait might indicate a similar occurrence in the other neighbouring Gulf Cooperation Council (GCC) states, which also impose unusually strict limitations on naturalisation. We will discuss this region later in more detail.

Some of the key problems identified with contemporary Muslim-majority countries such as the high incidence of statelessness and large refugee populations are closely associated with the granting of nationality. In addition to the officially stated naturalisation rules, practices with regard to marriage, adoption and freedom of religion are also relevant for the acquisition of nationality.

The world's Muslim population is geographically spread out, estimated at nearly a quarter of the global population in 2015 (Pew Research Centre 2017). Only about a fifth of the Muslim population lives in the Middle East and the North Africa regions. The largest number lives in the Asia-Pacific region. Indonesia has the highest number, followed by India.

The context is generally harsh for non-Muslims in Muslim countries especially as non-locals or newcomers, to enjoy equal rights in the host countries. At first glance, citizenship allocation in Muslim countries appears to suggest

1 The 1851 reform in France reinstated *Jus soli* for a child born of foreign parents in France, who themselves were born in the country (double *Jus soli*).

that *Jus sanguinis* is something natural or typical for them, confirming the wide perception that they are conservative societies. This is because predominant *Jus sanguinis* practice tends to point to closed societies. Muslim countries are presumed to be non-modern societies that explains this highly restricted access to citizenship. To what extent are their citizenship practices similar or antithetical to the more "liberal" practices elsewhere in the world?

The following analysis limits itself to the contemporary practice of Muslim states regarding non-Muslim residents and their access to citizenship, by looking at nationality legislation and the *Jus sanguinis* principle. First, we note the general trend among a cross-section of selected Muslim states. Next, we will explore the case in the Arab-Gulf states.

3.1 *The Wider Practice among the Muslim States: Strict Nationality Law Provisions*

In contemporary practice, the majority of the Muslim states clearly follow *Jus sanguinis* combined with a *Jus soli* variant, but where the stress is on the former (see Table 8.1).

TABLE 8.1 *Jus sanguinis* in selected muslim-majority states—access to naturalisation in the citizenship policies

State, Legislation	***Jus sanguinis; Jus soli***	**Naturalisation rules**
Morocco Nationality Code (last revised 2007)	*Jus sanguinis* via father (via mother if father unknown or stateless); No *Jus soli* (or if unknown parents)	Residency 5 years; Must be approved by Cabinet decree; Knowledge of Arabic
Tunisia Nationality Code 2011	*Jus sanguinis* via father or mother; *Jus soli* if father and grandfather born in the country	Residency 5 years; Knowledge of Arabic; Allows Dual
Niger Nationality Code 1984	*Jus sanguinis* via father	Residency 10 years
Somalia Citizenship Law 1962	*Jus sanguinis* via father (whose father is Somali); or who is ethnically Somali	Residency 7 years; Dual (2012 Constitution)
Turkey Law 2009 (revised)	*Jus sanguinis* via father or mother; No *Jus soli*	Residency 5 years; Knowledge of Turkish

TABLE 8.1 *Jus sanguinis* in selected muslim-majority states—access to naturalisation (cont.)

State, Legislation	*Jus sanguinis;Jus soli*	Naturalisation rules
Lebanon Decree No. 15, 1925 (revised 1960)	*Jus sanguinis* via father; *Jus soli* conditional (of unknown origin)	Residency 5 years
Iraq Law 2006	*Jus sanguinis* via father or mother (if born in Iraq; if born abroad could apply if father unknown/stateless or does not establish filiation)	Residency 10 years; Doesn't mention language/integration; Excludes Palestinians; Dual
Kazakhstan Law 1991 (revised 2013)	*Jus sanguinis*	Residency 5 years
Iran (*Islamic Republic of Iran*) Based on Civil Code 1928 (revised 2006)	*Jus sanguinis* via father; *Jus soli* conditional (one of the foreign parents also born in Iran; born to foreign father to confirm upon maturity, other)	Residency 5 years; Other acquired credit such as military service, Children in marriage to Iranian women; No dual
Pakistan Law 1951	*Jus sanguinis* via father or mother; *Jus soli*	Residence for a continuous period of one year before application and a period of four out of seven years prior to the one year period before the application; Dual
Indonesia Nationality Law 1946 (revised 1958)	*Jus sanguinis* via father; No *Jus soli* (only between January 1, 1946 and August 1, 1958)	Residency 5 years or 10 if not continuous

State legislation regulates the granting of nationality. In addition, norms relating to the nation-state's sovereignty and the local legal and regulation systems determine the nuances in the actual practice of *muwāṭana* or citizenship, resulting in variations in content and in practice. Table 8.1 shows the nationality policy of some states to observe important common elements: 1) *Jus sanguinis* is a predominant condition, while *Jus soli* is under very limited conditions such as when a child has unknown parents (except Pakistan).2) At least in the text, naturalisation eligibility provisions generally appear to meet reasonable standards, such as in the residence period requirement. 3) Gender hierarchy is at work as *Jus sanguinis* usually passes via the father. Women have limited ability to acquire nationality (other than via marriage) and to transfer it to their children or to foreign spouse. This is an important contributor to the extent of statelessness found in the region. 4) The laws normally demand language proficiency of the country but none explicitly mention religious affiliation. 5) Naturalisation rules are more applicable at the age of maturity; 6) Sometimes states confer citizenship on those who have given exceptional service to the country; and 7) These states mostly do not tolerate dual citizenship.

Despite the diversity among the Muslim-majority states we reviewed, *Jus sanguinis* evidently dominates as the language of belonging or the link to identity. From Morocco to Indonesia, the states extend from the west to the east in different regions. In Africa: Morocco and Tunisia, Niger and Somalia (also Egypt); in Central Asia and Caucasus: Turkey, Kazakhstan and Iran; in West Asia: Lebanon and Iraq (also Jordan, Syria, Yemen), and in Asia: Pakistan and Indonesia (also Malaysia).[2] In addition to the diversity in geography, the states represent diversity also in economic development, experience of colonialism, sectarian affiliation, political regimes, and popularity.

Should we conclude that the integration of migrants has less relevance in Islamic countries and that the citizenship concept is essentially associated with the liberal discourse, at least in the civic rights sense? Parolin (2009: 127) observes that citizenship attribution in an Islamic country is commonly via *Jus sanguinis* by paternal origin and that the sequence of membership is at three levels: in the kin group, the religious community and the nation-state. Further, "most Arab legislation provides for special naturalisation rules for nationals of other Arab countries (co-ethnic preference) and a few for foreign Muslims (co-religious preference) (usually they both imply the same, the confessional aspect)" (ibid.). In the larger picture, the religious lens, rather than the ethnic or the cultural one, appears to define the "other." Parolin concludes that the citizenship rights of minority-others in Islamic countries, "only imply residency rights and nothing more" (ibid.). We noted important similarities in our selected group. The larger evidence suggests that the co-ethnic or co-religious preference (or in combination) dominates in the allocation of citizenship to outsiders. However, it would be relevant to seek more nuanced explanations

2 Malaysia—*Jus sanguinis* requires both parents to be citizen; no *Jus soli.*

that reflect the complexity rather than merely the simplistic *dhimmi*-based logic for acts of closure.

It is beyond the scope of this paper to explore deeper, for instance, into the specific contexts and the political considerations about the choices of the Muslim states over time. Some factors that stimulated diversity in the policy practice (or convergence) of these states might include phenomena such as pan-Arabism, regional and internal conflicts often associated with the transformation tied to the nation-building processes, and ideological stance against perceived Western imposed standards or institutions. Perrin (2014: 230–1) highlights the relevance of the colonial experience with reference to countries in the Maghreb, "the political use and construction of ethno-religious determinants by the colonial powers during colonization and by the subsequent regime after independence." Some of these states for instance, followed the French model after their independence from colonization such as Egypt, Algeria and Morocco.[3] The affected population includes local minority groups (including co-religionist or co-sectarian) such as the *bidūn* (those without nationalities) of nomadic origin in Kuwait, as much as groups from the outside, such as the long-residing Afghans in Iran. She proposes further that, "Reluctance to grant citizenship is rather based on a mix of immaturity in nation-building, of a closed and 'naturalist'—if not ethno-religious—conception of the nation, and of suspicion and fear toward difference and aliens," but she notes that the rejection of diversity is increasingly questioned today (Perrin 2014: 234). Thus, citizenship practice was often a political gesture, linked to interstate relations, national balances and sensitive issues of belonging.

There has been a positive trend for reform in the national legislations in recent years. Two examples of positive reform include Egypt which, in 2004 modified its personal status law to allow women to confer citizenship to their children; and Algeria in 2005 provided that the double *Jus soli* provision to establish nationality origin applies to both males and females, although the individual must still hold Muslim personal status. The North African states in particular, took measures for granting nationality rights to reduce statelessness and gender inequality. At the broader level, however, we could observe discrimination in the naturalisation law practiced in the Muslim states based on gender, ethnicity (such as Arab race, or language) and religion. Van Waas (2014, 24–30) notes discrimination to be widely common on the grounds of gender, ethnicity, religion and disability in her study on the nationality laws in 17

3 Perrin notes: the French Protectorate used *Jus soli* (for the indigenous) and *Jus religionis* to distinguish between the settlers and the natives. The latter made it also possible to separate the Muslims and the Jews from the indigenous.

Middle East and North African countries (MENA). These violate the International Covenant on the Elimination of All Forms of Racial Discrimination, particularly that the state parties should guarantee the right of nationality to everyone, without distinction as to race, colour, or national or ethnic origin [Article 5 (d)(iii)]. Moreover, she emphasizes that the "letter of the law can be only half of the story" (p. 31) and that there is an effective gap between rights and the actual practice of granting nationality.

This is evident through the stringent naturalisation provisions that make acquisition difficult as an adult (for example, the use of language that provides for a generally large margin of discretion)[4] and the neglect of mechanisms for procedural safeguards (such as right to appeal, system of checks and balances and jurisdiction for the courts on nationality matters). As van Waas sums up, "in other words, MENA states' naturalisation practices can be highly challenging, often unpredictable and are especially problematic in those states with large stateless populations" (ibid.).

The religious denomination plays out as an important condition for naturalisation in most of the Muslim countries. Perrin (2014) remarks that although religion is quasi-absent from the citizenship laws of Libya, Algeria, Tunisia, Morocco and Mauritania, the constitutions from "the Great Maghreb" region proclaim a Muslim identity and a belonging to the Arab world (with the official language as Arabic). She adds, "in practice, it (religion) may be important in getting Citizenship through naturalisation and marriage" (p. 233). In our selected group, Lebanon, Iraq, Pakistan and Indonesia apply the *Shari'a* for the family law domain. Therefore, religion could have an indirect effect at least, where states constitutionally provide for an "officially favoured religion" and/or a religious/*Shari'a* law. Similarly, some states gave access to citizenship to individuals with an Arab origin, even though it was not a legal condition.

3.2 *The GCC's Citizenship Policies: "The Gate Is Not Open"*

We explore the Gulf Cooperation Council (GCC) states' practice in a closer detail in this section, which is a relatively extreme case in the contemporary context. The six member states namely, Oman, Saudi Arabia, the UAE, Qatar, Bahrain and Kuwait stipulate demanding conditions for naturalisation in the formal text as well. They define themselves as Islamic states and stand out for having large proportion of foreigners of diverse origin in their populations as

4 For instance, Lebanon applies it as a matter of clear policy: "it is not definite that a foreigner who meets [the conditions for naturalisation] will be granted Lebanese nationality" (cited in Frontiers Ruwad Association, *Invisible Citizens: Humiliation and a life in the shadows. A legal and policy study on statelessness in Lebanon*, 2011: 70; Ministry of Interior, General Questions).

TABLE 8.2 Nationality law in the GCC states and the length of residence for naturalisation

	Law	Residence requirement
Oman	2014 Nationality Law (repeals 1983 law)	Residence for 30 years
UAE	1972 Federal UAE Nationality Law	Residence for 30 years, 20 of those years occurring after January 1, 1972 (3 years residence for citizens of Qatar, Oman, and Bahrain; 7 years residence for citizens of Arab descent)
Bahrain	1963 Nationality Law (revised 1981)	Continuous residence for 25 years since September 16, 1963 (15 years for persons of Arab descent)
Qatar	2005 Law (revised 1961)	Consecutive residence for 25 years
Kuwait	1959 Nationality Law by Emiri Decree	Residence for 20 years (15 years residence for citizens of other Arab countries) *Required to be Muslim[a]
Saudi Arabia	1954 Nationality regulations (revised 2004)	Residence for 10 years but conditions vague

"temporary guests," who are indefinitely excluded from integration in the local society with the citizenry. As per their current nationality laws and practice, citizenship is almost impossible to acquire for the resident expatriates. All the GCC states introduced their nationality laws in the 1960s and the 1970s, with the exception of Saudi Arabia, which was the first to introduce them in 1954.

The Arab-Gulf states' citizenship policies are exclusionary and involve largely ambiguous provisions. They endorse an ethno-cultural model and in practice, they privilege affiliation to Islam. Table 8.2 underscores a key common element regarding the nationality laws of the Gulf states for naturalisation that are essentially applicable to males: that the primary condition requiring an unusually long period of residence in the territory[5] effectively discourages naturalisation. *Jus sanguinis* is the overarching principle in defining eligibility

5 Saudi Arabia, at least in the text specifies a shorter period, and its criteria for qualification including for permanent resident are not clear.

for naturalisation, by blood and descent only. *Jus soli* or nationality by birth does not apply, except for instance, if the child is born of unknown parents. In addition, the Arab Gulf states favour *Jus sanguinis* based on male lineage, where the father can pass on citizenship. The mother can transfer citizenship only in limited cases,[6] such as in the case of an unknown father or if the father is stateless.

The UAE in 2011[7] and Saudi Arabia in 2007[8] made positive reforms whereas Kuwait became more exclusionary.[9] The ascription of citizenship on the basis of gender is a common element under the prevailing logic of cultural tradition and is a broader practice also in other Muslim countries, as we saw earlier. Naturalisation access for a foreign woman is through marriage. Native men can pass nationality to foreign spouses, however conditions might vary in different GCC countries and the process is not always transparent. A native woman cannot pass her nationality on to a foreign husband.[10] The woman might also lose her Gulf-citizenship and privileges. In addition, the Gulf states do not tolerate dual citizenship unless specifically approved.

A review of some historical and socio-cultural factors might help us to understand the Arab-Gulf states' citizenship policies. As Longva (2000) suggests, "contributing to the way citizenship is conceptualized and put into practice is: history, tradition and above all, the circumstances under which the state is created and legitimacy is maintained" (p. 97). Longva writes that the notion of citizenship (her work concerns Kuwait but is broadly relevant to the rest of the Gulf region) "is implicitly but nonetheless inherently conceptualised by most Kuwaitis not on terms of universal and abstract rights and duties but in the deeply cultural and particularistic terms of identity and loyalty" (p. 196). The Gulf States were essentially tribal and traditional desert societies that transformed in a rapid fashion to wealthy, modern nations from the turn of the 1960s. Citizenship in the Arab-Gulf States is largely based on the *jinsiyya* principle, as "an identity or membership linked to the territorialized state/and a community" (p. 193). Citizenship and access to it in the Gulf is hence generally

6 Qatar does not let mother confer citizenship to children without exception, even if the result is statelessness.

7 UAE allows a child (boy or girl) of native mother and non-national father to apply for citizenship after 18 years.

8 Saudi Arabia allows sons of a native mother and non-national father to acquire citizenship at the age of majority.

9 E.g., it removed a clause that previously allowed children of Kuwaiti mothers and stateless fathers to acquire nationality.

10 Omani law reduced the residence period requirement for a foreign man married to an Omani to 15 years, but subject to the conditions that the marriage occurred with prior approval of the Ministry of Interior and there is a son born from the marriage.

conceptualised on creed/or a religious-ethno-cultural basis. In addition to this, important state-centred explanation of practices in the region, Longva (2000) further suggests that citizenship also implies entitlement rights in an "entitlement state" (including political rights in the case of Kuwait) (p. 193). The entitlement focus of citizenship in the GCC is an accrual of membership in an autocratic welfare state, in contrast to a participative model that is more prominent elsewhere.[11] The current Gulf regimes maintain the "ruling bargain" and sustain their political legitimacy, by maximal wealth distribution within a limited native membership to ensure citizen loyalty. Thus, the *Jus sanguinis* nationality laws effectively maintain citizenship as an exclusive privilege of the local-national.

An important problematic aspect with respect to naturalisation in the region is that the implementation of the nationality rules is a non-transparent process. The royal authority or the relevant agency (normally the Ministry of Interior) grants citizenship usually by a highly discretionary exercise. Even if the procedure for naturalisation exists in the legal text, its application in practice is hazy. In addition to the residency period, other general conditions include knowledge of Arabic language, good character and sufficient financial capacity. However, there is ample anecdotal evidence about numerous cases where expatriate applicants never succeeded in their applications for naturalisation. This was despite their qualifying on all the specified criteria as per the local rules including long term residence in the respective host country and Arab descent with affiliation to Islam. This was a familiar story during earlier fieldwork in the region. Typically, applicants for naturalisation waited for an unspecified number of years to receive a decision after the submission of their files.

On the other hand, there are also successful instances of citizenship acquired via the more discretionary exercise of authority, such as an Indian cook who had worked for an important family in Oman for many decades being rewarded with citizenship. Exceptions therefore, include hand-picked individual cases and by a selection process that is non-transparent. There are still no clear rules or practices[12] in the Gulf region as to qualifications and procedures for naturalisation. For example, naturalisation criteria in Saudi Arabia does not mention religion, the Basic Law requires a citizen to be Muslim. In Bahrain, the

11 Allegedly associated with the Western notion of the citizenship

12 2005 Amendment in Qatar introduced eligibility guidelines for naturalisation, prior to which, the law only provided that that the Emir would grant naturalisation at his discretion.

text mentions that the person must be of good character, with a good command of Arabic, and have real estate registered in his or her name in Bahrain. Permission can only be granted from the ruler of Bahrain. The lack of consistency and common rules for the granting of naturalisation is glaring. In contrast, there is a clear perception amongst both the expatriate and the national populations in the region that naturalisation is an unlikely phenomenon. Hence, stories, such as the Syrian in Kuwait cited earlier, of individuals resorting to indirect and false methods to acquire citizenship might not surprise us much. On the rare occasions of successful naturalisation, the process and the information remain a black box. The news is usually sensitive and kept confidential. Hence, information about the successful cases of citizenship acquisition in the Gulf is unclear. The applicable criteria, as well as the actual numbers in a specific period are rarely made accessible to the public.

Moreover, the Gulf States have also used naturalisation strategically as a selective instrument on several occasions, to manipulate the ethnic and nationality composition in the population on the basis of geo-political calculations. The Bahraini regime's controversial practice to grant nationality to some Sunni-denomination communities to undermine the Shia dominance in the local population is a prominent example. It supposedly gave nationality liberally to the expatriates of Pakistan and of other origins at specific times in the past decades. Kuwait also used this strategy in the 1960s and the 1970s to naturalize mostly Sunni tribes from other parts of the Arabian peninsula, "as a counterweight to the urbanised Kuwaiti liberals, leftists and Arab nationalists" (Kinninmont 2013, 53). The Palestinian population[13] spread throughout the Gulf region is another example of the selectivity of the nationality grant. Other instances of the GCC states' wide scope for arbitrary exercise over citizenship used against their own populations include, the cases of Kuwait's Bedouins and Bahrain's revocation of some its nationals' citizenship since the protests in 2011 (the Shi'a dissenters). Granting nationality is clearly the discretionary domain of the supreme authority vested in the executive power of the Ruler. In a more recent trend, the GCC states have extended "temporary citizenship" to sports-professionals from the African, Central Asian or other developing countries (including to individuals with desired talents in other domains). While the practice again exemplifies the instrumentalist aspect to grant citizenship to foreigners, it also underlines its essential exclusionary element. It is an example of selective citizenship as a temporary grant, in exchange for the

13 The Arab League put a ban on naturalizing Palestinian refugees in the Arab countries to avoid undermining the right of return cause.

individual's anticipated value to enhance the Gulf nations' performance and reputation records in the international arena. The state withdraws citizenship when the player leaves the sports team.

Therefore, the GCC states grant citizenship highly selectively. "No GCC country has made any significant policy changes addressing the situation of their long-term and second-generation migrants since the modest changes in citizenship law of Saudi Arabia" (Baldwin-Edwards 2011: 43). The GCC states have actually tightened their nationality rules.

4 Conclusion

Random comments such as, "In a Muslim country, citizenship is impossible to acquire as a foreigner!'" are indicative of a relatively pervasive impression as if it were a self-explanatory phenomenon. I heard it often from the expatriates of different nationalities during my doctoral fieldwork in the Gulf region, where naturalisation is especially arbitrary and the local regimes are authoritarian. This general impression that naturalisation is difficult and officially unwelcome to a non-Muslim resident applies to most Muslim-majority states.

We looked at naturalisation provisions from a mixed set of 18 Muslim-majority states. While the laws and provisions appear reasonably fair as per international norms (the six GCC states are an exception, which impose more extreme requirements), the actual citizenship acquisition for foreigners is difficult and unpredictable. In general, the naturalisation phenomenon in Muslim countries shows a less objective basis with an emphasis on *Jus sanguinis* and co-religious preference. Most nationality laws do not mention Islam in their official criteria, but apply it in effect. Perrin's (2014, 234) observation concerning the Maghreb states in North Africa is applicable to most of these states: "While express mentions of Arab ethnicity or Islam are scarce on the books, they seem to be important criteria when granting citizenship.'

However, we do not see a uniform rule or a consistent practice among Muslim states. Foreign Muslim residents are also not granted naturalization more liberally, except when the host state favoured for other reasons (for instance, to influence the demographic composition in the population). In addition, it might be easier to explain the Arab-Gulf states' much harsher rules as due to the nature of their absolute monarchies. Moreover, their policies and practices on naturalisation and citizenship emphasize a priority to exclude, and to maximize their flexibility and power over foreign workers. Yet, such discrimination is no different from examples that involve non-Muslim states both in the past

(Germany) and in the contemporary period (Japan) where restrictive naturalisation is on a highly selective basis.

The notion of citizenship and integration of the "outsider" in the classical texts have largely suggested that full membership should be limited to the adherents of Islam. However, the larger textual body and Muslim practices over time have shown some provision for flexibility and accommodation to reflect changing societal and ethical concerns. The *Al-Azhar Declaration* and significant scholarship have asserted that Islam or the *Sharīʿa* does not preclude plurality. Further, Islam in its practice is not monolithic and history gives us ample proof of its adaptation. Therefore, the invocation of Islam's supposed reluctance to integrate the Other to explain the contemporary Muslim states' proclivity for restrictive naturalisation policies would be insufficient. We observe an amount of commonality in the Muslim states' naturalisation practice with a tendency to exclude the outsider. However, a more careful look already suggests more consideration of politics in the discrimination.

States' choices in their local contexts, including for potential reform, reflect exigencies as much as doctrinal inspiration. For example, the Arab-Gulf region shows variations in the practice of granting citizenship and reflects the local regimes' delicate ruling bargain and their perceived imperative for greater control over the foreign population to maintain their legitimacy. We see evidence of randomness in granting citizenship involving, for instance, the native Bedouin in Kuwait as well as expatriates (whether Muslim, Arab, or other faith and identities). To conclude, this research affirms the evidence that Muslim states' naturalisation provisions incline towards highly selective practices, but they also show a certain receptivity to diversity.

Bibliography

Albarazi, Zahra and Laura van Waas. 2014. "Transformations of nationality legislation in North Africa." In *Routledge Handbook of Global Citizenship Studies*, edited by Egin Isin and Peter Nyers, Abingdon, Oxon: Routledge. Chap. 17

Baldwin-Edwards, Martin. March 2011. "Labour immigration and labour markets in the GCC countries: national patterns and trends." Research Paper, *LSE Kuwait Programme on Development, Governance and Globalisation in the Gulf States.* No. 15.

Fetni, Hocine. 2008. "Citizenship divided: Muslim subjects, Arab citizens, democratic dilemmas." In *The Future of Citizenship*, edited by Jose Ciprut. Cambridge, Massachusetts; London: MIT Press. pp. 167–189.

Hourani, A.H. 1947. *Minorities in the Arab World*. London: Oxford University Press.

Isin, Engin. 2012. "Citizenship after orientalism: an unfinished project." *Citizenship Studies* 16(5–6): 563–572.

Isin, Engin and Peter Nyers, eds. 2014. *Routledge Handbook of Global Citizenship Studies*. Abingdon, Oxon: Routledge.

Kanchana, Radhika. 2016. PhD thesis, Political Science. "The expediency of the contemporary guest worker migration policies that curb mobility: The Arab-Gulf countries and the Indian migrants." Institut d'Études Politiques de Paris (Sciences Po), France.

Kinninmont, J. 2013. "Citizenship in the Gulf." In *The Gulf States and the Arab Uprisings*, edited by Ana Echague. Spain: FRIDE & the Gulf Research Center. pp. 47–57.

Kiwan, D. 2014. "Emerging Forms of Citizenship in the Arab World." In *Routledge Handbook of Global Citizenship Studies*, edited by Engin Isin and Peter Nyers. Abingdon, Oxon: Routledge. pp. 307–316.

Longva, A. 2000. "Citizenship in the Gulf States: Conceptualization and Practice." In *Citizenship and the State in the Middle East: Approaches and Applications*, edited by Nils Butenschon, Uri Davis and Manuel Hassassian. Syracuse: Syracuse University Press. pp. 179–197.

Martin, R. 2005. "From Dhimmis to minorities: Shifting constructions of the non-Muslim Other from early to modern Islam." In *Nationalism and Minority Identities in Islamic Societies*, edited by Maya Shatzmiller. Montreal and Kingston: McGill-Queen's University Press. pp. 3–21.

Parolin, G. 2009. *Citizenship in the Arab World. Kin, Religion and Nation State*. Amsterdam: Amsterdam University Press.

Perrin, D. 2011. Immigration and citizenship law in the Maghreb: Turning aliens into citizens. *EUI Working Papers*. RSCAS, No. 40.

Perrin, D. 2014. "Citizenship struggles in the Maghreb." In *Routledge Handbook of Global Citizenship Studies*, edited by Engin Isin and Peter Nyers. Abingdon, Oxon : Routledge. pp. 230–239

Shatzmiller, Maya, ed. 2005. *Nationalism and Minority Identities in Islamic Societies*. Montreal & Kingston, London, Ithaca: McGill-Queen's University Press.

Van Waas, Laura. September 2014. "A comparative analysis of nationality laws in the MENA region." *Report of the Middle East and North Africa Nationality and Statelessness Research Project*. Tilburg University Statelessness Programme.

Other Documents

Asia News (March 3, 2017) "Al-Azhar: pluralism and citizenship at the basis of Islam. But a civic state is missing."

Pew Research Centre. April 6, 2017. Michael Lipka and Conrad Hackett. "Why Muslims are the world's fastest-growing religious group." <https://www.pewresearch.org/fact-tank/2017/04/06/why-muslims-are-the-worlds-fastest-growing-religious-group/>. Accessed August 2017.

Pew Report. 2013. *The World's Muslims: Religion, Politics and Society*. <http://assets.pewresearch.org/wp-content/uploads/sites/11/2013/04/worlds-muslims-religion-politics-society-full-report.pdf>. Accessed August 2017.

CHAPTER 9

The Obligation to Migrate and the Impulse to Narrate: Soviet Narratives of Forced Migration in the Nineteenth Century Caucasus

Rebecca Ruth Gould

In the year 622/3, ten years after he first heard the Qur'an recited to him, Muhammad was made an offer he could not refuse. The Quraysh of Mecca, a city where he had passed most of his life, had grown hostile to him on account of the popularity of his teachings with the poor, women, and other disenfranchised members of society. Muhammad's calls for social justice and purity of worship were perceived as a threat to the social order. The Meccan elite in particular saw Muhammad's growing popularity as a threat to their power. When the residents of nearby Yathrib offered Muhammad a sanctuary if he wished to relocate there, he agreed, on three conditions. First, he insisted that all of his followers, including his family, would be welcome to migrate to this new city. Second, that all the migrants would be given food and a place to sleep until they were able to look after themselves. Third, that he and his companions would become full-fledged citizens of Yathrib, so that if any of them were attacked by the Meccans, all of Yathrib would come to their defense.

Muhammad's stipulations were accepted and the migration began. So as not to arouse suspicion among the Meccans who preferred to see him and his followers harmed than to leave their city peacefully, the movement was gradual. As for Muhammad himself, after all of his followers had arrived safely in Yathrib, he escaped Mecca in the middle of the night accompanied by Abū Bakr, having spent three days in a cave in order to evade a plot to kill him. Throughout Islamic history, the narration of these events, well known to every Muslim in countless variations, has served as a perpetual reminder that conversion meant abandoning "one's home in order to fight for the cause" because "salvation lay in going forth for heroic ventures and a new world ahead, not patiently staying by one's fields or camels" (Crone 1994, 383).

Known as the *hijra*, from the Arabic root meaning "to cut off from friendly association" (Q 4:34) the migration to Yathrib is among the most important events in Islamic history (Watt 1941). In keeping with its allegorical style, the Qur'an makes no mention of the city to which Muhammad and his followers migrated. At the same time, the historical event of the migration is clearly reflected in the text, for it abounds in praise of the *muhājirūn* (emigrants) and in condemnation of those who did not migrate. "Whoever emigrates for the cause of Allah will find on the earth many spaces and abundance," reads one memorable verse (Q 4:100). By contrast, the angels of death will interrogate those who refuse to migrate. "Was not the earth of Allah spacious [enough] for you to emigrate therein?" (Q 4:97) will be asked of those who, contrary to the example of the Prophet, chose to stay at home. Through such verses, an historical event was rendered as allegory, and the stage was set for later memorializations of Qur'anic stories.

According to Islamic tradition, pious Jews and Christians prophesied Muhammad's *hijra* long before its occurrence. After conquering Yemen, the Himyarite king Tibān As'ad Abū Karib made his way to the Hijaz with the intention of leveling Yathrib, the city where his son had been killed, to the ground. The king was dissuaded from destroying this town by two Jewish rabbis who warned the king, "if you persist in your intention [to destroy Yathrib], something will happen to prevent your carrying it out and we fear that you will face speedy retribution" (*Kitāb Sīrat Rasūl Allāh*, ed. Wüstenfeld 1858–60, 14). At first, the rabbis were hesitant to divulge the reason for their warning. Finally, they explained that Yathrib was designated as the site of a future *hijra* for a prophet of the Quraysh, and that it would become his home and resting place. The use of the term *hijra* in this context by Muhammad's biographer Ibn Isḥāq (c. 704–770) is an anachronism, for the concept of *hijra* as migration was introduced with Islam. However, Ibn Isḥāq's anachronism is central for grasping the concepts elaborated here, for it demonstrates how, in Islam, *hijra* is a means through which history is transmuted into cultural memory. It is also an early illustration of the process through which the obligation to migrate has been made coterminous with the impulse to narrate throughout Islamic history.

Further adding to its epoch-making status, the year of the *hijra*, 622/3, marks the beginning of the Islamic calendar. The migration bisects the two major categories of Qur'anic revelations, those that were revealed to the prophet in Mecca, which pertain primarily to spiritual matters, and those that were revealed to the prophet in Yathrib, which pertain to politics and ethics. Finally and most importantly, the *hijra* marks the date when Islam became a religion with an institutional foundation. So long as Muhammad and his followers were based in Mecca, his teachings pertained primarily to personal piety, and could be rejected or accepted at will or in part, without any obvious social consequences. Following the migration, these same teachings came to be endowed with political as well as spiritual import. In recognition of the Prophet's new political orientation, Yathrib's name was changed to *Madinat al-nabi* ("the city of the prophet") following the arrival of Muhammad and his followers.

A constitution was drafted and laws were proclaimed (see: Arjomand 2009). Gradually, Islam was coming to be conceived of as a religion of the state, as well as a matter for the soul.

Muhammad's migration from Mecca to Medina was to play an unparalleled role in subsequent Islamic history, as an event in its own right, but particularly as a template for narrating subsequent migrations from lands under non-Muslim rule. At least a century passed before the event itself acquired its singular status, as a paradigmatic story rather than, as in the Qur'an, a perpetually recurring obligation. In its capacity as a narrative trope, the prophet's *hijra* provided a framework through which trauma and defeat could be made legible. Time and again, the traumatic journey of Muhammad and his *muhājirūn* was invoked by Muslim writers to give substance to the geographically and demographically more expansive displacements of later periods of Islamic history, including the Mongol invasions of the thirteenth century and the Spanish Reconquista (1492). Most notably for present purposes, the inaugural *hijra* from Mecca to Medina shaped local memories of the ethnic cleansings that scarred the former Soviet Union, particularly in the Caucasus, during the 1940s. For the displaced Muslims from the Caucasus discussed in this chapter, the ancient concept of *hijra* was used to address the traumatic legacies of Soviet deportations.

In its Qur'anic signification as migration away from a territory that has, whether through conquest or corruption, fallen outside the abode of Islam, *hijra* is obligatory on all believers. Several *hadith* attest to its compulsory status. The first, cited by numerous jurists, insists that *hijra* "will not end until repentance (*tawba*) does, and repentance will not end until the sun rises in the west" (Abū Dāwūd 1995/6: 3: 2479). Another *hadith* lists *hijra* among the five commandments that, along with acceptance (*samʿ*), obedience (*ṭaʿa*), striving (*jihād*), and unity (*jamāʿa*), is obligatory on all believers. (Ibn Ḥanbal 4: 130) And yet even in the context of these citations, *hijra* is often understood as a figurative rather than literal migration. As the tenth century jurist Qāḍī an-Nuʿmān put it, anyone who has made a journey to Islam (*man dakhala fī al-islām*) *is* a *muhājir* (an-Nuʿmān 1951, 1194). Another scholar, the Ḥanafī jurist al-Ṭaḥāwī (843–933), elaborated a concept of a "second *hijra* [*hijrat al-sūʾ*]" which the believer can perform while remaining physically at home, at any point in time, and under any type of rule (al-Ṭaḥāwī, 1533).

Although the division between the *muhājirūn* and those who remain behind is lucid in the Qur'an, the ethical and legal meanings of the obligation to migrate have been continuously contested within Islamic political thought. This debate raises questions such as: What constitutes an Islamic territory? How can we know when this territory has ceased to belong to the abode of

Islam (*dār al-islām*)? What is the relationship between the abode of unbelief (*dār al-kufr*) and the abode of faith? These unresolved questions have structured much of Islamic political thought across the centuries. They influence how migration generally, and *hijra* specifically, has been understood over the course of Islamic history. While serving as a reminder that "salvation lay in going forth for heroic ventures," *hijra* increasingly became a discourse on the condition of being Muslim in a non-Muslim world, and a commentary on the extent to which the Islamic community (*umma*) could be spatially imagined and materially mapped. *Hijra*'s meaning has accordingly shifted dramatically across time and space, along with the shifting boundaries of Islamic empires. Many different conceptions of *hijra* have animated and conditioned religious belief, for, in Muslim-minority societies, the believer's relations with the non-Islamic state substantially shapes the conditions under which the obligation to migrate is performed. These pages offer a perspective on *hijra*'s trans-historical meanings based on nineteenth and twentieth-century sources, while consider its role in the making of literary and cultural history in the Caucasus.

In light of its responsiveness to changes in history, the *hijra* concept illustrates the internal diversity of Islamic narratives and of Muslim cultural memory.[1] Patricia Crone calls *hijra* "one of the rare Islamic notions of which we can unequivocally say that they take us back to the beginnings" (Crone 1994, 383). And yet, even as the concept powerfully evokes Islamic beginnings, it is worth remembering the many radical transformations that *hijra* has undergone along its journey to the postcolonial present.

At every stage of its development, *hijra*'s meanings have been shaped by the political circumstances within which the concept was implemented, as well as by internal developments within Islamic political and legal thought. With the beginning of Muslim modernity, which almost always transpired under the aegis of colonialism (see Rabbat 2014), the ethical and legal content of the Islamic obligation to migrate underwent a dramatic shift. Whereas the Qur'an interprets the relation between the *muhājirūn* and those who remain behind allegorically, scholars during the Ummayad period (661–750) began to understand the *hijra* as a single event, referring to Muhammad's migration to Medina. Although it could be reenacted and commemorated in many different ways, *hijra* in this singular meaning could never fully be reproduced.

As the singular event of the *hijra* became a relic of the past during the Umayyad and particularly Abbasid periods, its contemporaneity faded from

1 Another instructive example of a modern resignification of a Qur'anic concept is *fitna* (temptation, discord, rebellion), which acquired in later periods of Islamic history an emphasis different from its earliest usages in the Qur'an (see Fisher 1994).

view. *Hijra* was transformed from a narrative for the present into a story about the past. In the words of Muhammad's beloved wife 'Ā'isha, "the believer used to flee with his religion to God and his Messenger, but as for today, God has made Islam victorious, and the believer can worship God wherever he wants" (al-Qāsim 1968, 254). While 'Ā'isha affirmed that the obligation to perform *jihād* remained, according to this tradition, the obligation to perform *hijra* had, to all intents and purposes, reached an end.

The dynastic concept of *hijra* as history prevailed over the Qur'anic concept of *hijra* as allegory for many centuries.[2] With the beginnings of modernity, 'Ā'isha's statement that "God has made Islam victorious" resounded with irony, since Islam was anything but victorious in political terms. The declining political status of Islam motivated a turn back to *hijra*'s Qur'anic meaning, as an open-ended and repeating journey incumbent on all believers. In addition to signifying the historical migration to Medina, as it had done since the earliest Islamic beginnings, *hijra* acquired a new meaning: the obligation to migrate away from lands that had been conquered by non-Muslims, many of which had previously been under Muslim rule. This obligation acquired greater political salience following the conquests by Mongols in the late medieval period, Spaniards in early modernity, and then, most irrevocably, by Russian, British, and French imperial armies and the anticolonial movements these incursions generated during the nineteenth century.

1 *Hijra* in the Caucasus

As a land removed from traditionally Islamic centers of power, the Caucasus did not figure centrally into Islamic legal or ethical discourse on *hijra* prior to the encounter with colonial modernity. Darband, Tiflis, and Shirwan were destinations for conquest, *jihād*, not for willed or forced migrations, prior to modernity. In keeping with Muhammad's widely-reported injunction to seek knowledge "even as far as China" (cited in al-Makkī ed. trans. Renard 2004, 119) individual Muslims from the Caucasus did migrate for religious reasons, as they did across the Islamic world. One of the most famous early modern seekers of knowledge was the eighteenth-century scholar Muḥammad al-Quduqi, who left Daghestan for Syria due to his frustration with local Muslims who in his view were uncritically imitating the customs of their ancestors

2 By "dynastic" I mean to imply what Crone (1994) calls the "classical" concept of *hijra* that prevailed in the first century of Islam. For the difference between the conceptualization of *hijra* in the two periods (also see Madelung 1986).

and ignoring the precepts of Islam (for al-Quduqī's biography see Gould 2015). When it came to mass migrations, however, and most notably in connection with the Safavid deportations of hundreds of thousands of Georgians and Armenians, mass population movements were organized by the state.

During early modernity, the populations in the Caucasus who experienced the most intensive forced deportation were primarily Christian Georgians and Armenians, not Muslims (Herzig 1990). Colonialism introduced new relations between Muslims and non-Muslims, and, in the Caucasus as elsewhere, these new relations grafted new meanings onto the old concept of *hijra*. In its various local adaptations, the concept was understood by Muslim and non-Muslim peoples across the Caucasus to signify "the mass migrations of Muslim populations from the Caucasus" (Manning 2012, 145) to Ottoman lands during the nineteenth century. *Hijra* from the Caucasus radically and permanently altered the demographic makeup of Circassia, Abkhazia, Chechnya, Ingushetia, Georgia, and Daghestan. From Amman to Damascus to Istanbul and all the way to the diasporic communities scattered across North America, the consequences of the colonial era migrations from the Caucasus to Ottoman lands are being lived, and mourned, to this day. (For a comprehensive account of colonial-era *hijra*, see Bīnū 2007. For recent engagements with these migrations in Anglophone scholarship, see Karny 2000 and Richmond 2013.)

Whereas the inaugural migration from Mecca to Medina is narrated as an act of piety performed under duress, colonial-era migrations from the Caucasus to Ottoman territories were undertaken in response to imperial mandates and threats. In Daghestan, among communities that sustained Islamic textual traditions dating back to the medieval period, the discussion of *hijra* directly engaged with—and to some extent adapted—Islamic legal theory. Beyond the Daghestani context, *hijra* more generally came to signify migration away from lands that had fallen under foreign rule. The concept was at once deeply rooted in Islamic traditions and dense with meaning beyond this context, including among Armenian Christian *muhājir*s.

By 1864, with the Circassian defeat, the entire Caucasus was officially incorporated into the Russian empire. Immersed as they were in the politics of Ottoman and Russian imperial collusion, the colonial government officials who coordinated and carried out the migrations frequently deceived the target populations concerning the terms of their displacement, and misrepresented the conditions they would face when they reached their destinations. In Soviet-era local literatures, these deceptions were memorialized as violations of the rights and humanity of those who migrated. Defeated mountaineers were forced to migrate and given only two possible destinations: to the Russian interior or to Ottoman lands (Toledano 2009, 83). Through such political maneuverings, *hijra* came for Muslim mountaineers to signify yet one more aspect of coercive colonial rule. Far from evoking the "heroic ventures" with which it was associated in the early days of Islamic expansion, *hijra* was now a handmaiden of colonial rule.

Pondering the reconfiguration of *hijra* that coincided with the global decline of Islamic sovereignty and the military ascendency of European empires sheds light on contemporaneous transformations in the Muslim understanding of migration. Looking backwards in time will help clarify the frameworks through which *hijra* came to signify in modernity. The schools of Islamic law responded to the challenges introduced by the declining fate of Islamic sovereignty in different ways. Given their different approaches to the legal and ethical dimensions of migration, Ḥanafī, Ḥanbalī, Mālikī, and Shāfiʿī interpretations of *hijra* each merit separate study in the context of their separate geographies. Without assaying a thoroughgoing treatment of *hijra* across the Islamic world, I will here focus on one specific Shāfiʿī trajectory, before turning to the literary transformation of *hijra* memory in Soviet-era depictions of forced migration in the nineteenth-century Caucasus.

2 *Hijra* as *Jihād*

Whereas *hijra* throughout the Caucasus signified primarily forced migration from the early modern period to Soviet rule, Daghestan presents an important exception to this general pattern. The territory of Daghestan overlapped with the polity in the Caucasus that most successfully withstood colonial rule Imam Shamil's imamate. This state functioned for a quarter of a century, from 1834–1859, as, among other things, a bulwark against Russian rule. The relative stability of the imamate generated internal splits within the Daghestan community concerning the obligation to migrate to lands under Muslim rule. The jurists in Shamil's service took the position that every Muslim in the region was obliged to migrate to his imamate. To reside outside the imamate was, in this view, to reside in *dār al-ḥarb* (the abode of war). In light of the less stringent understanding of *hijra* that was dominant in the Shāfiʿī legal school prevalent in Daghestan, this interpretation appears to represent an innovation, attesting to the new meanings the term acquired during the nineteenth century. And yet, as much as the rigorous, even literalist understanding of *hijra* was responsive to modern conditions, Daghestani historiography from the period also engaged increasingly with narratives of Islamic beginnings. Alongside reviving its Qur'anic associations, the jurists working under Shamil developed a concept of *hijra* that was closely bound up with his conception of *jihād*.

The poet and jurist Yūsuf al-Yakhsāwī (1795–1871), best known to history as one of Imam Shamil's most articulate opponents, tried to use the Shāfiʿī understanding of the obligation to migrate to his advantage. (For al-Yakhsāwī's biography, see al-Durgilī 2004: 64/88; al-Ghumūqī 2014: 624–5; al-Qarākhī 1946.) Once, while he was in Mecca for the purpose of performing the *hajj*, al-Yakhsāwī issued a request for a legal opinion (*istiftā'*) to a local mufti concerning the legitimacy of Shamil's imamate. Prior to the formation of the imamate, al-Yakhsāwī recollected that "the people of Daghestan did not live under anybody's power…they were Muslims, and their leaders and judges knew the contents of the book of God, and what had to be done." With the encroachment of the tsar's armies into Daghestan and the simultaneous appearance of a new imam, however, the situation changed. Daghestan was besieged on all sides. The new imam began demanding that Daghestanis must perform *hijra* by entering the region under his control. Wishing to remain independent of any ruler, al-Yakhsāwī marshaled the resources of Shāfiʿī legal theory to debate the obligation to migrate in a fashion that the new imam would have difficulty contesting:

> Do we have to perform *hijra*?… In our present condition, we are able to live according to our religion, and that we keep to the firm bond of God. This is possible either because we manage to keep apart from the Infidels, for we are a powerful people, or because the Infidels are generous to us, for they fear that we might associate with the *muhājirūn* [emigrants, in this case to Shamil's imamate]. Does he who abstains from *hijra* therefore become an unbeliever? Not performing the *hijra* is not counted among the things that lead to unbelief. (Kemper 2002: 268)[3]

Al-Yakhsāwī's insistence on the permissibility of living within territories that have fallen under colonial rule was contested by his Meccan correspondent, who, although also a Shāfiʿī, was persuaded of the necessity of residing in the core Islamic lands (*dār al-Islām*), and declared that all Muslims were duty-bound to engage in *jihād* against the infidels rather than to accept peaceful cohabitation with them. Al-Yakhsāwī's interpretation of *hijra* in terms that legitimated his preference for staying at home was repeated time and again in the nineteenth-century Islamic juridical discourse concerning migration and

3 Arabic manuscript labeled (in Russian): "Letter from Yusuf of Aksai to scholars in Mecca with the request to confirm whether the activity of Imam Shamil conforms to sharia" (Rossiiskaia Akademiia Nauk, Dagestanskii Nauchnyi Tsentr, Institut Istorii, Arkheologii i Etnografiia, Makhachkala, Daghestan), fond 16, op 1, No 174, p 1. Translated in Kemper 2002: 268.

mobility. Both among scholars who argued for migration and for those who argued for staying behind, banishment from the Islamic community was consistently treated as the greatest tragedy that could befall a Muslim.

Al-Yakhsāwī wished to remain in his native village rather than migrate to Shamil's imamate and become subordinate to what he regarded as its coercive forms of governance. Others did not wish to migrate to Ottoman lands or to Russia's interior. Few Muslims who wished to stay at home saw their wishes honoured. Even when it was not legally mandated, or enforced at the point of a gun, migration was incentivized and often coerced by the colonial state. Mountaineers who remained behind lived to regret their decision, if indeed they lived at all.

Given the region's long history of violent migrations, it is unsurprising that the Caucasus offers a particularly rich set of archives and literatures for the study of migration, and in a range of genres. In Arabic, Russian, Georgian, and Chechen, *hijra* texts—often invoking this specific term and variations of it—narrate many possible relations between literature and history. *Hijra* in the Caucasus encompasses the mountains in the north to the lower-lying regions of the south, the defeat of indigenous anticolonial resistance movements during the 1850s and 1860s and Daghestan's ill-fated uprising of the 1870s. The term acquired new meanings during the Soviet repressions of minority ethnicities, as well as during their memorialization. Of course, *hijra* was never a static concept. Yet even a scholar well-versed in its many meanings may be surprised by just how potent and flexible *hijra* imagery turned out to be over the course of the long nineteenth century.

Colonial-era *hijra* narratives are primarily in Arabic. They are composed by Muslim scholars who filter their personal experiences and opinions through the prisms of Islamic pasts. Soviet *hijra* narratives are primarily in Russian and Caucasus vernacular languages, including Georgian, Chechen, and Abkhaz. The nineteenth-century Arabic literature of *hijra* includes prosimetric autobiography, poetry, and political and legal theory. Soviet Russian and vernacular *hijra* literature is largely in prose, and includes historical novels that inaugurated their respective literatures.[4] Diasporic *hijra* literature, composed by migrants from the Caucasus once they reached their destination, proliferates to this day in Arabic, Russian, English, and French.[5]

Hijra narratives in the Caucasus comprise an internally variegated yet intertextually linked whole. In the process of (re)constructing this literary corpus, I build on prior efforts to develop an anthropological approach to literary

4 An exception to the general tendency toward verse is Galaktion Tabidze's poem, "Muxajiri."
5 In this category, fictional writing such as Idilbī 1991 can be included.

texts from the Caucasus (Gould 2016). My approach brings migration texts from a range of Caucasus literatures into conversation with each other, and uses these texts to shed light on two centuries of colonization and decolonization in the Caucasus. An anthropological approach to literature enables us to look beyond the construction and deconstruction of canons as literary systems isolated from the broader world, and to understand how texts impact and inflect the worlds to which they refer.

3 *Hijra* as Banishment

While *hijra* was regarded as a singular event in early Islamic history, parallels between the circumstances of Muhammad's migration and the experience of Muslim mountaineers in the aftermath of colonial conquest gave new meaning to the teaching concerning the obligation to migrate. These parallels were reinforced and intensified with repeated narration. As in the age of Muhammad, but in contrast to most of Islamic history, in colonial modernity, the regions to which a Muslim residing in territory under non-Muslim rule could migrate were rapidly contracting. The abode of Islam had radically contracted, and the social infrastructures that facilitated such migrations in prior eras had correspondingly deteriorated.

For Muslims in the nineteenth century Caucasus, *hijra* meant migration to lands under Ottoman rule, including present day Syria and Jordan, where many Daghestanis and Chechens reside to this day (Bīnū 2007). These lands were vast, but the constellations of power and authority that governed such migrations made them more traumatic than for any preceding period in Islamic history. Whereas *hijra* was classically an obligation for which the entire Muslim community shared the burden, Ottoman involvement in migrations from the Caucasus was driven by mercenary rather than spiritual concerns. For migrants to Ottoman lands during the colonial period, *hijra* was less an act of piety which connected them to the wider Islamic community, than a necessity imposed by colonial conquest.

In his Soviet-era reconstruction of these events, the Chechen historical novelist Abuzar Aidamirov (1933–2005) conveys the complex position of the migrants—whom he appropriately calls *muhajirs* (as the term was rendered in Chechen and Russian)—between Islamic norms and bereavement towards the homeland they were now compelled to abandon after it had come under colonial rule. "A faithful Muslim was performing a pious act—abandoning the land of the giaours," Aidamirov narrates, using the Turkic term for infidel, *giaour*. Even when these modern Chechen migrants recognize that their trauma was prefigured in the life of the Prophet, nonetheless "saying farewell to one's homeland left a tragic impression" (Aidamirov 1996, 409). While narrating these events through the narrative templates afforded by the migration of the Prophet helped migrants connect their plight to the founding narrative of early Islamic history, modern *hijras* were performed under conditions even more harrowing and more coerced than those undertaken by the Prophet and his companions.

The divided loyalties of the government officials who organized the migrations further complicated the meaning of migration from the Caucasus to Ottoman territories. The enigmatic life and legacy of Musa Kundukhov (1818–1889), who served both the tsar and the Ottoman sultan during successive stages in his career, illustrates these ambiguities well. The son of an Ossetian nobleman (*aldar*), Kundukhov entered the Pavlovskii Cadet Corps at the age of twelve (Kundukhov 1937). Before he reached the age of twenty, Kundukhov was already working as an interpreter to the Emperor Nicholas during his visit to the Caucasus in 1837. Over the course of the next two decades, this ambitious Ossetian officer rose to the rank of major general in the tsarist army. In 1860, a year following Shamil's surrender and thus of the end of his imamate, tsar Alexandre II (r. 1855–1881) created the Terek province, which included Chechnya and Ingushetia within its domain (figure 9.1). Kundukhov was appointed as the first governor.

During his tenure as a governor, Kundukhov began to make preparations for what would be his most durable and damaging legacy: the forced migration of many thousands of Circassians, Chechens, and Ingush to Ottoman territories. Although the land they were given to live on was, in contrast to the fertile land that they had been promised, barely habitable, the beleaguered mountaineers were powerless to contest decrees that originated in St. Petersburg, or even to ask for what they needed to survive. Although these forced migrations were a disaster for the *muhajir*s on all counts, they were a success for the tsarist administration, Kundukhov included. After he arrived in the Ottoman empire, Kundukhov soon parted ways with the mountaineers, changed his name to Musa Pasha, and embarked on a career in the sultan's army. Musa Pasha rose high in the ranks of the Ottoman army, and even commanded a battalion *against* the Russians during the Turko-Russian war of 1877.

For the early part of his life in the service of the tsar, sources agree concerning the general contours of Kundukhov's biography. It is only after Shamil's surrender, when Kundukhov began to organize mass migrations to the Ottoman empire, that the representation of Kundukhov and his legacy diverges depending on who is telling the story. When Kundukhov's story is told from the vantage point of official Russian sources, the narrative differs starkly from later

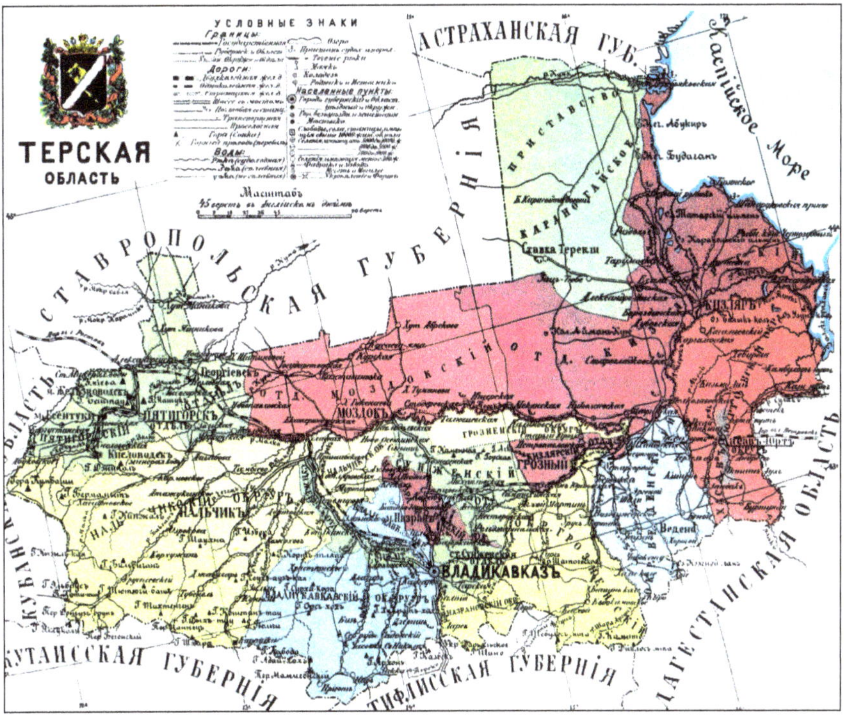

FIGURE 9.1 Map of Terek province

Ingush and Chechen reconstructions. In what, notwithstanding its partiality towards its subject, is among the most detailed accounts of Kundukhov's life on record, Kantemir describes the forced migrations of the 1860s as evidence that "this talented administrator and brave warrior had completely relinquished his political acumen" (Kantemir 1939, 10). Without acknowledging the tragic consequences of his actions or further clarifying their meaning, Allen and Muratoff argue that Kundukhov's organization of the forced migration marked a "break with the Russian authorities" (Allen, Muratoff 1953, 547). Most sympathetic of all is a modern scholarly account that identifies Kundukhov's "disgust with Russian policies towards the local population" as the stimulus behind his campaign for the departure of the mountaineers to Ottoman lands (Khodarkovsky 2011, 4).

If Kundukhov was in fact seeking to rectify the damage done by tsarist policies, it is telling that these noble efforts left no trace in local Caucasus literatures, historiography, or in local memory. In all of these contexts, Kundukhov is remembered in a negative, or at best ambiguous, light. The contemporary Chechen historian Ibragimova has documented in meticulous detail how in

1861, four years prior to the first major deportation, Kundukhov commandeered an expedition against the Chechen mountaineers that resulted in the destruction of fifteen mountain villages (*auls*), as well as the massive resettlement of Chechens residing in the mountains onto the plains (Ibragimova 2010). "All of the buildings, in the *auls* and the homesteads [*khutorov*] have been burned to their foundations," Kundukhov proudly informed his Russian superiors, "all the hay was charred, not only in the *auls*, but even in the mountain heights, which surprised the Chechens, who witnessed the conflagration of their inaccessible declivities and lofty heights" (Ibragimova 2010, 295).[6]

Adding to the portrayal of Kundukhov as a perpetrator of injustice, Ibragimova refers to an event in 1845 when Kundukhov publicly shot a Chechen elder who had killed a distant relative of his thirteen years earlier (Ibragimova 2010). As Ibragimova notes, the only punishment Kundukhov faced for this murder was a brief arrest. The colonial administration took the position that "for the sake of peace in the region, it was necessary to treat the event as a matter pertaining [only to] local custom" (Lapin 2008,156). Assessing his overall impact, Ibragimova sums up Kundukhov's legacy as one of "mercenary…careerism" (Ibragimova 2007, 36).

Historians widely acknowledge that Kundukhov acted in tandem with local Chechens who were in the service of the tsar, as when he organized the deportation of twenty-three thousand Chechens to Turkey in 1865 in cooperation with Usmi Saadulla, a former deputy (*nāʾib*) in Shamil's imamate (Khojaev 1998,172). Kundukhov also encouraged members of the mountaineer elite to simulate a desire to migrate to Ottoman lands in exchange for bribes, after having promised them secretly that they could return home if they were not pleased by the lands that were allotted to them (Ibragimova 2010). Needless to say, such promises were not extended to the impoverished mountaineers who comprised the vast majority of those forced to migrate. Adding to the irony, a Chechen named Arzu Chermoev—who features widely in subsequent fictional retellings—headed the battalion that destroyed fifteen *auls* under Kundukhov's command, and which was followed by resettlements (Muzaev 1992,3). Notwithstanding the broad acknowledgement of Chechen complicity by Chechen historians, Kundukhov is consistently treated as a major orchestrator of Chechen's suffering during the nineteenth century, and as the man

6 Otdel rukopisnyh fondov Severo-Osetinskogo instituta gumanitarnyh i social'nyh issledovanii im. V.I. Abaeva (Division of the manuscript section of the North Ossetian Institute of Humanities and Social Research named after V.I. Abaev) f. 33; op. 1; d. 1; l. 14, 21, 25. Cited in Ibragimova 2010: 295.

primarily responsible for the large-scale deceptions that were perpetrated regarding the terms of the proposed migrations.

These ambivalent memories tied to Kundukhov's legacy are even more forcefully evoked in vernacular literary representations of Kundukhov from the Soviet period. Significantly, the two major historical novels of Ingush and Chechen literature, Idris Bazorkin's *From the Darkness of Ages* (1968) and Aidamirov's aforementioned trilogy (1972–1999) both devote to Kundukhov a degree of space and attention that compares only with the attention lavished on another non-Russian tsarist official, Vorontsov's aide-de-camp the half-Armenian Count Mikhail Tarielovich Loris-Melikov (1826–1888). On both accounts, both Kundukhov and Loris-Melikov were instrumental in organizing the deportations. Bazorkin and Aidamirov however attribute the real agency behind these events to Kundukhov. As they construct an image of Kundukhov as the mastermind behind the mountaineers' tragedy, both novelists emphasize the distance between Kundukhov and the mountaineers. Bazorkin's irony-laden scene in which Kundukhov addresses a pair of Ingush mountaineers, Turs and Goitemir, who have come to plead for the right to access their land, renders this distance through the paradigm of linguistic difference. "I too am a mountaineer," Kundukhov says to a translator, by way of explaining his wealth, and of identifying with the impoverished mountaineers, "I am an Ossetian and a Muslim" (2001, 36). That this heartfelt speech takes place through the medium of a translator, with the self-proclaimed Muslim speaking Russian which the Nakh (the collective term for Chechen and Ingush) can only understand in translation, is indicative of Kundukhov's alienation from his environment.

As soon becomes apparent, Kundukhov's words have a hidden motive. He is trying to persuade his auditors to embark on a *hijra* to Ottoman lands. He says to his captivated listeners: "I am giving up everything to go to Turkey to live with my Muslim brothers. A man must think not only of his mortal life, but about his eternal life." Kundukhov then divulges his plans to relinquish his wealth in order to migrate to Turkey alongside his fellow mountaineers. Manipulating the spiritual, ethical, and legal discourse of *hijra* for the political ends of the colonial state, Kundukhov asserts that anyone who refuses to migrate will become "a slave to the tsar" and "will never see paradise," while those who migrate will be blessed with more land than they can harvest. Kundukhov succeeds in persuading at least one of his audience. After he finishes his speech, Turs exclaims gratefully, "Praise Allah! I'm so glad that I met you, Musa… I'll do everything in my power to help you. Thank you for everything."

As readers of the novel soon learn, Turs' gratitude is entirely misplaced. The many promises that were made from both the tsarist and the Ottoman side to the Muslim mountaineers who migrated to Ottoman lands went unfulfilled.

Instead of fertile land, the migrants were forced to survive on land on which crops could not be sown. Many died from starvation. It is on this juncture in the *muhajirs*' traumatic history that Aidamirov focuses in his literary treatment of Kundukhov. Whereas Bazorkin portrays Kundukhov from the viewpoint of his mountaineer protagonists, Aidamirov uses internal monologue to depict Kundukhov from within. Writing several years after Bazorkin, Aidamirov delves yet deeper into Kundukhov's enigmatic character, and explores how his desire for good was mixed with a willingness to sacrifice his fellow mountaineers' best interests for the advancement of his career.

Although Kundukhov's father makes no appearance in this or any other Chechen literary text, Aidamirov's chapter on the mastermind behind the migration is entitled "Musa Kundukhov, son of Alxas." In emphasizing his parentage, this label thereby stresses his roots among local mountaineers. The chapter "Musa Kundukhov, son of Alxas," consists mostly of a dialogue between Kundukhov, a Chechen emigrant named Arzu (Chechen for "eagle"), and his Ali. Arzu and Ali were leading a group of Chechens who, having given up on obtaining the land that had been promised, were returning to Chechnya. Although the Chechens knew that they would be stopped at the border by the authorities and forced to turn back, they felt that they had no other option. When Kundukhov crossed paths with the Chechen cavalcade headed for the Ottoman-Russian border, they were prepared to die if they could not make it across.

Although the encounter that subsumes this chapter is narrated primarily through the eyes of the Chechen brothers, Aidamirov's narrative technique polyphonically registers multiple points of view. The scene opens with an unnamed Kundukhov, an officer "dressed in Turkish clothing," whom Ali recognizes immediately as "a Caucasus mountaineer" (551). At this juncture in his rise to power, Kundukhov has become more adept at speaking directly to Chechens, for he addresses Arzu in broken Chechen, asking to speak with the eldest among the group.

Arzu recognizes Kundukhov before Kundukhov recognizes him. Addressing him as "Musa, son of Alxas," Arzu accuses his interlocutor of having a bad memory. By this he means to imply that Kundukhov's culpability has dulled his will to remember. As the modern literature of migration repeatedly affirms, memory acts as an ethical compass. According to this same literature, memory is sustained by an ethical capacity to withstand trauma, and, in the case of the Chechens, to survive. The ethics of memory are forcefully conveyed in Arzu's reflection on why the Chechens are perpetually forgotten by their persecutors. "Everyone tries not to recognize us these days," Arzu says, "Indeed, the executioner does not need to know whom he is decapitating." Following this ominous analogy, Arzu concludes with an equally incendiary topic, concerning the arson that Kundukhov perpetrated on fifteen Chechen *auls* while serving as the governor of the Terek district. In response to Arzu's accusation, Kundukhov launches into a defense of the colonializing project. "It was a bad idea to rise up against the tsar," he declares. "Everyone else submitted to their fate. Only you [Chechens] wanted that crazy freedom [*dikii svobodyi*]" (552).

In contradistinction to earlier periods of Islamic history, the concepts of freedom and *hijra* closely converged during the nineteenth and twentieth centuries, amid the struggle against colonial rule and for political autonomy. Whereas *hijra* originally signified a migration performed under duress but volitionally and in expectation of bigger and better things, the tension between the coercive aspects of the obligation to migrate and the yearning for freedom became evident once the pressure to migrate was imposed by the state rather than by ethical commitment or religious belief. Prior to this transformation, which can be said to have begun with the *Reconquista* and the expulsion of Muslims from al-Andalus in 1492, *hijra* was not coercively imposed by the state. As a result of the early modern expulsions, the relationship between *hijra* and freedom changed. Yet even amid this transformation, earlier *hijra* narratives appealed to Muslims during the colonial and Soviet periods due to their longstanding, if malleable, association with freedom. The desacralized understanding of *hijra* that shaped the experience of modern Muslims is apparent from the remark of another of Aidamirov's *muhajirs*, "Everywhere people are running away from poverty and injustice. It doesn't matter much whether it is the Russian tsar or the Turkish sultan [who causes the injustice]. Everywhere our brothers are being expelled" (416).

Given the tension between *hijra* and freedom generated by new forms of state coercion in colonial modernity, it is unsurprising that the climactic debate between Kundukhov and the Chechen migrants he encounters on their way back to Chechnya pivots on the issue of freedom, including its dangers and illusions. As a Chechen author, Aidamirov is keenly aware of the prominent status accorded to the concept of freedom in Chechen culture. This reverence for freedom penetrates so deeply that the majority of greetings in the Chechen language are morphologically related in one way or another to *marsho*, meaning both peace and freedom (Campana 2009, 45).[7] Even the word for greetings itself, *marshalla*, bears this morphological inflection (Jaimoukha 2005, 140). Finally, as the author of the Chechen national anthem which is

7 While Campana 2009 is right to point to the constructed status of Chechen freedom myths, the present example demonstrates that such myths longs predate the post-Soviet conflict and are arguably congruous with Chechen modernity itself.

included in the novel—a ballad known as "death or freedom" due to its refrain—Aidamirov was well positioned to make this the overriding theme of his text.

In response to Kundukhov's critique of the mountaineers who attempted to resist the tsar's military might, Arzu launches into a defense of freedom, a concept for which he is prepared to die. "Do you know what freedom is?" he asks Kundukhov, "We do. This is why we die for it. We have no regrets, even though [this knowledge] costs us dearly. But when you know what you are dying for, then it's much easier to die" (552). Impressing on Kundukhov the injunction to remember that his experience of banishment has imposed on him, Arzu recalls a statement Kundukhov made after destroying the Chechen *auls*. At that time, according to Arzu, Kundukhov had promised to never again harm another Chechen. Arzu confronts Kundukhov with the Ossetian proverb he uttered at the time to a group of Chechens that included himself: "when a tree falls, it falls on a neighbor" (535). This means both that the neighbor prevents the tree from falling to the ground as well as that the tree inevitably shoulders the burden of its neighbor's pain. Arzu counters Kundukhov's proverb by accusing Kundukhov of lying. "In order to remind you of your promise," Arzu says, "last winter two people travelled to Skut-Koh. One of them was me."

Tellingly, Kundukhov fails to remember the Chechens' visit, while it is permanently etched on Arzu's consciousness. When Kundukhov confesses, and half apologies for, this failure in his memory on account of the many visits he has received from unhappy *muhajirs*, Arzu explains what made his reasons for visiting distinct. "We wished to remind you," he states, "that you were obliged to keep your word." Disturbed by these unclaimed memories, Kundukhov deploys a familiar line of defense: he had no other option and was acting according to what he believed were the Chechens' best interests. He claims that the tsar intended to forcibly remove any Chechens who did not migrate to Ottoman lands in the depths of Russia, far from the Caucasus, and compel them, "like sheep, to adopt the [Christian] faith and the [Russian] language" (556). Under such circumstances, Kundukhov stresses, the inevitable outcome would have been genocide. Given that, as he admits, Muslim mountaineers would never agree to the conditions stipulated by the colonial administration, the result would have been war and even more violent banishments of the type that were later to be perpetrated by Stalin. With Kundukhov, colonial discourse merges with an Islamic ethical tradition concerning the obligation to migrate. New meanings are generated and new hypocrisies are forged.

4 Conclusion

Beyond its status as a core teaching and tradition within Islamic law and ethics, *hijra* is a story, and a method for narrating displacement. The narration of migration as *hijra* generates a language for grasping the trauma of forced displacement at the global as well as individual level. Much can be gained from inhabiting cognitively the prisms through which the *hijra* story has been told, from the Maghreb to the Mashreq, from the establishment of the first Islamic state in Medina to the period of dynastic expansion under the Umayyads and the Abbasids to the radical contraction of Muslim sovereignty in early modernity and its obliteration under Russian, French, Spanish, and British colonial rule.

As can be seen from these brief excavations of *hijra*'s meanings across time and space, the obligation to migrate is as variable as Islam itself. Seen from the vantage point of its complex historical trajectory, *hijra* bridges temporalities, geographies, and peoples. Originating in the severance, of kin from kin, husbands from wives, and of Muslims from non-Muslims, *hijra* is also paradoxically a unifying concept, a way of living with and through trauma, that gives meaning and structure to the experience of exile and displacement, including, for Chechens, the ongoing experience of the 1944 deportation (Gould 2012). Through the medium of memory, the *hijra* story is acted out repeatedly, each time with a different meaning yet familiar echoes, varying according to the literature in question, the people whom this literature concerns, and every text's genre and form.

Acknowledgements

This research was completed with the support of the European Union's Horizon 2020 Research and Innovation Programme under ERC-2017-STG [grant agreement number 759346].

Bibliography

Aidamirov, Abuzar. 1996. *Dolgie Nochi.* Moscow: Izd-vo "Agraf."

Arjomand, Saïd Amir. 2009. "The Constitution of Medina: A Sociolegal Interpretation of Muhammad's Acts of Foundation of the *Umma*," *International Journal of Middle East Studies* 41(4): 555–575.

Bazorkin, Idris. 2001. *Iz T'my Vekov.* Nazran: Seraldo.

Bīnū, Sa'īd. 2007. *Al-Shīshān wa-Hijratuhum ilā al-Urdunn* (n.p. Amman).

Campana, Aurélie. 2009. "Collective Memory and Violence: The Use of Myths in the Chechen Separatist Ideology, 1991–1994." *Journal of Muslim Minority Affairs* 29(1): 43–65.

Crone, Patricia. 1994. "The First Century Concept of "Hiĝra." *Arabica* 41(3): 352–387.

Dāwūd, Abū. 1995/6. *Sunan Abī Dāwūd.* Beirut: Dār al-Kutub al-'Ilmīya.

al-Durgīlī, Nadhīr. 2004. *Nuzhat al-Adh-hān fī Tarājim 'Ulamā' Daghistān.* Edited and translated by Michael Kemper and Amir R. Shikhsaidov. Berlin: Klaus Schwarz Verlag.

Fisher, Humphrey. 1994. "Text-Centered Research: *Fitna* as a Case Study and a Way Forward for Guests in The House of African Historiography." *Sudanic Africa* 5: 225–260.

al-Ghumūqī. 2014. "*Tarājim 'Ulamā' Dāghistān*," edited and translated by M.A. Musaev as "Biografii dagestanskikh uchyonikh-bogoslovov, protivnikov imama shamiliia," *Fundamental'naia issledovanie* (6): 624–5.

Gould, Rebecca Ruth. 2012. "Leaving the House of Memory: Post-Soviet Traces of Deportation Memory," *Mosaic, A Journal for the Interdisciplinary Study of Literature*, 45(2): 149–164.

Gould, Rebecca Ruth. 2015. "*Ijtihād* Against *Madhhab*: Legal Hybridity and the Meanings of Modernity in Early Modern Daghestan." *Comparative Studies in Society and History*, 57(1): 35–66.

Gould, Rebecca Ruth. 2016. *Writers and Rebels: The Literatures of Insurgency in the Caucasus*. New Haven: Yale University Press.

Herzig, Edmund. 1990. "The Deportation of the Armenians in 1604–1605 and Europe's myth of Shah. Abbas I." *Pembroke Papers* 1: 59–71.

Ibn Ḥanbal. 1984. *Musnad.* Edited by Aḥmad Muḥammad Shākir. Egypt: Dār al-Ma'ārif.

Ibn Isḥāq. Muḥammad. *Kitāb Sīrat Rasūl Allāh.* Edited by Ferdinand Wüstenfeld (1858–60). Göttingen: Dieterich'sche Universitäts-Buchhandlung.

Ibragimova, Z. Kh. 2007. *Chechentsy- XIX vek.* Moscow: Probel-2000.

Ibragimova, Z. Kh. 2010. *Chechentsy.* Moscow: Probel-2000.

Idilbī, Ulfat. 1991. *Hikāyāt Jaddī: Riwāya.* Damascus: Dār al-Talās.

Jaimoukha, Amjad. 2005. *The Chechens.* New York: Routledge.

Kantemir, A. 1939. *Moussa-Pacha Koundoukhov. Les Memoires du general Moussa-Pacha Koundoukhov (1837–1865).* Paris: Edition du Caucase.

Karny, Yo'av. 2000. *Highlanders: A Journey to the Caucasus in Quest of Memory.* New York: Macmillan.

Kemper, Michael. 2002. "Daghestani Legal Discourse on the Imamate." *Central Asian Survey* 21(3): 265–278.

Khodarkovsky, Michael. 2011. *Bitter Choices: Loyalty and Betrayal in the Russian Conquest of the North Caucasus.* Ithaca: Cornell University Press.

Khojaev, Dalkhan. 1998. *Chechentsi v Russko-Kavkazkoi Voiny.* Grozny: Seda.

Kundukhov, M. 1937. "O Vospominaniiakh Musa-Pashi." *Kavkaz* 8(44): 11–77.

Lapin, VV. 2008. *Armiia Rossii v Kavkazskoi voine XVIII-XIX.* St Petersburg: Evropeiskii Dom.

Madelung, W. 1986. "Has the *Hijra* Come to an End?" *Revue des Études Islamiques* 54: 225–237.

Manning, Paul. 2012. *Strangers in a Strange Land Occidentalist Publics and Orientalist Geographies in Nineteenth-century Georgian Imaginaries.* Brighton: Academic Studies Press.

Montgomery Watt, William. 1941. "Hidjra," *The Encyclopedia of Islam, first edition.* Leiden: Brill.

Muzaev, T. 1992. *Golos Chechenskoi Respubliki* 76.

al-Nuʿmān, Qādī. 1951. *Daʿāʾim al-Islām.* Edited by Asaf ibn ʿAlī Asghar Faidī. Cairo: Dār al-Maʿārif.

al-Qarākhī, Muḥammad Ṭāhir. 1946. *Bāriqat al-Suyūf al-Dāghistāniya fī baʿḍ al-Ghazawāt al-Shāmiliya.* Edited by AM. Barabanov and Krachkovskii IG. Moscow: AN SSSR.

al-Qāsim, Abū ʿUbayd ibn Sallām. 1968. *Kitāb al-Amwāl.* Edited by Muḥammad Khalīl Harrās. Cairo: Maktabat al-Kullīyyāt al-Azharīya.

Rabbat, Nasser. 2014. "Encounters with Modernity in the Arab World," Yale Law School, Occasional Papers, The Dallah Al-Baraka on Islamic Law and Civilization. New Haven: Yale Law School.

Renard, John and Karamustafa, Ahmet T., ed. and trans. 2004. *Knowledge of God in Classical Sufism: Foundations of Islamic Mystical Theology.* Mahwah, NJ: Paulist Press.

Riabchenko, A.E. 1913. *Geograficheskoe opisanie Rossiiskoi Imperii po guberniiam i oblastiam s geograficheskimi kartami.* Sankt-Peterburg: Tipografiia "Berezhlivost'"—Rossiia.

Richmond, Walter. 2013. *The Circassian Genocide.* New Brunswick: Rutgers University Press.

al-Ṭaḥāwī, Muḥammad. *Mushkil al-āthār* (1533/1915). Hyderabad: Maṭbaʿat Majlis Dāʾirat al-Maʿārif al-ʿUthmānīya.

Toledano, Ehud. 1998. *Slavery and Abolition in the Ottoman Middle East.* Seattle: University of Washington Press.

CHAPTER 10

Experiences of Uyghur Migration to Turkey and the United States: Issues of Religion, Law, Society, Residence, and Citizenship

Mettursun Beydulla

1 Introduction

At least one million Uyghurs now live outside their homeland Xinjiang, also known as the Xinjiang Uyghur Autonomous Region (XUAR) and East Turkistan. The experience of migration has been a reality for many years for these Diaspora Uyghurs. They reside in about 50 different countries around the world, but two locales where Uyghurs reside, Turkey and the US, will be the focus of this paper. First, I will describe the migrations to Turkey—when, why and how they were treated. Then I will focus on the US. Following that, I will describe and analyze the differing experiences of the various waves of migrants in light of five topics. The first topic is religion, where I will compare the traditional dichotomy of migration to a Muslim and/or a non-Muslim state, the *Dār al-Islām* and *Dār al-Kufr*. The second topic will be the issue of law and the implementation of changing laws during the periods of migration. The third topic is society, specifically the integration of migrants into their new home cultures. The fourth is residence, which encompasses both legal and illegal means of staying or residing in a country and how this impacts the fifth topic, citizenship. At every juncture, the relationship with the People's Republic of China (PRC), looms large, affecting integration, legal status, business and political factors that impact the Uyghurs in the Diaspora. In the concluding remarks, I will address the issues of identity and the maintenance of Uyghur culture in the Diaspora and how this has been affected by the factors above.

As well as published sources, I draw heavily upon my own experiences as a Uyghur in the Diaspora and the fieldwork that I pursued between June 2013 and September 2017. This fieldwork was carried out while working as an academic in Istanbul, Turkey and later in the United States. I interviewed 200 Diaspora Uyghurs who resided in Istanbul, Ankara, and Kayseri in Turkey as well as Washington, New York and Boston in the US. Also interviewed were Uyghurs currently residing in other countries. Questions asked included those about their migration, and specifically how they maintained their Uyghur identity in the Diaspora. They were asked about their use of language, religious practices, food, clothing, holiday celebrations, problems they faced and how they and their children identified themselves.

During the fieldwork research in Turkey, I interviewed the well-known Uyghur religious scholars Dr. Atavulla Karakas and Hebibulla Kuseni in Istanbul, exploring their view of immigration and how it can be interpreted from an Islamic perspective. Their views regarding Uyghur migration were located in the *hijra* as referring exclusively to flight and refuge or seeking asylum. *Hijra* has more often been used in relation to emigration to join a Muslim community elsewhere to ensure the safe practice of the Muslim faith, meaning for religious reasons. In the Qur'an there is no excuse for suffering under persecution when there are other places to seek refuge. Uyghurs have long been oppressed culturally, economically, socially and religiously. Currently they suffer severe restrictions on the practice of their religion. Because of this, thousands of Uyghurs have been forced to leave their homeland, East Turkistan, to safe places such as Turkey and Western countries. According to Islamic teaching, every part of the earth is Allah's land. Now, borders divide nations and block the flow of migration from one land to another. Yet it does not matter where Uyghurs migrate, as much as their ability to maintain their religious life.

2 Geography, History and Culture of the Uyghur

Uyghurs are the indigenous people in Xinjiang. Most of the world's Uyghurs, Turkic-speaking Sunni Muslims who belong to the *Ḥanafī* school of law, live in Xinjiang, the biggest province of China. Although the XUAR is home to 13 ethnic nationalities, the largest minority is the Uyghurs (about 11 million, based on official statistics) who make up 45.9 % of the total population of XUAR and about 1% of the total population of China. Some Uyghur scholars, writers and activists stressed that the total population of Turkic people in Xinjiang such as Uyghur, Kazakhs, Kyrgyz and Uzbek is 25 million, even some of them claim 35 million. Located in the center of the Eurasian continent, the total land mass of Xinjiang is 1,600,000 square km, making up 1/6 of China. Xinjiang shares international borders with Russia in the north, Kazakhstan in the north-west, Kyrgyzstan, Tajikistan and Afghanistan in the west, and Pakistan and India in the south-west (figure 10.1).

Xinjiang is rich in raw materials and natural resources. Oil reserves in Xinjiang total 23.4 billion tons, and gas reserves are roughly 13 trillion m^3 (Jinhui et al. 2016), making Xinjiang one of biggest oil and gas producing

FIGURE 10.1 The Xinjiang Uyghur Autonomous Region

regions in the world. It is also the gateway to the Silk Route, through which China not only exports to Central Asia and the Middle East, but also imports oil and gas for its economic development. Right now, China's major foreign policy initiative is the One Belt and One Road Initiative. Xinjiang is right in the middle, the hub of that infrastructure development plan.

The geographic foundations that constitute the divisions according to culture and ecotype in the north, south and east are the patterns of the dominant landforms of mountains and deserts. North Xinjiang includes the arid steppe grassland of the Jungarian basin, surrounded by mountains and high pastures. East Xinjiang includes the cities of Turfan, and the large oases around it. South Xinjiang consists of the oases surrounding the Tarim basin and the Taklamakan Desert. Known variously as Kashgaria or Altishehir (six cities), this region has a long and complex history of interaction with Iran and the lands to the south.

3 Brief History of Uyghur and Xinjiang (from Ancient Times up to Chinese Communist Rule)

An outline of Uyghur history is essential in understanding modern Uyghur consciousness and identity. Existing before the eighth century, Chinese historians reported them as Hui-he or Hui-hu. At this time, the Uyghur were just one of a number of nomadic tribes, who in 740 A.D, confederated with other nomads, defeated the Second Turkish Khanate, established a Uyghur empire and then dominated the federation. The traditional shamanistic Turkic-speaking Uyghur came increasingly under the influence of Persian Manichaeanism, Buddhism and eventually Nestorian Christianity. In the year 840 A.D., the Kyrgyz destroyed Uyghur power in Mongolia and the Uyghurs split into two major groups. One moved into the Gansu Corridor region and the other took over the oases north and south of the Tianshan Mountains, establishing the Idiqut Buddhist Uyghur Kingdom in Turfan and the Karakhanli Khanate in Kashgar. These migrant Uyghurs, as well as the indigenous people (such as Scythians, Saks, Tokharians, Sogdian, Hun, and Turks who lived in Xinjiang since 2000 BC) with whom they assimilated, make up the stock of the current Uyghur population.

Most of the Tarim Basin and Jungaria were ruled by Gengiz (Genghis) Khan, his son Chaghatay and his descendants from the early thirteenth to the mid-fourteenth century, when the Mongol rulers separated from the Ulus of Chaghatay. As a result, Xinjiang was ruled by the Turkic-speaking Mongols until the seventeenth century, when Qalmaq Mongols grabbed control of the northern part of Jungaria. They helped establish the White Mountain Khoja clan's rule of the Kashgar Kingdom (Brose 2007; Light 2008).

The Manchu Qing emperor Qianlong had success against the Muslims in western Xinjiang in 1758 and south of Lake Balkhash in 1795, once and for all bringing the entire area within Chinese rule (Hsü 1995). In 1865 a second attempt at establishing an independent Muslim state in southern Xinjiang was made by a leader from Kokand. Within five years, Yakub Beg ruled over a large area of Xinjiang from his base in Kashgar, uniting Muslims across the entire region. After the defeat of Yakub Beg by Zuo Zong-tang in 1878, the region passed into the hands of a Han dominated administration. It was at this time that the name Xinjiang was given to the region on November 18, 1884. Xinjiang means "new borderlands" or "new frontier." In 1911, the Nationalist Chinese overthrew Manchu rule and established a republic.

The Uyghurs staged several uprisings against the nationalist Chinese rule during this period. Twice, in 1933 (in Kashgar) and 1944–1949 (in Ghulja), the Uyghurs were successful in setting up a short-lived independent Eastern

Turkistan Republic. The 1759 Qing occupation, the 1879 Zuo Zong-tang reconquest of Xinjiang and those two secular independent East Turkistan Republics are symbols for most Uyghurs of the illegitimate outsider domination and a legitimation for their cause. The mere mention of the term Sherqi Türkistan (Eastern Turkistan), the preferred term of Uyghurs, especially Uyghur nationalists and diasporas, is enough to draw accusations of separatism or even terrorism from the Chinese government.

4 Uyghur under Control of the Peoples Republic of China (1949 to Present)

Communist China, with the collaboration of the Soviet Union seized Xinjiang in 1949, and the second Eastern Turkistan Republic (ETR) collapsed. The Uyghurs were (yet again) incorporated into China. In October 1955, Xinjiang was officially made the Xinjiang Uyghur Autonomous Region and the Uyghurs were designated as the titular nationality of the region, thus making Xinjiang the homeland of the Uyghur. From 1950 to 1958, the government's mission was to create national unity and establish loyalty among all the minority populations by promoting patriotism and socialist ideology. A tightened control of religion, underpinned by the atheistic principles of Marxism/Leninism, suppressed Islam and ethnic consciousness, alternated with periods of more lenient policies. The Great Leap Forward (1958–62) and the Cultural Revolution (1966–76) were two periods of the greatest intolerance. Many religious holy places including mosques were destroyed or changed into warehouses or pigsties. Intellectuals or secular nationalists who played a role in the clergy were labeled "counter revolutionary." Many members of the clergy such as sheikhs and ishans (religious clerics), or believers suspected of disloyalty, were persecuted, sent to re-education camps, or executed.

The end of the Cultural Revolution ushered an era of reform policies characterized by an expansion of the school system, a drop in illiteracy, and an official softening towards religion and the use of minority languages in education. There were more opportunities for education and a moderate return of religious practices. Churches, mosques, and temples began to reopen in the years following official reauthorization in December 1978. The decade of 1980 to 1990 saw a progressive opening of borders that made Uyghur youth better able to travel more freely and provided opportunities for spiritual exchange and revival. Until the mid-1990s, hundreds of young Uyghurs attended religious schools in Pakistan, Egypt, Turkey, and Saudi Arabia, and a few of them also headed to Yemen, Qatar, and Malaysia for the same reason.

During this period, hundreds of Uyghur immigrated to Central Asia, North America, Europe, and especially to Turkey. Domestic (1989 Tiananmen protest) and international (collapse of the Soviet Union) events made the Chinese government change their policy toward Uyghurs. Policy changes that date from 1989/1990 include changes in religious tolerance, which were mirrored in a crackdown on religious education. Attitudes towards Uyghurs involved reforms or reinterpretations of official policies towards religion, education, and cultural expression. The government began to issue licenses for legal mosques, reviewed appointments of imams and started an "education in atheism" campaign (Amnesty International 2002). Thus began a Sinicization by educating Uyghurs into Chinese culture. Legally, neither the Qur'an nor religion could be taught to students younger than eighteen. Chinese schools and television reinforced this Sinicization by teaching "patriotism" at the expense of other cultural expressions. Restrictions also included banning religious practices during Ramadan, increasing control over Islamic clergy, and the detention or arrest of religious leaders who had been labeled "hypocrite," "unpatriotic" or "subversive" (Human Rights Watch 2005). Restrictions included the annual pilgrimage to Mecca. "In contemporary Xinjiang, the power of the state to regulate religion, including Islam, has brought the forces of law and order into direct conflict with Muslims who are trying to live according the tenets of their faith" (Fuller and Lipman 2004, 323). Since September 2017, Chinese officials have confiscated religious items including prayer mats and copies of the Qur'an in Xinjiang. These copies were taken as part of a Xinjiang-wide campaign that bans "illegal" publicity materials, religious activities and religious teachings that officials consider to be tools of terrorism (Radio Free Asia 2017b).

Education is the key to Sinicization. In order to speed up assimilation, in 1997, the government provided a new model for compulsory Chinese language education and the marginalization of the Uyghur language as well as other minority languages in Xinjiang. By using the term bilingual education, the government is implementing a monolingual language education system that undermines the linguistic basis of Uyghur culture. Chinese has become the only official language and is now the language of instruction in all levels of Uyghur schools including kindergarten (Dwyer 2005). The government has exerted more and more control over every aspect of life in Xinjiang. Now, Uyghurs have become strangers in their own land. (Bovingdon 2010). China bans the Uyghur language in schools in Hotan (Radio Free Asia 2017a), as well as other places.

Ethnic tensions have clearly increased in Xinjiang, especially since the 2009 Urumqi riot and that worries Chinese government officials. As a result of Chinese repressive policies, Xinjiang has become the largest outdoor prison in the world. (Xiang, 2019). In August, 2018, a United Nations panel reported that China had turned Xinjiang into "a massive internment camp." United Nations human rights experts have expressed alarm at what they said were many credible reports that China had detained a million or more ethnic Uyghurs in the western region of "Xinjiang" and forced as many as two million to submit to re-education and indoctrination. Gay McDougall, a member of the UN Committee on the Elimination of Racial Discrimination has described this as, "something resembling a massive internment camp, shrouded in secrecy, a sort of no-rights zone," (Cumming-Bruce, 2018). The government has intensified the crackdown on Uyghurs inside Xinjiang with increased pressure on Uyghurs outside Xinjiang. For example, the Chinese government has forced thousands of Uyghur students abroad to return home since January 2017. Under pressure from the Chinese government, the Egyptian government arrested hundreds of Uyghur students in July 2017 (Aljazeera News, 2017). Some of them are still in jail, some have been released and some repatriated to China. Hundreds of Uyghur students fled to Turkey and a few to Europe.

5 The Uyghur Diaspora in Turkey

After the PLA (Peoples Liberation Army) entered Xinjiang in 1949, a number of Uyghur leaders managed to escape, finally settling in Turkey. Since then, the migration has continued in waves. At first, they fled China to neighboring countries, mainly to India (Kashmir), Pakistan and Afghanistan, but also to Kyrgyzstan and Kazakhstan. While most of them stayed, in the second stage many Uyghur refugees left their host country and re-migrated to a second host country, usually for economic reasons but also, as in the case of Turkey, for cultural and political reasons. In the third stage, Uyghurs migrated yet again, from a second host country to a third host country—Australia, Western Europe and North America—primarily for economic, but also for political reasons.

In this migration process, Turkey became a terminal destination as well as a transit or junction to other destinations. Of the one million Uyghurs who make up the Uyghur diaspora, the largest concentration outside Xinjiang can be found in the "West Turkestan" central Asian states of Kazakhstan, Kyrgyzstan, Turkmenistan and Uzbekistan, as well as significant clusters in Pakistan and Afghanistan (Chung 2002; Wang 2003). The largest Uyghur population resides in Kazakhstan, where 300,000 have lived for several generations (Golovnina 2009; Leonard 2009). After Central Asia, the next largest diaspora community resides in Turkey, where Uyghurs claim ancestral links to the Turks. Because of Turkey's ancestral, historical, linguistic and cultural ties, it has been the most attractive destination for Uyghurs looking to escape the influence of Communism. As a result, Turkey has been the most influential node in the Uyghur diaspora during the twentieth century. This may also explain why Turkey, since the 1950s, has provided Uyghur activists a primary haven to help shape an East Turkestan independence movement (Shichor 2007). Of the total population of Uyghur living in Turkey, estimated to be 35,000–45,000 about 10,000 of them are refugees.

Already in the nineteenth century Turkey served as a model for Turkistan nationalism. Although Turkey could not extend its assistance to Xinjiang's Turkic nationalities, they have always regarded Turkey as a model and a source of moral support and ideological inspiration. Indeed, following the flight of Uyghur refugees from Chinese Communism in March 1952, Turkey, supported by the United Nation High Commissioner for Refugees (UNHCR), offered sanctuary (in fact, political asylum) to 2,000 Eastern Turkistan refugees who had fled Xinjiang to India and Pakistan following the communist occupation. In 1953, Turkey accepted an additional 900 Eastern Turkistan refugees from Kashmir and Pakistan. This Turkish policy, offering temporary or permanent residence, persists to this day. In 1965, Turkey accepted 235 from Yarkand, one third of a group of Uyghur refugees who had fled to Afghanistan in 1961. Their absorption was made possible by a special resettlement program financed by UNHCR, at the request of the Turkish government. Like their predecessors, they were given citizenship and provided with housing. Uyghur have continued to arrive in Turkey since the late 1960s, mostly on an individual basis. Since the 1980s Open Door policy, many Uyghurs have left China to study abroad or go on pilgrimage (hajj) to Mecca, never to return. In August 1982, Turkey accepted another group of several thousand Uyghur refugees who had come from Afghanistan and Pakistan. Many of them had escaped from Xinjiang by crossing the border, now more open and less guarded.

Thus, the Turkish experience created two groups of Uyghurs, called "yerlik" (local) or "kona" (old) who were descendants of those migrating at earlier times, and "yengi kelgenler" (newcomers), those immigrants since 1980. At first the cultural differences between these groups were significant. The "yerlik" were more Turkicized, more religious and looked down upon the newcomers because of their ignorance of religion. The newcomers, those who arrived since 1980, have more relational ties with the Uyghurs of Xinjiang. Most newcomers saw their new life in Turkey as a temporary solution to the political and economic turmoil transpiring in their "homeland." They felt they would be able to return and reclaim their "homeland" once the Chinese communists left Xinjiang or the regime changed.

Isa Yusup Alptekin and Mehmet Emint Bugra, who, after spending a few years in Kashmir following their flight from Xinjiang, had finally settled in Istanbul, led the Uyghur community in Turkey. After Bugra's death in 1965, Alptekin remained the uncrowned leader of Eastern Turkistan until his death in 1995, aged 94. Their activities had always been aimed at two interconnected targets and at two different audiences simultaneously. Alptekin was particularly active in raising awareness for the Uyghur causes and paid visits to many organizations such as the Muslim World League and the Arab League as well as attending the Bandung Conference in 1955, the Afro-Asian Conference in 1965 and the World Congress of Islam in 1964 (Landau 1995, 118, 150; Shichor 2003, 290). The Uyghur diaspora community in Turkey has also worked closely with the Turkish government, and in return, Turkey remains highly critical of Beijing's Xinjiang policy and is sympathetic toward the plight of the Uyghurs. In the 1980s and since, especially since 2009, there has been a new wave of migration that crossed the international borders in order to visit relatives, engage in trade, to study and for many, to flee from Chinese persecution. Initially, most Uyghur migrants who had arrived tended to settle together, creating special quarters such as Zeytinburnu, Sefakoy, Aksaray, Kaya Sehir, and Selim Pasa in Istanbul or Yasevi in Kayseri. There, residential concentrations can also provide networking opportunities for new immigrants. Those with professional skills have many opportunities in Turkish society, but Uyghurs who do not have qualifications are often trapped in specific labour markets. Occupation plays an important role in shaping identity and giving a sense of difference. One's identity may limit or increase not only one's employment opportunities but also one's social integration.

The interaction between the various communities of Uyghurs has helped shape the current concept of a common Uyghur identity. A sense of a unique community has begun to dissolve as the younger generations have become Turkicized and lost their Uyghur cultural and linguistic identity. They have tended to leave their traditional communities seeking accommodation, education and employment. For similar economic and professional reasons, since the 1960s, many of Turkey's Uyghurs began immigrating to third countries, such as Canada, Holland, and Scandinavia, but primarily to Germany. Paradoxically, it has been more difficult for them to assimilate and easier to maintain their identity in these countries compared to Turkey. Germany has become the central outpost and the most important base for promoting the cause of East Turkistan independence and Uyghur nationalism. Some of the factors are related to the collapse of the Soviet Union in 1991. The independence of the Central Asian countries, with whom Uyghurs share a common religion, culture, language and history, created hopes among Uyghurs and contributed to their seeking of a greater autonomy or even independence from the PRC. China, since the 1990s, has pressured the Turkish government to restrict Uyghur national activism as it has become more sensitive to separatist activity within its borders. This, combined with growing economic relations between the two countries, has dampened Turkey's enthusiasm in hosting the Uyghur community (Shichor 2007). Pro-Uyghur, pro-independence and anti-Chinese government mobilization in Turkey has attracted the attention of Chinese authorities, and this attention has in turn affected and shaped this mobilization.

Since 2009, especially after 2017, China intensified persecution of Uyghurs leading to human rights abuses in Xinjiang. Shortly after the mass arrest of Uyghur students in Egypt and hundreds of arrests and imprisonment in Turkey, Uyghur groups felt the need to move westward again, this time to Europe and eventually the United States. All these developments, along with changes in communications, contributed to a renewed phase of Uyghur diaspora activism. Diaspora members can now share information about news and events and coordinate more easily (Brinkerhoff 2006, 31–32, Bernal 2006, 163). According to Bernal, the internet is a transnational space where diaspora members "produce and debate narratives of history, culture, democracy and identity" (Bernal 2006, 161). Thus, the internet has had the capacity to transform the diaspora.

6 Uyghur Diaspora in the United States

During the 1990s, many Uyghurs migrated to the United States. Some of them came as students, visiting fellows/researchers and recently came as tourists and later sought asylum. Many of them came as political refugees, fearing prolonged and ruthless Chinese suppression. The Uyghurs from Turkey and the Central Asian region also fled to safer countries like the United States. Many Uyghurs in the US have ensconced themselves in middle class America and are one of the most educated immigrant groups in the US. Those with limited linguistic and professional skills usually work in lower-class, low-wage jobs in restaurants, grocery stores, delivery services, drive taxis or work for Uber. The majority of Uyghur immigrants are first generation foreign-born and came as young singles. Currently, they number around 5,000 to 6,000 and growing. They are mostly concentrated in metropolitan areas such as Washington D.C., New York, Boston, Los Angeles and San Francisco. First-generation Uyghur Americans prefer to live in a Uyghur neighborhood because of language difficulties. For many unskilled Uyghur immigrant workers, staying in the same neighborhood with fellow Uyghurs can provide important advantages for better survival in the "strange land." Relatives or friends who already live in the area may provide them with places to stay and work, thus speeding up the process of acculturation.

The Uyghur immigrants in the US have remained attached to their culture, which finds expression in the traditional festivals, ceremonies and socio-cultural activities. They remember the two East Turkistan Republic foundation days, several incidents such as the 1990 Barin incidents, the 1997 Ghulja demonstration and the 2009 Urumqi riot (Millward 2009). These are seen as protests to the Chinese government, where Uyghurs were cruelly suppressed, hundreds were killed, thousands injured and scores of people were disappeared after each event. They also celebrate New Year and religious holidays like Ramadan and Qurban Eid and organize a couple of protests in front of the Chinese embassy in Washington each year. They engage in traditional Uyghur dance theatre, drama, stage shows, and organize picnics and prayers. These activities are organized by the Uyghur American Association and the Uyghur Human Rights Project in Washington DC., who work along with the World Uyghur Congress.

7 Issues and Factors of Religion, Law, Society, Residence and Citizenship

7.1 *Turkey*

As has been mentioned above, Turkey hosts Uyghur separatist activists and human rights organizations. Since the mid-1990s, Beijing has been applying pressure on Ankara to curb Uyghur separatist activism in Turkey. Beijing has used its relations with the Kurds, who claim Turkish territory, to twist Ankara's arm (Kuang Shengyan 1995). Beijing has used an analogy between Uyghurs and Kurds, saying that if Ankara continues to support Uyghurs, Beijing will support Kurds. When President Jiang Zemin visited Turkey in April 2000, he indicated that both countries were faced with the task of protecting national unity and territorial integrity and both opposed all kinds of international terrorism, national separatism and religious extremism (Si, 2000).

These days, Turkey hosts thousands of Uyghur refugees and immigrants, but their situations are precarious. Aside from those who are citizens, many do not have legal or social protection and live on the charity of Turkish people (*zakat*). In pursuit of work and residence permits, they have to deal with various authorities. Many live in constant insecurity, stress and fear, and are forced to remain in such a state of limbo for years. Ethnic tensions have clearly increased in Xinjiang and this worries Chinese government officials. The Uyghurs (40%),

Kazakhs, Kyrgyz and other Turkic groups (15%), who currently make up 55% of the population in Xinjiang, are closer culturally and linguistically to Turkish people than they are to the Han Chinese. Beijing has planned to combine its intensified crackdown of Uyghurs inside Xinjiang with increased pressure on them outside Xinjiang, through the Turkish government.

In an interview, one of my informants touched on many of these factors at the nexus of law, society, residence and citizenship. He said:

> The Chinese government and investors have an interest in Turkey and they have been providing technology and expertise for the development of Turkey and they are promising more. One of my friends, who works for a Turkish company as a translator, told me that $40–50 billion deals (joint funds) have already been made or are being discussed. When the Turkish foreign minister visited Beijing this summer he promised to restrict all pro-Uyghur activity in Turkey. At the same time, a number of Uyghur religious leaders, activists and public figures such as Adukadir Yapchan, Canadian citizen Ibrahim Haji, and about a thousand Uyghur refugees were arrested and they are in jail now. I do strongly believe that Turkey is under pressure from the Chinese government. As Turkey receives more economic and technologic assistance from China, there will be more pressure on Uyghurs in Turkey. These is no such thing as a free lunch... I was kicked out in my last year of medical school in Xinjiang, because of my peaceful pro-Uyghur activity. Later, I was able to manage to flee from further Chinese persecution in 2000 and I came to Turkey. I found a safe haven here in Turkey. I went to medical school in Turkey and I earned my degree. Then I worked for a government family care center for the last 10 years. I also married and am raising two children in Turkey. But now I am nervous and do not feel safe anymore here in Turkey. Especially, I don't see a bright future for my children. So first I planned to immigrate to the US or Canada, but based on my knowledge, the US and Canada do not accept my medical degree and experiences. It means an extremely difficult time for me to find a job there. Later, I learned that it will be easy for me to adjust and settle in Europe, especially Germany because I can certify my degree and experiences easily and in a short time. After all, my family and I decided to immigrate to Germany and we have already started the paper work." (Personal communication, September 4, 2017).[1]

1 This informant became a Turkish citizen in 2009, his two children were born as Turkish citizens and his wife is an ethnic Uyghur with Chinese citizenship. She applied for Turkish

On September 25, 2017, Abdulkadir Tumturuk (Deputy Director of the Uyghur association in Kayseri, Turkey) expressed in social media (WhatsApp) that 125 Uyghurs had been released from jail and the Uyghur scholar and activist Abduwali Ayup (exiled in Turkey for the last two years) expressed in a Facebook post that "370 Uyghur are jailed in Turkey, because of terror suspect." Unofficially, yet quite obviously, China's strategy in Turkey is aimed at gaining political influence, security guarantees, economic presence and natural resources as China has wanted to become one of the main economic powers in Turkey. China's strategy and foreign policy in Turkey is firstly determined by its need to consolidate control of "Xinjiang" and restrain the Uyghur independence movement in Turkey. Next in importance is China's trade and economic investments in Turkey, especially its "One Belt, One Road" initiatives. These are not just increasing its influence; they are making Turkey far more reticent to speak out about Beijing's abuses and oppression in Xinjiang. (Gunes, 2019). China's geo-economic strategy has resulted in political influence in Turkey that profoundly affects its Uyghur population.

7.2 *The United States*

Religion is the main difference between Turkey and the US for Uyghur immigrants. Turkey is a predominantly Muslim country, and the US, a secular country (but mostly Christian). This obviously colors much of the reception by the local population. Many Uyghurs find themselves socially and legally marginalized by United States' restrictive asylum policies. They cannot lead an independent life or plan a future and they are severely restricted in their settlement, movement, employment and educational opportunities. In pursuit of work and residence permits, they have to deal with various public authorities. Thus, many live in constant insecurity, stress and fear, and are forced to remain so for years, with the threat of expulsion hanging over their heads. In such a situation, it is nearly impossible to establish a home in United states and develop a sense of national belonging.

In a study of attitudes towards immigrants in America, Canada and Europe over the past two decades, Hainmueller and Hopkins looked at two approaches, one of political economy and the other of a socio-psychological orientation. Political economy approaches are characterized as follows: "Frequently starting from formal models of immigration's economic impacts, this theoretical approach explains immigration attitudes with reference to native-born

citizenship in 2016, but she has not yet received any response. He and his family finally immigrated to the UK on March 25, 2019 and are now living in London (Personal communication, March 27, 2019).

citizens' individual self-interest" (Hainmueller et al. 2014, 2). By contrast, socio-psychological inquiries frequently look at cultural responses based on perceived threats to national identity or prejudices generated by local group contact. The research shows that a country's regime policies have important implications for the populations' intolerance of immigrants. In the US, that has translated into legal and cultural concepts of citizenship, and the general attitude towards immigrants has also become more negative especially since the Trump administration. US President Trump has already cut refugee admissions by more than half, from more than 100,000 down to 50,000. In fact, just 22,491 refugees were resettled in the US in fiscal year 2018, roughly half the 45,000 cap. The number of Muslim refugees is down by 90 percent since fiscal year 2017. Drastic budget cuts and staff layoffs began in 2018 and are expected to continue through 2019. Secretary of State Mike Pompeo announced in September, 2018 that the US would admit no more than 30,000 refugees in fiscal year 2019; he also said the lower refugee ceiling would help improve national security (Amos, 2018).

However, others have disagreed. Writer, the US homeland security secretary from 2005–2009, proposed that, "Cutting refugee admission hurts Americans and this would be a mistake. Cutting refugee admission would not only be a moral failure but also damage our national interest abroad and our economy" (Chertoff, 2017).

Uyghurs acquiring Turkish or US citizenship cannot be taken as an indication of a loosening ties to their homeland, East Turkistan. There are two main reasons why Uyghurs distinguish between citizenship and national identity. The first is that permanent and inborn identities and belongings are considered more important than those acquired. A second major reason for the non-identification with the US nation is the strong belief that "natives" will never perceive naturalized Uyghurs as being American and continue to identify them as "others," because of, according to Uyghurs, their different physical appearance, religion and culture. These two reasons are likely to reinforce one another. Several scholars (Barnes 2001, 410; Kumar Behera 1999, 76; Valtonen 1998) suggest that the experience of social exclusion from the mainstream society is likely to cause ethnic revitalization and a withdrawal of social and emotional commitment to the host society.

Meeting America, as some of my respondents express it, has often been the first meeting with a democratic system and with political freedom. Meeting America has also meant meeting other Uyghur and the Uyghur movement's organizations and institutions. It has also meant opportunities to meet the larger world, intensified interactions, identifications as well as differentiations. All of my informants appreciated American society very much for the political freedom that they experienced. They also appreciated the possibilities and perquisites that society allows them as citizens. However, in the US, they also face racism, otherness and an inferior identity as immigrants. A number of informants encountered overt racism and many believe they have fewer chances of finding employment and housing. Some informants stressed that at work and when they apply for jobs, they experienced disrespect, humiliations, rejections and blocked opportunities. A number also complained about the United States banking system. They stressed that in the United States there is no governmental encouragement for citizens to help immigrants. The US banking system is based on personal credit history. If an immigrant does not have a good history, he cannot get a loan. It takes a long time to develop a credit history and, consequently, this makes the lives of immigrants miserable. As well, visual religious differences, such as the Muslim headscarf, can also greatly influence employment opportunities for immigrant communities. Since 9/11, some Uyghur women have faced discrimination when they apply for jobs. The feeling of marginalization is probably strengthened by the fact that many refugees used to belong to the better-off and educated sections of their country of origin. Some respondents believe that foreigners have to work much harder and prove themselves more in order to reach the same level as Americans. Feelings of not belonging and being different seem to have increased since 2001 and especially since the current administration.

Men tend to have more contact with formal religious structures and other Muslims both in Turkey and the US than women, especially older women, since they attend mosques with greater frequency and work outside the home. Islam may well offer both a structure within which they can find meaning and purpose in their lives, and certain rights and privileges in private life that they do not have in public life. Some young women in Turkey and U.S have chosen to adopt the *hijab*, or more "orthodox" veil, which they would not have worn in Xinjiang. This is seen as similarly empowering, in that it allows them to project the importance of their identity as Muslims and enables them to honour Islamic morality while moving in non-sex-segregated and non-Muslim spaces.

Differences between the generations are undoubtedly exacerbated in the US because the younger generation moves with greater ease in the "foreign" land. They are generally more proficient in English than their parents, and they sometimes act as translators when their parents have to deal with US institutions. They have gone to school and spent more of their formative years in the US than their parents. Some of them have non-Uyghur friends (as their parents are less likely to), and they are more familiar with technology.

Even those Uyghurs who are not particularly religious, though, still insist on the importance of marrying Muslims. For men, and less so for women, marriages are sometimes arranged with Uyghurs outside of the US and occasionally young Uyghur men marry outside the group. Still, there is considerable pressure to marry within the community or, at least, to marry another Muslim. The most important consideration, perhaps, is the Uyghur fear of losing their identity as Muslims, usually expressed as the fear of raising children who are "confused" by conflicting religious messages or fear of their children becoming "*kāfir*" (unbelievers). Many Uyghurs said that they believe they will be judged guilty and will be punished on judgment day for their children's "deviant" behavior and "sins."

8 Searching for Identity among the Uyghur Diaspora in Turkey and the United States

Uyghur identity-construction spaces are those in which Uyghurness is formed, celebrated, and promoted and in which the values of the community are transmitted to the next generations. Uyghur spaces can be seen in five categories: cultural, labour/market, residential, institutional, and organizational/political spaces. These spaces are not independent of one another, for they all function in an interrelated manner to preserve Uyghur identities and to increase the power of the Uyghur community in the sociopolitical space. The diversity of Uyghur institutions (especially in Turkey) and locations reflects the diversity of the community. Although mosques, for example, are important sites for conservative Muslims, strict seculars distance themselves from such institutions and form their own organizations. Therefore, religion is not only an important boundary between Uyghur immigrants in Turkey and the U.S (and the larger American culture as well), but also a significant boundary within the Uyghur community

Many Uyghurs are very critical about the images of Muslims and of Islam portrayed in the media in the aftermath of 9/11. As non-Western immigrants, they are particularly exposed to discrimination and exclusion in American society. Besides these problems, the category of forced migrants and exiles suffer the traumatic experience of having no access to the places to which they are emotionally and socially related. My informants viewed their Uyghur identity as inborn and inescapable. This biological inheritance through blood and genes must, however, be accompanied with cultural inheritance.

Immigrants are to a large extent pushed back into their own communities and therefore do not always have the same relationship towards the "outside." As the "first generation" they have memories, lived experiences, and connections with a place to which they can relate when they are excluded from the receiving societies, while the "second generation" do not always have these in the same way. We are located not only in ethnic categories but also in other intersectional categories such as gender, class, generation, lifestyle, origin, history, nationality, culture, education, sexuality, politics, etc. Uyghur social institutions include schools, mosques, associations, Uyghur restaurants (both in Turkey and the US), social media such as Facebook, WeChat and WhatsApp. They function as identity-construction spaces because they provide sites for Uyghur's distinct experiences and expressions of identity. They help Uyghurs find a special place in the larger Turkish or American space. These institutions represent the Uyghur to "others" and ensure that their voices are heard. Worship places, churches, synagogues, and mosques, serve as sacred spaces where meanings, ethics, and values of a particular nation or culture are transmitted through religious discourse and interaction (Barot 1993). As spaces of gathering, sharing, and interacting, they also function to preserve identities and produce a community based on religion and nationality (Ernst 1987). Places of worship provide boundaries of difference to resist the dominant culture and celebrate cultural uniqueness. They are territories where a certain degree of autonomy is practiced (Barot 1993).

Due to the importance of cultural practices and memories in conceptions of Uyghurness, Uyghurs are afraid that their "natural" identity as Uyghur will fade away if they do not do the things that make them Uyghur and do not remember "where they came from." Children, and young Uyghurs in particular, are considered susceptible to change due to their lack of memories of Uyghur society. Their exposure to different values and lifestyles has resulted in the older generation not considering them to be "real" Uyghur and they themselves often struggle to define their identity. In their new environment, they begin a process of being forced to revalue and negotiate their sense of themselves, their experiences and knowledge, in order to orientate themselves and find continuity in their identity.

Claims of roots play an important role among the diaspora, but they are weakened by the recognition that roots also have had an influence on their identity, culture and attachment to territory. Paradoxically, it was these experiences of change, displacement and uncertainties about identity themselves that generated the longing to cling to an anchor of roots in the first place.

For diasporic Uyghurs, their identity is formed in direct contact and contrast to non-Uyghurs. Practices and beliefs that used to be simply a part of life have become conscious symbols of Uyghurness, even if these have had to be moderated and adapted to the new environment. To be a Uyghur means belonging to a family that has been broken up and scattered all over the world. It means having been displaced from one place to another, and having memories of childhood, landscapes, loss and flight.

9 Conclusion

The aim of this study was to explore the experience of Uyghur immigration to Turkey and the U.S, in relation to issues of religion, law, society, residence, and citizenship. Their experience in Turkey and the US provides a cogent example of the complex and contested geographies of home and identity and the multiple experiences of displacement. Uyghurs, as refugees, migrants, residents and citizens and in liberal Western democracies, have obtained the possibility to enjoy general human rights and citizen rights, although in different degrees in different countries. In spite of the diversities and differences that divide the Uyghur diasporic community, the Uyghur refugees' relation to Turkey and the US can be analyzed within a context where they all encounter Turkish and US multiculturalism—which implies on the one hand democracy and tolerance, and on the other hand exclusion, inferiority and otherness. Diaspora Uyghurs, especially those living in Turkey (depending on government restrictions), the US and Europe, have played a major role by their contribution to the development of the Uyghur cause by maintaining language and identity. Many significant Uyghur cultural and political activities, which do not take place in "Xinjiang," have found a home in exile.

Global migration is an irreversible historical process and is also a component of the contemporary global system. However, it challenges the concept of citizenship and belonging and demands for adapting to new global conditions. Global migration has become an issue of security and is highly political. The politics of Turkey and the US are gradually changing in order to encompass this shift. Hall claims that a growing number of people "are beginning to think of themselves, of their identities and their relationship to culture and to place, in more "open" ways" (Hall 1995, 207). I consider it incorrect to focus solely on roots and hybridity, because such concepts do not reflect the way that ordinary people and nation states themselves think and speak about identity, culture and place. A few decades of globalization have not led to the development of cosmopolitan hybrids and a post-national world of limitless mobility, but rather to the reinvention of nationalism, boundaries and distinct identities. Immigrants are not viewed or treated as equals by the host society. Hence, there is a gap between formal and "substantive" citizenship. The social relations between refugees or migrants and the rest of society are determined by the position of the immigrant "Other" within the global distribution of power and dominance.

My research has indicated that ideas about an inborn and unchangeable identity connected to a certain territory and culture remain very much alive among both Uyghur-Turks and Uyghur-Americans. When Uyghurs use language about their roots, they refer to a culture that is in their blood, a connection to East Turkistan's holy soil, and they compare East Turkistan with a nurturing mother figure. When I speak of roots, I do not mean to say that these are naturally and primordially given. Ideas of roots rest upon inventions and imaginations. It is important to realize, however, that they appear to be natural and authentic in the minds of people. The first generation of Uyghur diaspora in Turkey and the US and adults of a young diaspora community are still very affected by the Uyghur movement and politics. They have experiences of, as well as existing and intense social and emotional bonds to, their "homeland" and the Uyghur diaspora community. As the "first generation," they encountered much greater difficulties and obstacles in becoming a part of Turkish and US society.

Classifying Uyghurs on the basis of national origin as East Turkistan or Uyghur reveals nothing about the actual relationships Uyghurs form on the ground, where shared language, culture, and especially religion is key, while shared national origin is a reminder of historical opposition and persecution. In the multicultural landscape of the US, Islam offers a means through which Uyghurs can establish themselves in a larger, community of Muslim Americans. It is an identity that seeks to assert its independence from forces abroad, one that combines the essential elements of Islam and the values of American constitutional democracy.

Acknowledgements

I very much appreciate the efforts of Dr. Ray Jureidini and the CILE team for organizing the CILE Migration Seminar and for their invitation. I also would like to say thanks to Dr. Ray Jureidini; Dr. Said Hassan and Dr. Wachob for their helpful comments and the editing of this article.

Bibliography

Amos, Deborah. 2018. "2018 Was A Year of Drastic Cuts to U.S. Refugee Admission." NPR, December 27. Available at: <https://www.npr.org/2018/12/27/680308538/2018-was-a-year-of-drastic-cuts-to-u-s-refugee-admissions>.

Aljazeera News. 2017. "Egypt arrests Chinese Muslim students amid police sweep." July 7. Available at: <http://www.aljazeera.com/news/2017/07/fear-panic-egypt-arrests-chinese-uighur-students-170707051922204.html>.

Amnesty International (2002). Peoples Republic of China's Anti terrorism Legislation and Repression in the Xinjiang Uighur Autonomous Region.

Barnes, Diane. 2001. "Resettled Refugees" Attachment to their Original and Subsequent Homelands: Long-Term Vietnamese Refugees in Australia." *Journal of Refugee Studies* 14(4): 394–411.

Barot, Rohit. 1993. *Religion and Ethnicity: Minorities and Social Change in the Metropolis.* Kampen, Netherlands: Kok Pharos Publishing House.

Bernal, Victoria. 2006. "Diaspora, Cyberspace and Political Imagination: the Eritrean Diaspora Online." *Global Networks* 6(2): 161–179.

Bovingdon, Gardner. 2010. *The Uyghurs: Strangers in Their Own Land.* New York: Columbia University Press.

Brinkerhoff, Jennifer M. 2006. "Digital Diasporas and Conflict Prevention: The Case of Somalinet.com." *Review of International Studies* 32: 25–47.

Brose, Michael C. 2007. *Subjects and Masters: Uyghurs in the Mongol Empire.* Center for East Asian Studies, Western Washington University.

Chertoff, Michael. 2017. "How Cutting Refugee Admissions Hurts America." *Washington Post, September 15.* Available at: <https://www.washingtonpost.com/opinions/cutting-refugee-admissions-hurts-americans-heres-how/2017/09/14/c7c8b5e6-9987-11e7-b569-3360011663b4_story.html?utm_term=.442ed60581ac>.

Chung, Chien-Peng. 2002. "China's 'War on Terror': September 11 and Uighur Separatism." *Foreign Affairs* 81(4): 8–12.

Cumming-Bruce, Nick. 2018. "UN Panel Confronts China Over Reports that It Holds a Million Uighurs in Camps." *New York Times.* Available at: <https://www.nytimes.com/2018/08/10/world/asia/china-xinjiang-un-uighurs.html>.

Dwyer, Arienne M. 2005. "The Xinjiang Conflict: Uyghur Identity, Language Policy, and Political Discourse." *Policy Studies* 15. Available at: <http://www.eastwestcenter.org/fileadmin/stored/pdfs//PS015.pdf>.

Ernst, Eldon G. 1987. *Without Help or Hindrance: Religious Identity in American Culture.* 2nd ed. Lanham, Md.: University Press of America.

Fuller, Graham E and Jonathan N. Lipman. 2004. "Islam in Xinjiang." In *Xinjiang, China Muslim Borderland,* edited by S. Fredrick Starr, 320–352. Armonk, NY: M.E. Sharpe.

Gernet, Jacques. 1982. *A History of Chinese Civilization.* Cambridge: Cambridge University Press.

Golovnina, Maria. 2009. "Asia Uighurs Harbour Revenge for Xinjiang Kinfolk." *Reuters*, 16 July.

Gunes, Gokan. 2019. "Turkey Treads Tricky Path with China's Muslim Minorities." AFP News, March 21. Available at: <https://sg.news.yahoo.com/turkey-treads-tricky-path-chinas-muslim-minorities-032439406.html>.

Hainmueller, Jens and Daniel J. Hopkins. *Public Attitudes Toward Immigration*. Centre for Research and Analysis of Migration. Department of Economics, University College London. Available at: <http://cream-migration.org/publ_uploads/CDP_15_13.pdf>.

Hall, Stuart. 1995. "New Cultures for Old." In *A Place in the World? Places, Culture and Globalization*, edited by Massey, Doreen and Jess, Pat: 175–211. Oxford: Open University / Oxford University Press.

Hsü, Immanuel C.Y. 1995. *The Rise of Modern China Fifth Edition*. New York: Oxford University Press.

Human Rights Watch. 2005. "China: Religious Repression of Uighur Muslims." Available at: <http://www.hrw.org/en/news/2005/04/10/china-religious-repression-uighur-muslims>.

Jinhui Duan, Shuying Wei, Ming Zeng, and Yanfang Ju. 2016. "The Energy Industry in Xinjiang, China: Potential, Problems, and Solutions. Power." Available at: <http://www.powermag.com/energy-industry-xinjiang-china-potential-problems-solutions-web>.

Kuang, Shengyan and Zhihong Chen. 1995. "Kuerde gongrendang wenti ji qi dui Tuerqi neiwai zhengce de yingxiang (The Question of the Kurdish Workers Party and Its Impact on Turkey's Domestic and Foreign Policy)." *Xiya Feizhou* (West Asia and Africa) 4: 19–24.

Kumar Behera, Deepak. 1999. "Ethnic Identity and the Adjustment Pattern of British-Born Sikh Children in the United Kingdom." In *Roots and Routes. Ethnicity and Migration in Global Perspective*, edited by Shalva Weil: 65–84. Jerusalem: The Magnes Press.

Landau, Jacob. 1995. *Pan-Turkism: From Irredentismto Cooperation*. Bloomington: Indiana University Press.

Leonard, Peter. 2009. "Kazakh Uighurs Hold Mass Protest." *Associated Press* 19 July.

Li, Yuanging. 1990. "Population Changes in the Xinjiang Uyghur Autonomous Region (1949–1984)." *Central Asian Survey* 9(1): 49–73.

Light, Nathan. 2008. *Intimate Heritage, Creating Muqam Song in Xinjiang*. Piscataway, NJ & London: Transaction Publishers.

Millward, James A. 2007. *Eurasian crossroads, history of Xinjiang*. New York: Columbia University Press.

Millward, James A. 2009. "Introduction: Does the 2009 Urumchi Violence Mark a Turning Point?" *Central Asian Survey* 28(4): 347–60.

Radio Free Asia. 2017a. "China Bans Uyghur Language in Schools in Key Xinjiang Prefecture." (July 28). Available at: <http://www.rfa.org/english/news/uyghur/language-07282017143037.html>.

Radio Free Asia. 2017b. "Chinese Police Order Xinjiang's Muslims to Hand in All Copies of the Quran." (September 27). Available at: <http://www.rfa.org/english/news/uyghur/chinese-police-order-xinjiangs-muslims-to-hand-in-all-copies-of-the-quran-09272017113203.html>.

Shichor, Yitzhak. 2003. "Virtual Transnationalism: Uyghur Communities in Europe and the Quest for Eastern Turkestan Independence." In *Muslim Networks and Transnational Communities in and across Europe*, edited by Stefano Allievi and Jørgen S. Nielsen: 281–311. Leiden, Boston: Brill.

Shichor, Yitzhak. 2007. "Limping on Two Legs: Uyghur Diaspora Organizations and the Prospects for Eastern Turkestan Independence." *Central Asia and the Caucasus* 6(48): 117–125.

Si Liang. 2000. "China and Turkey Made Joint Efforts to Curb 'Xinjiang Independence' Activities," Zhongxun She News Agency (Hong Kong), in *Guangzhou Ribao* (Gauangzhou Daily), 21 April.

Troop, Stanley. 2004. "The Demographic of Xinjiang." In *Xinjiang: China's Muslim Borderland*, edited by Federick Starr, 241–263. Armonk, New York: M.E. Sharpe.

Tyler, Christian. 2003. *Wild West China: The Taming of Xinjiang*. London: John Murray.

Valtonen, Kathleen. 1998. "Resettlement of Middle Eastern Refugees in Finland: The Elusiveness of Integration." *Journal of Refugee Studies* 11(1): 38–60.

Xiang, Yi. 2019. "Xinjiang: The Largest Outdoor Prison in the World." March 29. Available at: <https://bitterwinter.org/xinjiang-the-largest-outdoor-prison-in-the-world>.

CHAPTER 11

Arab Immigrants under Hindu Kings in Malabar: Ethical Pluralities of "Naturalisation" in Islam

Abdul Jaleel P.K.M.

1 Introduction

The process of "naturalisation" by immigrant Muslims in modern nation states has often been examined within the light of Islamic legal parameters drawn by Muslim scholars in the heartlands of Islam.[1] The plethora of legal opinions that support naturalisation of Muslims in non-Muslim polities has deliberately been ignored to sustain an anti-immigrant fervor in Europe and to reject Middle Eastern Muslim refugees. The vilifying medieval religious notions of "*Dār al-Ḥarb*" is used to evoke suspicion of Muslim immigrants particularly regarding loyalties to their homeland or to the host country. Against such generalizing legal opinions, often aired in anti-immigrant campaigns in Europe, this chapter reflects some historical anecdotes of naturalisation by Muslims in far-flung peripheral lands of non-Muslim political settings and examines varying but marginalized aspects of critical legal opinions regarding the naturalisation of Muslims.

Recent studies show that a majority of Muslim immigrants are easily adaptive to European values (for e.g., Haug, Müssig and Stichs 2010; Inglehar and Norris 2009) and the ethical doctrines of Islam endorse the grounded principles of liberal democracy (March 2007).[2] Adducing to such ethical debates, the historical anecdotes from amicable livelihoods that Arab immigrants nurtured in the peripheries such as the Indian Ocean provide better understanding of the process of naturalisation in non-Muslim lands. These historical accounts counter the tarnished images of Muslim immigrants, demanding a re-think of anti-immigrant politics that shut doors against abject refugees. In fact, the

1 The concept "heartlands of Islam" is geographically assumed as centred around the two cities of the Prophet, Mecca and Medina. However, the concept is loosely used in this chapter to indicate the entire Arab world in contrast to non-Arab centres of Islamic inhabitancy in distant regions of the Indian Ocean.

2 The inherent deep philosophical rift within the liberal Western democracy since the Enlightenment is rearticulated by the current anti-immigrant anti-Muslim debates (O'Brien 2013).

question of living and naturalisation under non-Muslim polities loomed large among Muslim trading communities who wanted to sojourn or settle in regions far flung from the heartlands of Islam. Centuries prior to the medieval re-conquests of Muslim habitats by Christian regimes and the subsequent colonization of Muslim lands by Europeans, these traders had traversed waters and lands beyond the heartland Arab Muslim localities and domiciled among pagan believers in India, Africa, Southeast Asia and among the Buddhists of China. The trading communities, along with their indigenous co-religionists, participated in the social, economic and political settings of host societies in these regions, naturalizing themselves and adapting their religious ethics to the cultural and religious settings of the new localities. Living aloof from the varied and dynamic experiences of Muslims in these distant non-Muslim peripheries, medieval Muslim scholars, mostly in the central lands of Islam, often demanded their demarcation into distinct ethical abodes of *Dār al-Islām* and *Dār al-Ḥarb*.[3] This chapter offers historical anecdotes of Muslim communities in the Indian Ocean to argue that the legal-ethical demarcations of habitats by scholars were mostly de-contextualized general assertions removed from the real experiences of naturalisation of Muslims and thus Islam in these lands.

The historical anecdotes of naturalisation of Muslim immigrants are mainly taken from the sixteenth century anti-Portuguese battle fought jointly by Muslim immigrants and Hindu cavalry under the Hindu kings in Malabar. As explained below, these historical accounts of the war in Malabar were narrated in the Arabic historical texts by indigenous scholars (and in the fatwa compilations such as *al-Fatāwa al-Kubrā*), but from the central regions of Islam such as Mecca and Cairo. While the contextual accounts in Malabar are detailed as questions in the fatwa literature, the consideration of contexts was naïve in the answers provided by heartland scholars such as Ibn Ḥajar. However, such fatwas in no way indicate that the scholars of heartlands were completely ignorant of the amicable situations in the periphery. Nor does it deny that such demarcating scholarly opinions regarding habitats had existed among scholars living in the peripheries. Rather, reflecting upon these historical accounts

3 However, it would not be true to assign exclusively opinions regarding the classification of habitats as distinct abodes to scholars in the heartlands of Islam, as the fatwas from the heartlands analyzed in this paper recall the significance of peripheral contexts to be taken into account in determining the nature of Muslim social lives among non-believers. Regarding scholarly opinions on demarcation of abodes into distinct lands, see Abou El Fadl (1994) and Al-Juday‘ (2007). The narrow medieval banal demarcations have later on been expanded into making these boundaries blurred and making amicable co-existence possible through novel concepts such as *Dār al-Da‘wa* (Abode of mission) and *Dār al-‘Ahd* (Abode of accord) (Bilici 2011).

against the fatwas issued from heartlands helps to revisit medieval anti-naturalisation fatwas.

To understand the process of naturalisation—a feature intrinsic to the concept of citizenship in modern nation states—in comparison to medieval historical anecdotes there are certain analytical limitations. First, the modern conceptualization of "nation states" and the rights and duties it provides for political subjects through the acquisition of citizenship could not be imagined fully in sixteenth century provincial kingdoms. Thus, the concept "naturalisation" in this paper is loosely defined as a socio-political process of engaging in local social and political settings— in the present case the sixteenth century Hindu kingdoms of Malabar. Likewise, the value-loaded terms of "centre" and "periphery" regarding scholarly figures in the region are intentionally used not only to indicate the larger Asian scholarly networks that extended from the Levant to Southeast Asia and beyond, but also to signify the largely Muslim-populated yet mostly neglected regions in the study of Islam (Ahmed 2016).

Second, to argue with these historical anecdotes against textual scholarly opinions from distant lands requires decisions about what one has to focus upon while studying Islam and Muslims as an historical phenomenon: whether textual traditions or human practices or the integration of both can be seen as discursive traditions (Asad 1984), or as a hermeneutical engagement with the Pre-Text, Text and Con-text (Ahmed 2016). The process of naturalisation that Malabar Muslims achieved historically, despite divergent rulings from the heartlands of Islam, was not entirely devoid of textual scholarly legitimation produced locally in the region. Conversely, the socio-historical accounts of naturalisation under the Hindu Kings in fifteenth and sixteenth century Malabar were compiled by well-known scholars who also had written jurisprudential texts like *Fatḥ al-Muʿīn* that often accommodated possibilities of living under the non-Muslim rulers. The presence of such indigenous textual rulings for naturalisation of Muslims provides ample scope for an alternative understanding of the process of naturalisation as hermeneutical engagements with the Textual forms or as discursive traditions employed. The scholarly rulings of heartlands often contradicted writings from peripheries that sought an easy naturalisation with distant non-Muslim contexts. These diverse historical experiences from peripheries signify what Shahab Ahmed argued for shifting the locus of attention in Islamic studies from the heartlands of Islam to the Bengal-Balkan peripheries (Ahmed 2016).

The first part of the chapter discusses the migratory settlement of Arab traders and the spread of Islam in Malabar along with wider Arab maritime networks in the Indian Ocean that not only enabled the spread of diverse religious forms but also made trans-regional scholarly exchanges possible. Two historical texts of *Tuḥfat al-Mujāhidīn*, written for advocating the holy war of Jihad against the Portuguese, and *Fatḥ al-Mubīn*, that celebrates the joint victory of Muslims and Zamorin's Hindu cavalry in conquering the Chaliyam fort from the Portuguese, will depict the socio-religious and political aspects of Muslim naturalisation in sixteenth century Malabar. The historical images from these two texts will enhance our understanding of how the community became part and parcel of the indigenous polity under the Hindu King Zamorin and how they developed political integrity despite being not under any formal treaty with Hindu Zamorins.

In the second part, these amicable historical images will be contrasted with the fatwas issued from scholars in the heartlands of Islam in Mecca and Egypt. These fatwas, written far away from Malabar, were often cast in terms of conventional legal demarcations of lands into separate abodes to prevent moral degradation in non-Muslim social realms. While the historical realities in the peripheries speak loudly for exemplary naturalisation of Muslims in non-Muslim cultural settings, the scholarly opinions from heartlands often vitiated such historical realities into relegating the land and its non-Muslims into the category of Ḥarbīs.

2 Arab Immigrants under Hindu Kings

Due to its geographic significance in East-West trade and the natural spices it produced, the region of Malabar on the west coast of India (now Kerala) had been receiving maritime people of different religions and cultures for centuries (Arasaratnam 2004, 33–39; Gupta 2001; Bouchon 1987, Abu Lughod 1989). The earliest treatise of *Qiṣṣat Shakrawat Fermāḍ* that tells the story of the coming of Islam to Malabar names a delegation under the aegis of Mālik ibn Dīnār, who approached the local Hindu king for a place to settle down and established a number of mosques in different parts of Malabar (*Qiṣṣa*, n.d., 10). Despite being the delegates of the converted king who demised while returning from Mecca, this missionary did not seek any political share in the territories of the old king. Instead, settling in the territories of local Hindu kings, the missionary became part and parcel of the local social setting by becoming involved in social, political and commercial activities. The missionary appointed members of the Muslim community as Shabandars or port leaders in various regions of Malabar (ibid., 10–13) and enriched seaborne trade profits by acting as agents for Arab-speaking maritime traders. Since the community accepted the prevailing political orders of Zamorins, Muslims such as the Kunjali Marakkars were bestowed with high positions including "admiral of the navy" (Nambiar

1863). Thus, through whole-hearted participation in the economic and social activities, they became naturalized into their host Malabari society. Developing certain geographies as centres of Muslim habitation through the establishment of mosques was another significant step to develop an indigenous community in the region. With the support and involvement of local Hindu rulers, the missionary built eleven mosques across the coast of Malabar (*Qiṣṣa*, n.d., 9–13). Thus, from the early centuries of Islam, a distinct Muslim community was developed within Malabar. At the same time, they emerged as strong defenders of the existing political system of the Hindu kings.

As will be seen in the texts below written in Malabar, the Hindu rulers treated their Muslim subjects with dignity and ensured a social environment that enabled them to perform their religious duties. Muslims adopted their Hindu rulers as legitimate holders of law. The scholars in Malabar gave legitimacy to the *qāḍīs* appointed by non-Muslim political authorities. This might be explained in terms of "*ḍarūra*" or political and economic necessity where Muslims and their Hindu political rulers cooperated with reciprocity for mutual benefit. The legal recognition rendered by the indigenous scholars in Malabar provides an interesting outlook in understanding the process of naturalisation of Muslims in non-Muslim lands. However, this does not mean that communal harmony permanently prevailed in Malabar following the Arab settlement; nor did it negate the political and economic relations of Malabari Muslims with other Muslim rulers in the far-flung areas. For example, the Rasulid court ledgers in 1290 show that the *khaṭībs* (those responsible for delivering sermons and leading prayers, i.e. *imams*) in the nine mosques of Malabar received stipends from the Rasulid rulers in Yemen (Lambourn 2008; Prange 2008, 208–213). The Rasulid ledgers also contain a letter sent by Muslims in Calicut to the then Rasulid Sultan al-Ashraf II in 1393 requesting his permission to recite his name in the Friday *khuṭba* of Calicut (al-Khazrajī 1911, 244–7; Prange 2008, 213–5).

These attempts to seek affiliation in *khuṭbas* with the Rasuild Sultans of Aden, though seemingly political, were more framed for the commercial benefits of traders in Aden and Calicut than forging political affiliations with distant lands (Prange 2008, 215; Lambourn 2008, 82). This observation can be substantiated with the request of Zamorin himself through his emissary sent to Timurid, prior to 'Abd al-Razzāq's visit to Calicut in 1442, to recite Timurid Sultan's name in *khuṭbas* in his region (Thackston 1989, 304). Prange explains that this might also have been initiated by some unofficial influential merchants in Calicut, for trade benefits from the Timurids. These merchants also proposed to the Sultan that Zamorin would convert if they sent a suitable ambassador, a futile task carried out by 'Abd al-Razzāq (Prange 2008, 215–7).

Generally, however, the Muslim inhabitancy in the region was cordial since the community pursued amicable naturalisation with the local Hindu society and other inhabitants in the cosmopolitan city of Calicut, along with other communities such as Buddhist Chinese, Jews and Christians.

Malabar was a peaceful multi-cultural cosmopolitan society before the advent of the Portuguese, who introduced a Mediterranean style of trade along with war (Chaudhuri 1985, 64; Ho 2004, 215; Gupta 2001, 423). As Geniza records indicate, out of sixteen ship owners in Malabar, seven belonged to Muslims, three to Jews and four to Indians (Goitein 2008, 142–8). Such a harmonious state of affairs in Malabar is well depicted by the Moroccan traveller Ibn Baṭūṭa in the early half of the fourteenth century, when Calicut was maintaining its maritime zenith in the Indian Ocean. Despite Ibn Baṭūṭa's analysis of religious scholarly engagements of Muslims in the regions, his description of the social and commercial state of affairs provides light into the nature of peaceful Muslim settlement in Malabar. For example in Mangalore, where Muslims numbered about four thousand, he narrates that inter-communal issues were mediated by the Hindu ruler Ramdev (Ibn Baṭūṭa 1905, 137). He was also keen to note the warm reception Muslims and other maritime players received in the region. When he reached Calicut, Ibn Baṭūṭa noted that Qulaj, the deputy of the King, welcomed him and that he enjoyed hosting the Hindu ruler for around three months until his departure for China (ibid., 139–41). In the northern town of Eli (Ezhimala), a *masjid* (mosque) was revered by both Muslims and non-Muslims, with votive offerings made by all sea voyagers. The income for this Masjid was spent as stipends for students who studied in the mosque and as food for visitors and poor Muslims (ibid.). The next town of Dharamadam, ruled by the Hindu ruler Kolathiri Raja, had a mosque where notables of Muslims and non-Muslims sat together under its revered tree, expecting its leaf written with the name of God and the Prophet Muhammad. While half of the leaf was for Muslims, the other half was kept in the treasury of the local Hindu ruler for healing purposes (Ibn Baṭūṭa 1905, 138). These narratives by the Moroccan traveller indicate the warmth of inter-communal relations and indigenization that Muslims adopted under non-Muslim rulers of the Malabar coast.

3 *Tuḥfat al-Mujāhidīn* and *Fatḥ al-Mubīn*: Two Texts Celebrating Naturalisation

Tuḥfat al-Mujāhidīn, the well-known sixteenth century history text written by Shaykh Zayn al-Dīn al-Makhdūm al-Maʿbarī, depicts vivid aspects of naturalisation that Malabari Muslims achieved under the non-Muslim Zamorins. *Tuḥfa* clearly mentions the Muslim community in Malabar as subjects of non-Muslim rulers and their ruler Zamorin as the one who loves Muslims (Nainar 2005, 15; al-Maʿbarī, n.d., 9). The text, written as an inspiration to wage religious Jihad against the Portuguese, describes the strange customs of Hindu non-believers in an entire chapter (Nainar 2005, 36–46; al-Maʿbarī, n.d., 26–34; al-Maʿbarī 1931, 18–22). The broader ethnographic and historical picture of Hindu society and customs in *Tuhfa* paints a civic, multicultural and peaceful urban society under attack by the Portuguese (Ho 2004, 222–3). *Tuḥfa* also wonderfully exclaims the fair treatment of Muslims by the Hindu Zamorin stressing that the remunerations for the Muslim religious judges and prayer leaders were borne by the Hindu king. He made arrangements for implementing their own Muslim religious laws. Those neglecting the Friday prayer were punished or made to pay a fine (Nainar 2005, 45–6).

Al-Makhdūm al-Ṣaghīr, who also wrote many jurisprudential works such as the famous *Fatḥ al-Muʿīn* and other scholarly works in Sufism and Arabic language, was keen to note in *Tuḥfa* that the legitimate rulers of Malabari Muslims were Hindus who enjoyed their judicial and political authority. "Muslims throughout Malabar have no leader possessed of power to rule over them. But their rulers are Hindus, who exercise judicial authority and organize their affairs by enforcing payment of debt or fine if anyone is subjected to such a payment" (Nainar 2005, 45). The jurisdictional executions made by non-Muslim rulers were also legitimized by Muslim scholars and their community. *Tuḥfa* makes it clear that the death penalty of a Muslim offender was to be carried out by the Hindu ruler, while others were handed over to Muslims for their ritual punishments. *Tuḥfa* also illuminates other inter-communal relations and social etiquette. For example, the people of other communities would not enter a Muslim house without seeking permission, even if they search for a wanted criminal; and those who converted to Islam were treated with equal respect, even if they were from the lower castes (ibid., 46).

There were also socio-economic and political reasons behind the earnest naturalisation showed by Muslims under the Zamorins of Calicut. As *Tuhfa* observes, it was thanks to Muslims that the construction and development of the country largely took place. The text explicates this reciprocal amicable socio-political and economic scenario: while the Arab traders brought prosperity to the region, the Hindu rulers, in turn, facilitated and protected Arabs' commercial and religious activities (ibid., 45–6). This mutual reciprocity that Arabs and Hindu rulers developed in Malabar was not perceived by scholars like al-Makdūm al-Ṣaghīr as a part of the jurisdictional necessity of "*ḍarūra*." Rather, *Tuḥfa* introduces the entire region as an abode of Islam despite being under a Hindu ruler. The dynamic approach of regional scholars in Medieval Malabar, who recognized the real living conditions in the region, is helpful in understanding the naturalisation of Muslims in modern nation states also, where they have become increasingly exposed to non-Muslim contexts.

Like *Ṭuḥfat al-Mujāhidīn*, the amicable living conditions of Muslims under the Hindu rulers were celebrated in another historical poem, *Fatḥ al-Mubīn*, composed by a contemporary scholar from Calicut, Qāḍī Muḥammad al-Kalikūtī (d. 1616). Qāḍī Muḥammad's poetic and other scholarly works discourse a number of disciplines such as Sufism, Shāfiʿī jurisprudence and Arabic grammar. Thus, he also can be reckoned among one of the renowned scholars of the time who lent a dynamic approach to the process of naturalisation in Malabar. The Arabic poem *Fatḥ al-Mubīn* that generously celebrates the friendly co-existence of different communities under the Zamorins was written primarily to advise the Muslim rulers in other regions of the world not to succumb to the Portuguese invasion. The poem tells the stunning story of conquering the Chaliyam fort in Malabar from the Portuguese in a year-long battle in 1571, fought by the joint army of Muslims and the Nayar cavalry of Zamorin. Qāḍī Muḥammad wanted to convey the joyful news of victory to remind the Muslim rulers like ʿAlī ʿĀdil Shah of Bijapur (who retreated and made treaties with the Portuguese) that a non-Muslim ruler (Zamorin) had conquered the Chaliyam fort for the cause of Islam. He spent all his wealth for this cause, while Muslim rulers in distant lands were indulging in luxurious life, forgetting all their responsibilities (al-Kalikūtī, n.d., 2).

The poem is entitled "The Opulent Victory for Zamorin, the one who loves Muslims" (ibid., 1). The character of the king as a sympathiser with Muslims is repeated at the beginning of the poem that goes on to describe the king's admiration for Muslim subjects and fair arbitrations in Malabar. Like *Tuḥfa*, the poem *Fatḥ al-Mubīn* also calls Muslims in Malabar as the subjects of Zamorin wherever they are (ibid., 3). Boasting that the Muslim port leader or Shahbandar is honoured with the prestigious chance of standing at the right side of the king in the royal festival of Mamankam, the poem exclaims that Muslims were politically naturalized and totally reliable subjects of Zamorin. *Fatḥ*'s description regarding the king's choice of Muslims as his naval chiefs reiterates the level of naturalisation Muslims made in the region. Calling the community of Muslims as Zamorin's beloved subjects, the text appealed to the community to pray for the betterment of all the king's matters. His staunch support for a non-Muslim king is that Zamorin did fight for the sake of Muslims while other Muslim rulers gave in to political treaties with the Portuguese (ibid., 4–5).

The poem moves on with the narrative of the Portuguese incursion into Malabar, their attempt to build a fort at Cochin and the atrocities they inflicted upon local inhabitants, especially on Muslims. When the Portuguese attack became unbearable, Zamorin with inspiration from his Muslim subjects sought assistance from Sultans in the far-flung regions of Sumatra, Bijapur and Hyderabad. Receiving no positive reply, Zamorin was compelled to cordon off the Chaliyam fort. The local Muslim community joined the movement under their local leaders, such as Sīdī Aḥmad al-Kumāmī, 'Umar al-ʿAntābī, ʿAbd al-ʿAzīz al-Makhdūm al-Maʿbarī, Sufi Shaykh ʿAbd al-Wafā Shams al-Dīn Muḥammad (d. 980 A.H.), and the naval admiral Kunhāli Markkār. Among the flamboyant narratives of the war zone are cordial inter-communal relations bounding two distinct local communities, as both observed separate ritual prayers for the victory in war at their respective religious centres. Muslims made votive offering to the mosques of Mecca and Medina, invoked chants from the Qur'an and supplicated Shaykhs. Hindus brought their astrologists and prayed to their idols for victory. The dignity Zamorin bestowed upon Muslims is obvious, as the poem quotes him comparing the loss of one Muslim in battle to the loss of ten non-Muslims (al-Kālikūtī 1996, 68). Likewise, when the joint army completely vanquished the fort, Zamorin allocated a part of the booty to repair the mosque demolished by the Portuguese army (ibid., 69).

Why are such aspects of Muslim naturalisation under the Hindu ruler being celebrated in a poem addressed to Muslim rulers in faraway regions? Utilizing the vivid pictures of honourable treatment of Muslims by the Hindu king in Malabar, the poem seeks to remind the Muslim rulers of their political duties which they default due to selfish living habits. It also shows that a local Muslim community would be ready to accept a non-Muslim ruler if he renders justice and respect to the community and helps them to fulfil their religious obligations. It proclaims that a just non-Muslim ruler committed to the cause of his subjects is better than an unjust Muslim ruler and that the non-Muslim Zamorin had spent his treasury for the sake of a harmonious society (al-Kālikūtī 1996, 74–5).

The above two texts that provide vivid pictures of amicable naturalisation enjoyed by Muslims under the non-Muslim lands were written by two indigenous scholarly figures; Shaykh Zayn al-Dīn al-Makhdūm al-Ṣaghīr of Ponnāni and Qāḍī Muḥammad ibn ʿAbd al-ʿAzīz (d. 1616) of Calicut. Despite the rich historical countenance these texts provided, the religious and ethical values mainly regarding the social and political localization that the Malabari Muslim community maintained under non-Muslim rulers cannot be ignored, because the authors of both texts were renowned jurists and erudite scholarly figures in a number of religious sciences. The author of *Tuḥfa* is a famous scholar renowned for his magnum opus, the Shāfiʿī jurisprudential work, *Fatḥ al-Muʿīn*, which has been taught and accepted widely across the Indian Ocean. The second author was a legal jurist based in Calicut who adorned the post of *qāḍī* under the Zamorin. He wrote not only the famous Sufi text of *Muhyiddīn Māla* but also *fiqhī* texts like *Maqāṣid al-Nikāḥ*. Despite their expertise in various Islamic disciplines, they did not record any dissenting note on the political and social naturalisation of Muslims in Malabar. These scholars vindicated the unconditional support to non-Muslim Zamorin and declared the naturalisation under him as a necessity for the Muslim community's survival. Rather than bringing the conventional legal classification of abodes of Islam and war and related polemics, they assumed Malabar as a peaceful place for Islam and Muslims. They recognized the serious political and economic precariousness of the community in the region, while scholars in the heartlands invoked the general polemics of abodes without delving into the contextual practical necessities.

4 Countering Fatwas

Against the viewpoint of indigenous scholars of Malabar favouring naturalisation under the Zamorin non-Muslim rulers, scholars such as Ibn Ḥajar al-Haytamī of Mecca cast contrasting scholarly fatwas from the heartlands of Islam. From the scholarly centres of Mecca and Cairo to the peripheries of the Indian Ocean, Muslim scholars reified a rampant religious network of scholarship. They connected the regions of the Indian Ocean to the heartlands of Islam, where scholars, students, shaykhs and disciples travelled, visited and exchanged ideas and goods.[4] These maritime networks enabled students and scholars in the distant peripheries such as Malabar to connect with scholarly stalwarts based in the heartlands of Islam. Such trans-regional connections of Malabari students with erudite scholars in Mecca and Cairo are praised in local historical and biographical texts such as the brief biography of al-Makhdūm

4 For a seminal study of the Indian Ocean scholarly networks see Azra (1999). The application of Braudelian perspective in the study of the Indian Ocean brought a chunk of literature from Chaudhuri (1985), McPherson (1993), Pearson (2003) and a number of studies based on diasporic communities such as the Hadramis. See Freitag and Clarence-Smith (1999), Freitag (2003), Boxberger (2002), Bang (2003) and Ho (2006).

al-Kabīr (d. 1522) in *Maslak al-Atqiyāʾ* (al-Maʿbarī, n.d., 2–3).[5] *Maslak* mentions Yemeni, Egyptian and Meccan scholars among the teachers of al-Kabīr. Besides Fakhr al-Dīn bin Ramaḍān al-Shāliyāthī of Malabar, Makhdūm al-Kabīr studied with Yemenis such as Shaykh Aḥmad Shihāb al-Dīn ʿUthmān bin Ab al-Ḥill al-Yamanī in Ḥadīth and Fiqh, with Egyptians such as ʿAbd al-Raḥmān al-Adamī al-Miṣrī, Shams al-Dīn al-Jawjarī (d. 1484), Shaykh Zakariyya al-Anṣārī (d.1520/926), the author of *Fatḥ al-Bārī*, and with Shaykh Kamāl al-Dīn Muhammad bin Abu Sharīf (d. 1500/905) (ibid.).

Since these maritime connections with the distant peripheries were flourishing, issues of the peripheries such as Malabar must have been known to scholars in the central lands. However, these scholarly networks often failed in assessing the real contextual situations in the peripheries, mainly due to the geographical remoteness and communication difficulties. Thus, fatwas issued by scholars in the central Arab knowledge centres were articulated in strict legal terms, without delving deeper into the real social and political contexts existing in far-flung non-Muslim settlements. For example, on the issue of naturalisation, while indigenous scholars encouraged a gradual and complete naturalisation process in Malabar, the edicts from the centres were mostly concerned about the socio-political degradation caused by settlement in non-Muslim polities. The indigenous scholars imagined an Islam suitable to the local ecological and social contexts, while scholars of the centres dealt with the monolithic, universal and distinctive Islam that they were acquainted with in the Arabic heartlands.

The text we take, as a case for analysis is a collection of scholarly opinions of fatwas by Ibn Ḥajar al-Haytamī of Mecca (d.1566), entitled as *al-Fatāwa al-Fiqhiyya al-Kubrā*. Born in Cairo, Ibn Ḥajar moved to Mecca after his graduation from al-Azhar to develop the city, under his tutelage, as a renowned knowledge centre of the sixteenth century, recognizing the social and political significance it assumed with the Ottoman ascension (Kooria 2016). The text, compiled by his disciple ʿAbd al-Raʾūf al-Wāʿiẓ al-Zamzamī (d.1568) contains a number of questions raised by various contemporaries with answers provided by Ibn Ḥajar. Malabar is mentioned in about twenty cases where its ecology, trees, language, inter-communal issues, insects, war booties shared with non-Muslims, trade activities and gender issues are discussed in detail.

Among many questions raised to Ibn Ḥajar in *al-Fatāwa al-Fiqhiyya al-Kubrā*, a number of issues are related to migratory settlement and naturalisation

5 The trans-regional connections of al-Makhdūm al-Ṣaghīr, the author of *Tuḥfa*, are detailed in the brief introduction provided in *Maslak* and can be inferred from his frequent mentioning of the phrase "Our Shaykh Ibn Ḥajar" in *Fatḥ al-Muʿīn* (al-Shafiʿī 2006).

under non-Muslims in Malabar. For example, under the general questions about booty from battles where it is assumed that war booties would not be distributed according to the recommendations of Shariʿah, a sub-question was raised specifically about the non-Muslim rulers of Malabar who helped Muslims implement their religious duties, acknowledging that the development of that country was generated by the maritime trade activities of Muslims. It was argued that although there was no written or oral treaty between Muslims and their non-Muslim rulers, the Muslims lived as their subjects; they resided in their territories and built cordial relations with other communities. After this explanation, the final question was whether these friendly non-Muslims are *ḥarbīs* who ought to be fought or not? The answer given by Ibn Ḥajar was: "the above mentioned non-Muslims are *ḥarbis*. However, transactions with interest or duping them in weight or size is not permitted" (al-Haytamī n.d. vol. 4, 245).

The answer regarding friendly non-Muslims of Malabar as *ḥarbis* might be suitable to the conventional legal criteria as the region kept non-Islamic laws and remains without written or verbal contracts with non-Muslim communities (Mawsūʿa 1990, 201–219). However, the term "*ḥarbi*" was in contradiction to the indigenous scholars of Malabar who wrote of the Malabari kings and non-Muslim communities as friendly rulers and fellow co-citizens. They introduced themselves explicitly as the naturalized subjects of Hindu Zamorin. The answer given from the centre was a more generalized demarcation of *ḥarbi* and *dhimmī*. It did not consider the possibilities of mutual faith and the informal accord that Muslim trading communities and indigenous Muslims in Malabar invested in the non-Muslim political system. The real socio-political dignity that Muslims enjoyed in Malabar and the forms of naturalisation about which the indigenous scholars depicted in their aforementioned historical works, such as *Tuḥfa* and *Fatḥ al-Mubīn*, also have to be taken into account while categorizing the Muslim settlements into distinct abodes.

However, it is noteworthy that the scholars in Malabar did not always categorize non-Portuguese as friendly non-*ḥarbis*. Many questions raised in *al-Fatāwa al-Kubrā* by Malabar scholars introduced non-Muslim Malabaris as *ḥarbis*.[6] Likewise, the scholars of the centre were not always blindly refusing the possibility that Malabari non-Muslims could be included as non-*ḥarbi*s. For example, a question in *al-Ajwiba al-ʿAjība*, asked by Shaykh Zayn al-Dīn al-Makdhūm in Malabar, introduced the non-Muslim Malabari debtor as *ḥarbi*, while the replying scholar, Ibn Ḥajar of Mecca, included the chance of the debtor being a *dhimmī* also. The question was:

6 For example, see the question raised from Malabar: is it allowed to join one of the battle sides if a battle is going on between two groups of *ḥarbis* (al-Haytamī n.d. vol. 2: 25).

> One of the *ḥarbis* is owed an amount to a Muslim and the custom among non-Muslims of Malabar is that they inherit property through matrilineal side, from aunts to children of sisters. Is it allowed for this Muslim to incur the debt from such inheritors and to procure it by force or not? If it is allowable, is the creditor eligible to demand an oath if they would deny leaving any inheritance by the demised debtor? The answer provided by our Shaykh ibn Ḥajar is: if they are *ḥarbis* the creditors can own whatever they conquer. Also, their repayment of debt and other transactions are legal. If they are *dhimmīs* it is not allowed to take more than what they owe to the Muslim. (al-Ṣaghīr n.d., 1–60)

The answer by Ibn Ḥajar does not consider an option other than the usual *ḥarbi* and *dhimmī*. In another answer, Ibn Ḥajar recommends not to flee Malabar to protect a new convert Muslim from his non-Muslim master. He suggests that if Muslims fail to protect their fellow believer or if sheltering the new convert would imply that Muslims should leave their homes, they should not give him shelter (al-Haytamī, n.d. vol. 4, 249).

The previous question in *al-Fatāwa al-Kubrā* on booties in Malabar provides the possibility to consider non-Muslim rulers of Malabar beyond the conventional binary of *ḥarbi* or *dhimmī*. In that question, the fatwa seeker introduced the Zamorin kings as assisting rulers and their non-Muslim subjects as friendly co-subjects who help Malabari Muslims even in their religious activities, despite the absence of formal treaties between them. The question also reiterates that the Malabari Muslims consider themselves as subjects of this friendly ruler Zamorin—a stand that was demonstrated by most local scholars such as al-Makhdum al-Ṣaghīr in his *Tuḥfa* and Qāḍī Muḥammad al-Kālikūtī in his *Fatḥ al-Mubīn* (Nainar 2005, 15; al-Maʿbarī, n.d. 9; al-Kālikūtī, n.d., 3). In *Fatḥ al-Mubīn*, it was explained that the meeting led by Muslim scholars such as ʿAbd al-ʿAzīz al-Makhdūm al-Maʿbarī, Sufi Shaykh ʿAbd al-Wafā Shams al-Dīn Muḥammad (d. 980 A.H.), the Muslim merchants and leaders such as Sīdī Aḥmad al-Kumāmī and ʿUmar al-ʿAntābī and the naval admiral Kunhāli Markkār had lent support to Zamorin in his military attempt to conquer the Chaliyam fort from the Portuguese (al-Kālikūtī, n.d., 28–29).

The Malabari scholars, in the early question, did provide the option of having treaties with non-Muslim rulers—a condition considered in another political category of *Dār al-ʿAhd* (the abode of accord). When a formal treaty is ratified, the abode of war moves to the abode of treaty (Verskin 2013, 12). Since there was no treaty with Malabar's non-Muslim rulers, the land of Malabar cannot be included in the abode of accord as the above fatwa in *al-Fatāwā al-Kubrā* suggests. However, the early jurists like al-Māwardī (d. 1050) attempted to mitigate the contrast between abode of Islam and abode of war by opining that the difference is not based upon one ruled by Muslim or non-Muslim. For him, like many of the later scholars such as Ibn Ḥajar al-Haytamī himself, the land ruled by non-Muslims also come under the category of abode of Islam provided that Muslims are permitted to publicly practice their religious rituals (Abou El Fadl 1994, 150). Ibn Ḥajar, the author of *al-Fatāwā*, like his predecessor Shafiʿī scholars, considered staying in *Dār al-Kufr* as recommended as long as his stay would help the religion (Sharawanī and al-ʿAbbadī, n.d., 9, 268–9).

Such a fluid category of abode of Islam, like the later category of abode of missionary (*Dār al-Daʿwa*), was also legally possible in the non-Muslim region of Malabar. But these categories were absent from the fatwa asked by the indigenous scholars and answered by heartland experts. Why did the indigenous scholars of Malabar omit such viable options, even after they acknowledged the ruler as very friendly and helpful by implementing Islamic religious laws? Did it indicate that they were yet to accept full naturalisation under the Hindu Zamorin? Or was it because such fluid categories were not broad enough to be applied in distant lands? A profound answer to such questions seems difficult here. However, since fatwas usually address particular issues raised by the fatwa seeker, the fatwa answers cannot be generalized to other contexts. Despite these scholarly polemical debates regarding the abode of land, it is clear that the Muslims of Malabar historically continued making amicable settlements as subjects of non-Muslim Zamorins.

Reading the historical accounts and fatwas together explains that although there had been scholarly polemics about the character of naturalisation of Muslims under the Hindu Zamorin, the indigenous Muslims were ready to become part of the non-Muslim Malabari settings, even fighting for its political stability. While the questions asked by scholars from Malabar often recognized the political and social significance of a friendly non-Muslim ruler, the scholars from the centre insisted they were *ḥarbīs*, disregarding the amicable socio-political conditions that existed in Malabar. Although indigenous scholars from Malabar had used the "*ḥarbi*" category to indicate particular anti-community figures in other questions, they had assumed a pragmatic political position of complete naturalisation under Zamorin. The indigenous scholars such as Shaykh al-Makhdūm al-Ṣaghīr provided legitimacy even for the religious judges appointed by the Hindu king, Zamorin. Al-Ṣaghīr writes that "if a Sultan, even if he is a non-Muslim, appoints an ineligible judge it would be legal" (al-Ṣaghīr 2000, 215). The clause "even if the Sultan is non-Muslim" was unprecedented in the earlier parent texts such as *Tuḥfat al-Minhāj* of Ibn Ḥajar al-Ḥaytamī, offering a political legitimacy to a non-Muslim ruler's appointments in religious matters of Islam. By endowing religious legitimacy for appointments of *qāḍīs* made by a non-Muslim ruler, the scholars like Zayn al-Dīn accepted the non-Muslim political system for his fellow Muslims in Malabar. Such particular issues discussed in *Fatḥ al-Muʿīn* regarding the non-Muslim contexts made the text more acceptable in the peripheries of the Indian Ocean (Kooria 2016).

5 Conclusion

Abou El Fadl (1994) has outlined how the scholarly positions in determining territories as distinct abodes of Islam and non-Islam have changed over centuries according to historical junctures that the Muslim community faced. It was in the wake of the Mongol invasion of Baghdad that the Shāfiʿis reached a position that Muslim territories remain as an abode of Islam even after it was conquered by non-Muslims (ibid., 183–5). The above historical pictures that shed light on the economic, political and social conditions in the peripheries such as Malabar, where non-Muslim settings were amicably absorbed by Muslims, must also be examined along with the legal texts while we analyse the issues of migration and naturalisation of Muslims.

The analysis of the legal and historical texts produced in the peripheries like Malabar shows that Muslims in the region unequivocally wanted to become a part of the indigenous local settings under the Hindu Zamorins. While indigenous Malabari scholars gave due attention to the actual socio-political circumstances, the scholarly discussions in the heartlands mostly overlooked such contexts, sliding into the binary categories of peace and war. The Malabari scholars, through their historical texts, conveyed that the Muslim community in Malabar not only had considered themselves as subjects of the Hindu king and enjoyed dignified political positions under the Zamorins but they had also fought Holy Jihad under the Hindu king against the Portuguese invaders. The entire leadership of the Muslim community, from affluent merchants to scholars and *Sayyids*, had lined up in the forefront of the Chaliyam battle, when both Muslims and Zamorins' Nayar army joined together to conquer the Chaliyam fort. Such a particular political and social setting fetched unprecedented legal challenges that induced indigenous scholars to think distinctively to enable their religious lives under Hindus, rather than invoking the traditional categories of abodes. That is why Malabaris asked the scholars in the heartlands whether these friendly rulers were *ḥarbīs* as they did not made any formal accord with Zamorins. The scholars in Malabar transcended such demarcations into making Islam suitable to the particular context that they happened to live. Therefore, unlike the early jurisprudential texts, we see that

Fath al-Muʿīn written by a Malabari scholar legitimized the religious judges appointed by non-Muslim rulers. The particular contexts and questions he addressed in this jurisprudential text were an attempt to reconceptualise Islamic lives according to the distinctive social political and ecological situations of non-Muslim settings.

Therefore, the above historical accounts of ardent socio-political and economic participation played by Arab traders and their Malabari co-religionists under the Hindu Zamorins in the fifteenth and sixteenth centuries not only vitiates the pure legal ethical demarcation of habitats into distinct abodes but also urges for a process of naturalisation by reformulating Islamic life-worlds appropriately to the local socio-political and cultural settings. The Muslim immigrants and indigenous scholars in the peripheries like Malabar reconceptualised Islamic life worlds into conducive inter-subjective realms that enabled their earnest political, economic and social participation in non-Muslim habitats. The legitimacy that the local scholars gave to the political appointments made by the Hindu kings in the region was one significant step of the community being indigenized. Such a naturalisation of Muslims and Islam through these immigrants granted the religion the potential to grow with vivid and diverse forms.

With the increasing number of refugees and other Asian communities in western countries, the question regarding the process of naturalisation by Muslim immigrants in secular nation states looms large. Sadly, in order to retain an anti-immigrant tendency, the legal scholarly articulations emerged in the heartlands that have lesser historical experience of non-Muslim settings often dominate the debates. The historical accounts such as the one brought above from the peripheries like Malabar often skip the conventional scholarly attention with their focus on Arab Islam. Shahab Ahmed signifies peripheral societies of his Bengal to Balkan complex as "in a post-formative stage of being Muslim," where Muslims are able to strike out for new constructions, trajectories and expressions of what it means to be Muslim (Ahmed 2016, 81). Although the pre-modern historical challenges and the consequent scholarly responses analyzed above would not be able to adequately resolve the tensions in the naturalisation process of current modern secular nations, the dynamic images from the periphery give supple threads to approach the process of naturalisation quite distinctively from the Euro-centric anti-immigrant viewpoints.

Bibliography

Abou El Fadl, Khaled. 1994. "Islamic law and Muslim minorities: the juristic discourse on Muslim minorities from the second/eighth to the eleventh/seventeenth centuries." *Islamic Law and Society* 1(2): 141–187.

Ahmed, Shahab. 2016. *What is Islam: The importance of Being Islamic*. Princeton and Oxford: Princeton University Press.

Arasaratnam, Sinnappah. 2004. *Maritime India in the Seventeenth Century*. New Delhi: Oxford University Press.

Asad, Talal. 1986. *The Idea of an Anthropology of Islam*. Washington D.C.: Center for Contemporary Arab Studies, Georgetown University.

Azra, Azyumardi. 1992. "The Transmission of Islamic Reformism to Indonesia: networks of Middle Eastern and Malay-Indonesian Ulama in the seventeenth and eighteenth century." PhD diss., Columbia University.

Bang, Anne K. 2003. *Sufis and Scholars of the Sea: Family Networks in East Africa, 1860–1925*. London: Routledge-Curzon.

Bilici, Mucahit. 2011. "Homeland insecurity: how immigrant Muslims naturalize America in Islam." *Comparative Studies in Society and History* 53(3): 595–622.

Bouchon, Genevieve. 1987. "Sixteenth century Malabar and the Indian Ocean." In *India and the Indian Ocean 1500–1800*, edited by Ashin Das Gupta and M.N. Pearson, 71–93. Calcutta: Oxford University Press.

Boxberger, Linda. 2002. *On the Edge of Empire: Hadhramawt, Emigration and the Indian Ocean, 1880s–1930s*. New York: State University of New York.

Chaudhuri, K.N. 1985. *Trade and Civilization in the Indian Ocean: An Economic History from the Rise of Islam to 1750*. Cambridge: Cambridge University Press.

Freitag, Ulrike and Clarence-Smith, William G., eds. 1997. *Hadhrami Traders, Scholars and Statesmen in the Indian Ocean 1750s–1960s*. Leiden: Brill.

Freitag, Ulrike. 2003. *Indian Ocean Migrants and State Formation in Hadhramaut: Reforming the Homeland*. Leiden: Brill.

Goitein, S.D. 2008. *India Traders of Middle Ages: Documents from the Cairo Geniza ("India Book")*. Leiden: Brill.

Gupta, Ashin Das. 2001. "Malabar in c. 1740." In *The World of the Indian Ocean Merchant 1500–1800*, edited by Uma Das Gupta, 421–456. New Delhi: Oxford University Press.

Haug, H.S., Müssig, S. and Stichs, A. 2010. *Muslim Life in Germany*. Berlin: Federal Office of Migration and Refugees.

al-Haytamī, Aḥmad ibn Muḥammad ibn Ḥajar. n.d. *Al-Fatāwā al-Fiqhiyya al-Kubrā*. 4 vols. Beirut: Dār al-Kutb al-ʿIlmiyya.

Ho, Engseng. 2004. "Empire through diasporic eyes: a view from the other boat." *Comparative Studies in Society and History* 46(2): 210–246.

Ho, Engseng. 2006. The Graves of Tarim: Genealogy and Mobility across the Indian Ocean. California: University of California Press.

Ibn Baṭūṭa, Abū 'Abd Allāh Muḥammad ibn 'Abd Allāh al-Lawātī. 1905. *Riḥla ibn Baṭūṭa al-Musammā Tuḥfat al-Nudhdhār fī Gharā'ib al-Asfār wa 'Ajā'ib al-Amsār*. Egypt: al-Maṭba' al-Khayriyya.

Inglehar, R. and Norris P. 2009. "Muslim Integration into Western Cultures: Between Origins and Destinations." *Faculty Research Working Paper Series RWP09–007*. Cambridge, MA: Kennedy School of Government, Harvard University.

al-Juday', 'Abd Allāh ibn Yūsuf. 2007. *Taqsīm al-Ma'mūra fī al-Fiqh al-Islāmī wa Atharuhu Fī al-Wāqi'*. Dublin: Al-Majlis al-Awrubbī li al-Iftā' wa al-Buḥūth.

al-Kālikūtī, Muḥammad ibn 'Abd al-'Azīz. 1996. "Qaṣīda Fatḥ al-Mubīn li al-Sāmirī al-ladhī Yuḥibbu al-Muslimīn." In *Fatḥ al-Mubīn Paribhasha*, edited by Mankada Abdul Aziz, 1–36. Calicut: Al-Huda Book Stall.

al-Kālikūtī, Qāḍī Muḥammad ibn Qāḍī 'Abd al-'Azīz. n.d. *Qaṣīda Fatḥ al-Mubīn li al-Sāmirī al-ladhī Yuḥibbu al-Muslimīn*. Manuscript no. 85. Chaliyam: al-Maktaba al-Azhariyya.

al-Khazrajī, Shaykh 'Alī ibn al-Ḥasan. 1911. *Al-'Uqūd al-Lu'lu'iyya fī Tārīkh al-Dawla al-Rasūliyya*. Edited by Shaykh Muḥammad Basyūnī 'Asal. Egypt: Maṭba'at al-Hilāl.

Kooria, Mahmood. 2016. "Cosmopolis of Law: Islamic legal ideas and texts across the Indian Ocean and eastern Mediterranean worlds." PhD diss., Leiden University.

Lambourn, E. 2008. "India from Aden": Khutba and Muslim urban networks in late thirteenth-century India." In *Secondary Cities and Urban Networking in the Indian Ocean Realm c. 1400–1800*, edited by K.R. Lanham Hall, 55–98. MD: Lexington.

al-Ma'barī, 'Abd al-'Azīz ibn Zayn ibn 'Alī ibn Zayn al-Dīn Aḥmad. n.d. *Maslak al-Atqiyā' wa Manhaj al-Aṣfiyā' fī Sharḥ Hidāyat al-Adhkiyā' 'la Ṭarīq al-'Awliyā'*. Calicut: Tirurangadi Books.

al-Ma'barī, Shaykh Zayn al-Dīn ibn 'Abd al-'Azīz ibn Zayn al-Dīn ibn 'Alī. n.d. *Tuḥfat al-Mujāhidīn fī Ba'ḍ Akhbār al-Burtughāliyyīn*. Manuscript not numbered. Chaliyam: al-Maktaba al-Azhariyya.

al-Ma'barī, Shaykh Zayn al-Din ibn 'Abd al-'Azīz ibn Zayn al-Dīn ibn 'Alī. 1931. *Tuḥfat al-Mujāhidīn fī Ba'ḍ Akhbār al-Burtughāliyyīn*. Edited by Shams Allāh al-Qādirī. Hyderabad: Maṭba't al-Tārīkh.

March, Andrew F. 2007. "Islamic foundations for a social contract in non-Muslim liberal democracies." *American Political Science Review* 101(2): 235–52.

McPherson, K. 1993. *The Indian Ocean: A History of People and Sea*. Delhi: Oxford University Press.

Nainar, S. Muhammad Husayn. 2005. *Shaykh Zainuddin Makhdum's Tuḥfatul Mujāḥidīn: A Historical Epic of the Sixteenth Century*. Translated from Arabic with Annotation by S. Muhammad Husayn Nainar. Calicut: Other Books.

Nambiar, O.K. 1863. *The Kunjalis: Admirals of Calicut*. Calcutta: Asia Publishing House.

O'Brien, Peter. 2013. "Clashes within western civilization: debating citizenship for European Muslims." *Migration Studies* 1(2): 131–55.

Pearson, M.N. 2003. *The Indian Ocean.* London: Routledge.

Prange, Sebastian Raphael. 2008. "The social and economic organization of Muslim trading communities on the Malabar Coast, twelfth to sixteenth centuries." PhD diss., University of London, SOAS.

Qiṣṣat Shakrwatī Farmāḍ. Manuscript, n.d. Nellikuth: Muḥammad 'Alī Musliyār's personal library.

al-Ṣaghīr, Shaykh Aḥmad Zayn al-Dīn al-Makhdūm al-Malibārī. n.d. *Al-Ajwiba al-'Ajība 'alā al-'As'ila al-Gharība.* no place: Kunhi Muhammad al-Kodanchery and V.K. Mūsān Kutty Musliyār.

al-Ṣaghīr, Shaykh Aḥmad Zayn al-Dīn. 2000. *Fatḥ al-Mu'īn bi Sharḥ Qurrat al-'Ayn*, Tirūrangādi: Tirurangadi Book Stall.

al-Shāfi'ī, Aḥmad Shaykh Zayn al-Dīn ibn 'Abd al-'Azīz al-Ma'barī al-Malibārī al-Funnānī. 2006. *Fatḥ al-Mu'īn bi Sharḥ Qurrat al-'Ayn bi Muhimmāt al-Dīn.* Calicut: Tirūrangādi Book Stall.

al-Sharawāni, 'Abd al-Ḥamīd and al-'Ibādī, Aḥmad ibn Qāsim. n.d. *Ḥawāshī Tuḥfat al-Minhāj bi Sharḥ al-Minhāj Ta'līf al-Imām Shihāb al-Dīn Aḥmad ibn Ḥajar al-Haytamī.* Egypt: al-Maktaba al-Tujāriyya al-Kubrā.

Thackston, W.M. 1989. "Kamaluddin Abdul-Razzaq Samarqandi: Mission to Calicut and Vijayanagar." In *A Century of Princes: Sources of Timurid History and Art*, edited by W.M. Thackston, 299–321. Cambridge: Agha Khan Program for Islamic Architecture.

Verskin, Alan. 2013. *Oppressed in the Land: Fatwās on the Muslims Living under Non-Muslim Rule from the Middle Ages to the Present.* Princeton: Markus Wiener Publishers.

Wazārat al-Awqāf wa al-Shu'ūn al-Islāmiyya. 1990. *Al-Mawsū'a al-Fiqhiyya.* Vol. 20: 201–219. Kuwait: Wazārat al-Awqāf wa al- Shu'ūn al-Islāmiyya.

Index

1951 Convention Relating to the Status of Refugees (Refugee Convention) 18
1967 Protocol Relating to the Status of Refugees 18

ʿAbd al-Raḥmān al-Adamī al-Miṣrī 206
ʿAbd al-Razzāq 200
ʿAbd al-Raʾūf al-Wāʿiẓ al-Zamzamī 206
ʿAbd al-Wafā Shams al-Dīn Muḥammad 204, 208
ʿAbd al-ʿAzīz al-Makhdūm al-Maʿbarī 204, 208
ʿĀbidín, Muḥammad Amīn Ibn 42
Abkhazia 159
abode of inequity 15
abode of Islam (see also *dār al-Islām*) 15, 21–22, 156, 163, 203, 205, 209–210
abode of unbelievers (see also *dār al-kufr*) 15
abode of war (see also *dār al-ḥarb*) 21, 160, 208–209
Abū Dāwūd 156
Abū Hurayra 71
access to citizenship 137, 141, 145
acts of aggression 19
Aden 200
al-Adi, Hawari 112
advent of Portuguese 201, 203–204
Afghanistan 2–3, 18–19, 48, 175, 180–181
agency 8, 31–32, 34, 60, 68, 70, 73, 76, 79, 81–84, 88, 96, 148, 167
ahl al-kitāb (People of the Book) 138
Aḥmad Shihāb al-Dīn ʿUthmān bin Ab al-Ḥill al-Yamanī 206
Ahmed, Shahab 198, 211
Aidamirov, Abuzar 163–164, 167–170
ʿĀʾisha 158
ajīr khāṣ (private employee) 98
Akmeer, Abdel Wahid 118
AKP 32, 37, 48–49
Aleppo 31
Alexandre, Emperor of Russia 164
Algeria 112, 144–145
ʿAlī ibn Abī Ṭālib 20
ʿAlī ʿĀdil Shah 203
Alptekin, Isa Yusup 182
Altishehir 176
amān (pledge of security or safe conduct) 19
amān (providing safety) 1, 19–20, 35, 213
Amman 159
Ankara 10, 174, 184
anṣār (helpers) 119
anti-immigrant fervor 196
anti-Islamic political discourse 116
anti-Portuguese 197
Arabic grammar 203
Arabic language 148, 202
Arabic literature of hijra 162
Arabic poem 203
Arab immigrants 11, 122, 196–197, 199, 201, 203, 205, 207, 209, 211
Arab maritime networks 198
Arab Revolt 22
Arab traders 198, 202, 211
Arab world 37, 51, 112, 121, 123, 137, 145, 196
al-ʿArifī, Muḥammad 70
Asad, Talal 28–29, 38, 47
al-ʿĀṣ ibn al-Rabīʿ 20
Al-ʿĀshir 74
al-Ashraf II, Rasulid Sultan 200
al-Assad, President of Syria 48
asylum 2, 6–8, 19, 25, 35, 49, 51, 60, 123–124, 175, 181, 183, 186, 213
asylum-seekers 6, 8, 49, 60
Athens 56, 58, 60
Australia 2, 180
Ayup, Abduwali 186
al-Azhar 136, 151, 206
al-Azhar Declaration 136, 151

Baghdad 55, 210
Bahrain 92, 138, 145–146, 148–149
Bangladesh 18, 123
al-Banna, Hany 33
al-Bannā, Ḥassan 30
Barin incidents (1990) 184
Barzegar 7, 28, 30, 32, 34, 36, 38, 40, 42, 44, 46, 127
Battle of Badr 14

Bava, Sophie 115
Bazorkin, Idris 167–168
Bedouins 24, 149
Belgium 122–123
bidūn (those without nationalities) 144
Bijapur 203–204
binary categories (social sciences) 110–111, 210
Boston 10, 174, 183
breach of contract 100
brotherhood 1, 3, 7, 15–16, 19, 21, 24–25, 52, 58, 99
Bugra, Mehmet Emint 182
Butler, Judith 81–82

Cairo 11, 74, 136, 197, 205–206
Calais 58–59
Calicut 200–205
Caliphate state 21
Canada 2, 88, 182, 185–186
Casanova, José 117
Caucasus 10, 143, 154–165, 167–171, 173
Çelik, Faruk 49
Central Asia 139, 143, 176, 179–180
central lands of Islam 197
Chad 18
Chaghatay 177
Chaliyam 199, 203–204, 208, 210
Chaliyam fort 199, 203–204, 208, 210
Chechen literature 167–168
Chechnya 159, 164, 168–169
Chermoev, Arzu 166
China 86, 158, 174–176, 178–181, 183, 185–186, 197, 201
Chinese Communism 181
Chinese culture 179
Christendom 22
Christians 138–139, 155, 201
Circassia 159
citizenship acquisition 140, 149–150
civil war in Syria 50
clash of civilizations 23
Cochin 204
co-ethnic preference 143
Cold War era 18
colonialism 22
communal harmony 200
communitarian solidarity 118–119
communities of interpretation 118
Connolly, William 117
contracts in Islamic law 99
Convention Against Torture and Other Cruel, Inhuman and Degrading Treatment 17
converts to Islam 14
conviviality 54–55
coreligious preference 143
costs and fees of visa and recruilment 100–101
Crone, Patricia 157
Crusades 22
Cultural Revolution (1966-76) 178

Daghestan 158–162
Damascus 50, 56–59, 62, 74, 76, 159
dār al-daʿwa (abode of mission) 197, 209
dār al-fisq (abode of inequity) 15
dār al-ḥarb (abode of war) 1, 11, 21, 160, 196–197
dār al-Islām (abode of Islam) 1, 11, 15, 21–24, 138, 157, 161, 174, 197
dār al-kufr (abode of unbelief) 15, 21, 157, 174, 209
*dār al-*ʿadl (abode of justice) 15
*dār al-*ʿahd (abode of accord) 197, 208
Darband 158
ḍarūra (necessity) 200, 203
daʿwah (missionary activity) 35
decline of Islamic sovereignty 160
Deniz Feneri 29, 32–33
Derrida 52, 60
Dharamadam 201
dhimmīs 139, 208
dhimmī (under the "protected" status) 137–139, 144, 207–208
diaspora studies 115, 119
diasporic hijra literature 162
discord 157
discourse on human rights 16
discourse on migration 16
discursive tradition 28–29, 38, 47, 53
displacement 18–19
ḍiyāfa (hospitality) 1, 7, 15–16, 19, 24–25
dual citizenship 143, 147
duty of hospitality 15
ḍuyūf (guests) 57

Eastern Turkistan Republic (ETR) 178
East Turkistan *see also* Xinjiang, 174–175, 178, 181–182, 184, 187, 192, 215
East-West trade 199
Egypt 8, 24, 67, 69, 71, 73–79, 81, 83, 85, 87, 89, 91, 136, 143–144, 178, 183, 199
Eli (Ezhimala) 201
Emon, Anver 42
Emre, Yunus 33
entitlement rights 148
Erdoğan, Recep Tayyip, President of Turkey 30, 48
ethical doctrines of Islam 196
ethic of conviction 9, 112–114, 125
ethic of responsibility 9, 112–114
ethnic consciousness 178
ethnic revitalization 187
ethnocentrism 23
ethno-cultural model 146
ethno-nationalist citizenship 41
eurocentrism 69
Europe 2–5, 23, 28, 33, 53, 60, 86, 110, 116, 118, 121, 123–124, 139, 179–180, 183, 185–186, 191, 196
European miracle 23
European secularism 118
European Union 4, 49, 60, 123, 125, 171
European values 196
exit visa 102–104
exploitable labour 49
exploitation 6, 18, 69, 77, 81, 84–86, 88, 92, 95–96, 104–105, 124
exploitation of migrant workers 96
extremism, religious 123

failure of integration 121
faith-based humanitarianism 28, 35
faith-based humanitarian organizations 28
Fakhr al-Dīn bin Ramaḍān al-Shāliyāthī 206
al-Fatāwa al-Fiqhiyya 206
Fatḥ al-Bārī 206
Fatḥ al-Muʿīn 11, 198-208, 210
Fatwa Center 70
fatwa seeker 208–209
Feneri 33
fiqh al-wāqiʿ 127
fitna (temptation) 157
fiṭra (sacredness and dignity of human life) 36
forced labour 96
forced marriage 88
forced migrants 1, 17, 19, 25, 34–35, 51–52, 60–61, 69, 86, 189
forced migration 2, 10, 16–19, 28–29, 34, 41, 45, 68–69, 77, 80, 83, 154–155, 157, 159–161, 163–165, 167, 169, 171, 173
foreign workforce 8, 102
freedom of movement 13–14, 21, 102
Friedmann, Georges 112

Gansu Corridor 177
Gaza 25, 32
Gaza Freedom Flotilla 31
Gaziantep 49
gender-based violence 83, 85, 87
gendered approach to fatwa 69, 88
Gender relations 68–69
Gender roles 69–70, 81, 83
Gengiz (Genghis) Khan 177
Gentiles 22
Georgia 159
Germany 18, 112, 118, 121, 125, 151, 182, 185
al-Ghazālī 44, 51, 53
Ghulja demonstration (1997) 184
Ghys, Jacques 125
giaour (infidel) 163
global/universalistic moment 111, 126
Great Leap Forward (1958-62) 178
Greece 60, 116
Gulf Cooperation Council (GCC) 2, 92, 96, 101–102, 104, 140, 145–150
Gulf States 5, 8, 92, 96, 102, 106, 139, 147, 149

Habermas, Jürgen 117
Hadramis 205
Ḥanafī school of law 175
Han (Chinese) 177, 185
ḥarbī (belligerent) 207–209
heartlands of Islam 11, 196–199, 205
al-Hifnāwī, Hala 121
Hijaz 24, 155
hijra (migration) 3–4, 10, 15, 19, 31, 51–52, 154–163, 167, 169, 171, 175
hijra texts 162
Hindu kings 196–201, 203, 205, 207, 209, 211

homesteads (*khutorov*) 166
hospitality 1, 7, 15–16, 19–21, 24–25, 48–52, 55, 57, 60–61
Hotan 179
Hui-he 177
Hui-hu see *Hui-he*
human dignity 7, 13–14, 16, 21, 36
humanitarianism 7, 28–29, 31–33, 35, 37, 39, 41–45, 69, 127
humanitarian relief 28
Humanitarian Relief Foundation 29, 31
human rights 1, 6, 8, 13, 15–17, 19, 21, 23–25, 27, 30, 32, 34, 36–37, 45, 68, 83, 102, 114, 123–124, 126, 179–180, 183–184, 191
human trafficking 18, 24, 86, 88
Hun 177
Hyderabad 204

ibn al-balad (son of the land) 57
ibn al-Qayyim 99
ibn Baṭūṭa 201
ibn Ḥajar 11, 197, 205–209
ibn Masʿūd 44
ibn Nujaym 43
ibn Taymiyyah 105
Ibrāhīm (Abraham) 35
Idiqut Buddhist Uyghur Kingdom 177
ʿIffa (chastity and modesty) 70–72
IHH (Humanitarian Relief Foundation) 29, 31–32
ijāra (providing protection and support) 1, 7, 19–20, 24–25, 95, 98, 104–105
ijmāʿ (consensus) 43
Ijtihad and jurisprudential culture 87–88
ijtihād (autonomous critical approach) 39–40, 42, 87, 97
illegal migration 121, 123
Imam Shamil 160
inborn identities 187
India 3, 18, 139–140, 175, 180–181, 197, 199
Indian Ocean 11, 196–198, 201, 205, 210
indigenization 201
indigenous paradigms for social science 110
Indonesia 37, 118, 140, 143, 145
Ingushetia 159, 164
Ingush literature 167
(local) integration 3-5, 9, 11, 49, 52-57, 114, 117-125, 137, 143, 146, 151, 174, 182
Inter-Agency Task Force on Religion and Development 34
inter-communal relations 201–202, 204
international labour law 98
International Labour Organization 95, 102, 104
international law 16–18
International Sociological Association 112
international terrorism 184
internment camp (Xinjiang) 180
intimate relations 83
iqāma (residency) 96, 103
Iqbal, Muhammad 30
IR *see also* Islamic Relief, 33–36
Iran 18, 22, 143–144, 176
Iraq 2, 18–19, 22, 55–56, 59, 67, 121, 142–143, 145
Iraq/Iran war 22
Iraqi refugees 62
ISIS 21, 123
Islamic citizenship 138
Islamic hermeneutics 38
Islamic legal traditions 1
Islamic moral impulses 13
Islamic normative ethics 38
Islamic political ethics 41
Islamic Relief 29, 33–36
Islamic Relief Worldwide 29, 33
Islamic revival 38
Islamic textual tradition 159
Islamic theology 16
Islamic theology and law 15–16, 38
Islamist 32, 48
Islamization of knowledge 110, 126–127
Islamophobia 111, 122
Islamophobic practices 28
Israel 19
Istanbul 10, 31–32, 62, 94, 159, 174–175, 182
istiḍʿāf (state of oppressive injustice due to disempowerment) 6, 14, 19, 25
iẓhār al-dīn (free practice of faith) 15

Jews 22
Jiang Zemin (President of China) 184
jihād 158
Jihad against the Portuguese 199, 202
Jihād al-Nikāḥ (Jihad of marriage) 70–73
Jinsiyya (nationality) 138, 147

jiwār (neighborliness) 51
jizyā (poll tax) 41, 139
Jordan 2, 18, 67, 143, 163
Judaism 22
Judeo-Christian tradition 23
Jungaria 177
Jungarian basin 176
Jus domicile 137
Jus religionis 144
Jus sanguinis 5, 9, 118, 136–137, 140–143, 146–148, 150
Jus soli 5, 136–137, 140–144, 147

kafala (*kafāla*: sponsorship or guarantee) 1, 5, 8, 24, 92–105
kafala system 8, 24, 95–96, 98–100, 102, 104–105
kafīl al-iqāma (the residency sponsor) 103
kafīl al-khurūj (the exit sponsor) 103
kafīl (guarantor, sponsor) 8, 93–96, 100–105
Kamāl al-Dīn Muhammad bin Abu Sharīf 206
Kamali, Hashim 42
Kamali, Mohammad Hashim 42
Karakas, Atavulla 175
Karakhanli Khanate 177
karāma (dignity) 61
Kashgar 177
Kashgaria 176
Kashmir 180–182
Kashyap, Ridhi 116
Katz, Marion Holms 87
Kayseri 10, 174, 182, 186
Kazakhs 175
Kazakhstan 143, 175, 180
Kerala 199
kharāj (tax) 139
al-Khatib, Mutaz 84
Khomeini, Ayatollah 30
Khoury, Elias 125
Kilis 30–32
Kokand 177
Kolathiri Raja, Hindu ruler 201
Kundukhov, Musa 164–170
Kunhāli Markkār 199, 204, 208
Kurds 138, 184
Kuseni, Hebibulla 175
Kuwait 94, 96, 138, 140, 144–145, 147–149, 151
Kyrgyz 175, 177
Kyrgyzstan 175, 180

labour contract 98, 105
Lake Balkhash 177
Latrach, Abdelkader 121
Lebanon 2, 18, 67, 142–143, 145
Leninism 178
Levitt, Peggy 114–116, 118–119
Lewis, Valerie A. 116
liberalism 114, 124, 127–128
Libson, Gideon 42–43
Libya 145
living fiqh 7, 29, 36, 38, 44
local/normative moment 9, 111–112, 126
Loris-Melikov, Mikhail Tarielovich 167
Los Angeles 6, 183
low-skilled workers 104

Maghreb 121, 144–145, 150, 171
Mahmood Hudayi Vakfi 32
Mahmood, Saba 82
makfūl (guaranteed person) 8, 94–96, 100–105
al-Makhdūm al-Kabīr 205–206
al-Makhdūm al-Ṣaghīr 11, 202–204, 206, 208–209
Malabar 11, 196–211
Malabari Muslims 200, 202, 208
Malabari society 200
Malabar Muslims 198
Malaysia 18, 143, 178
Mālik ibn Dīnār 199
Mamankam 203
Manchu 177
Maqāsid al-Shariʿa (aims and objectives of the Shariʿa) 36
marginalization of immigrants 120
marginalized groups 70, 88
marriage 1, 8, 67–89, 91, 101, 139–140, 143, 145, 147
Marxism 178
maṣlaḥa (public interest) 93, 97
Massey, Doreen 54
Mauritania 145
Mawdūdī 30
Mawlana (Rumi) 30
McDougall, Gay 180

Mecca 3, 11, 14–15, 24, 31, 51–52, 154–156, 159, 161, 179, 181, 196–197, 199, 204–207
medieval history 22
Medina 3, 14, 16, 20, 24, 31, 119, 136, 156–159, 171, 196, 204
Mejelle (Ottoman codified Shariʿa law) 42–43, 94
MENA (Middle East and North Africa) 28, 34, 45, 139, 145
mental health (of refugees) 85
Mercy Corps 34
migration studies 2, 9, 12, 111–112, 114, 120, 126–128
military ascendency of European empires 160
mobility 13
modern-day slavery 24
modernization 110–111
Mongolia 177
Mongol invasions 156
moral agency 81–82
Morocco 112, 143–145
mountain villages (*auls*) 166
Mubashar, Hasan 123
muhājirūn (migrants) 3, 48, 52, 119, 155–157, 161
Muḥammad ibn Aḥmad al-Sarakhsī 43
Qāḍī Muḥammad ibn ʿAbd al-ʿAzīz 204
Muhammad, Prophet of Islam 3, 10, 14–15, 20, 31, 48, 51–53, 58, 61, 63, 71, 136, 155, 158, 164, 196, 201
Muhyiddīn Māla 205
mujāwir (servant of sanctuary) 20
multiculturalism 11, 55, 114, 120, 126–127, 191
Mūsā (Moses) 35
Musa Pasha *see* Kundukhov, Musa
Muslim Brotherhood 33
Muslim civic engagement 38
Muslim civil society 29
Muslim communities in the Indian Ocean 197
Muslim humanitarian sector 29, 33, 36, 38, 41, 44
Muslim immigrants 122, 196–197, 211
Muslim localities 197
Muslim mountaineers 160, 163, 167, 170
Muslim peripheries 197
Muslim scholars 1, 4, 11, 68, 162, 196–197, 202, 205, 208
Muslims in Calicut 200
Muslim World League 23, 182
mustaʾman (person enjoying a protected status) 19
mustaʿmin (allowed to conduct business) 139
al-Muṭʿim ibn ʿAdiy 52
Muwāṭana (citizenship) 138
muʾākha (brotherhood) 15–16, 19, 23–25

Nahda Party 37
An-Naʿim, Abdullahi Ahmed 110, 128
Nakh 167
nationalism 7, 23–24, 62, 138, 181–182, 191
Nationalist Chinese 177
national separatism 184
nation-state 1, 4, 11, 22, 47–49, 51, 53–59, 62–63, 68, 95, 115, 138, 142–143, 191, 196, 198, 203, 211
naturalisation 1, 4, 9–11, 124, 136–138, 140–151, 196–207, 209–211
naturalisation as a selective instrument 149
naturalisation through marriage 147
Nayar Cavalry of Zamorin 203
neighbourliness 7, 50, 52–53, 55–56, 58, 60, 62
neo-enlightenment 9, 114, 126–127
Nepal 18
The Netherlands 121–122
New York 10, 174, 183
NGO 33
Nicholas, Emperor of Russia 164
Niger 143
non-Muslim communities 35, 207
non-Muslim lands 11, 196, 200, 204
non-Muslim political authorities 200
non-Muslim political system 207
non-Muslim polities 196–197
non-Muslim rulers 198, 201–205, 207–211
non-Muslim subjects 208
non-Muslim Zamorin 204–205
non-secular humanism 29–30, 33, 35, 41–42
non-secular humanistic discourse 29, 36–37
non-secular Islamic humanism 41
non-secular universal humanism 28
North America 159, 179–180
nuclear family 82–83, 86

Oman 2, 138, 145–146, 148

One Belt and One Road Initiative 176
Open Door policy 181
oppressive injustice 14
orientalism 68, 83, 87
orphans 31, 71–72, 78–79, 101
Oruc, Huseyin 32
Ottoman empire 164
Ottoman lands *see also* Ottoman empire, 159, 162–163, 165–167, 170
The Overseas Development Institute 34

Pabst, Adriana 118
Pakistan 3, 18, 143, 145, 149, 175, 178, 180–181
Palestinian refugee crisis 19
Palestinian refugees 2, 62, 67, 126, 149
Palestinians 18
Palestinian Syrians 56
pan-Arabism 144
Papal states 24
Partnership for Religion and Development 34
patriarchy 80
Pavlovskii Cadet Corps 164
People's Republic of China (PRC). *see* China
peripheries 55, 196–199, 205–206, 210–211, 220
Piché 115
PLA (Peoples Liberation Army) 180
polygamy 86–87
Pompeo, Mike 187
Portuguese incursion 204
Portuguese traders 197, 199, 201–204, 207–208, 210
postcolonial peminism 68
post-colonialism 12, 110
post-nationalist paradigm 23
post-secularism 117–118
post-secularity 118
pre-Islamic Arabian culture 51
Prosperous Justice Party 37
public religion 117

Qāḍī an-Nuʿmān 156
Qāḍī Muḥammad al-Kalikūtī 203
Qāḍī Muḥammad al-Kālikūtī 208
Qāḍī under the Zamorin 205
Qalmaq Mongols 177
Qaradawi 127
Qatar 5, 70, 100–104, 138, 145–148, 178
qaṭʿī (certain, definitive) 39
qawāʿid (legal maxims) 43–44
Qianlong, Manchu Qing Emperor 177
Qiṣṣat Shakrawat Fermāḍ 199
qiyās (analogy) 43
al-Quduqi, Muḥammad 158
Quraysh 52, 154–155
Qur'anic narrative on migration 14
Quṭb, Sayyid 30

racial hierarchy 24
racism 23, 111, 121–122, 188
Raḥūma, ʿĀshūr 123
Ramadan, Tariq 4, 29–31, 37–41, 43–44, 68, 84, 87, 179, 184
Ramdev, Hindu ruler 201
rape victim 73
Rasulids 200
reformist theology 41
refoulement 17–18
Refugee Convention 2, 17–18
Refugees 2, 4, 6–7, 11, 18, 30, 47–50, 55–57, 59–62, 67, 69, 73–74, 80, 85, 113–114, 123–126, 137, 149, 180–181, 183–185, 187–188, 191, 196, 211
Refugee women 67, 69–71, 80, 83–88
Relational autonomy 81, 88
religiosity 116–117, 119, 122
religious extremism 122–123, 184
religious pluralism 136, 138
religious pluralization 118
ribā (usury) 95
Riḍā, Rashīd 42
Rozakou, Katerina 60
Russia 3, 18–19, 162, 170, 175, 212, 220, 222
Russian empire 159

Saadulla, Usmi 166
Safavid deportations 159
Şahin, Fatma 49
al-Sahlī, Nabīl 123
Saidi, Mohamad 122
Sakellariou, Alexandros 116
Sakib, Chaaban 115
Saks 177
San Francisco 183
Sari Hanafi 9, 110

Saudi Arabia 19, 24–25, 74, 97, 100, 123, 138, 145–148, 150, 178
Scott, David 47
Scythians 177
Second Turkish Khanate 177
sectarianism 41
securitization of migration 123
Senegal 18
sexual violence 85
Shabana, Ayman 42
shahbandar (Muslim port leader) 203
Shams al-Dīn al-Jawjarī 206
shaqīq (full brothers) 57
Shariati, Ali 30, 128
Sherqi Türkistan 178. *see also* East Turkistan
Shirwan 158
Sīdī Aḥmad al-Kumāmī 204, 208
Silk Route 176
Sinai 24
sinicization 179
social exclusion 122–123, 187
socialist ideology 178
social justice 73, 154
social media 67, 70, 123, 128, 186, 190
Sogdian 177
Somalia 2, 48, 143
Soroush, Abdolkarim 58, 128
South Asia 139
South Darfour 123
South East Asia 139
Soviet hijra narrative 162
Soviet Union 156, 178–179, 182
Spanish Reconquista 156
statelessness 140, 143–145, 147
St. Petersburg 164
studying Islam 11, 198
Sufi orientation towards migration 15
Sumatra 204
*Surat al-Isrā*ʾ 13–14
*Surat al-Nisā*ʾ 13–14
Survival 58, 86, 184, 205
sutra marriage 67–71, 73–75, 77–81, 83–85, 87–89, 91
sutra (protection, esp. in case of marriage) 1, 8, 67–81, 83–85, 87–89, 91
Syria 2, 7, 19, 31–32, 48–50, 56, 67, 76, 88, 123, 143, 158, 163
Syrian displacement crisis 48
Syrian refugees 2, 7, 30, 49, 56, 62, 74, 125

al-Ṭaḥāwī 156
Tajikistan 175
Taklamakan Desert 176
taqwā (faithfulness) 99, 105
Tarim Basin 176–177
Tawḥīd (unity and oneness) 35–36
al-Ṭayyib, Aḥmad 136
Thailand 18
Third world women 68
Tiananmen protest 179
Tianshan Mountains 177
Tibān Asʿad Abū Karib, Himyarite king 155
Tibi, Bassam 118
Tiflis 158
Timurid 200
togetherness 55, 58
Tokharians 177
Torture Convention 17
trading communities 197, 207
Transitional Religion 115
transnational religious movements 115
travel notice 104
Trump, Donald, President of the United States of America 187
Ṭuḥfat al-Mujāhidīn 11, 199, 202–203, 205–208
Tumturuk, Abdulkadir 186
Tunisia 37, 143, 145
Turfan 176–177
Turkey 2, 7, 10–11, 18, 29–33, 37, 49, 62, 139, 143, 166–167, 174–175, 178–186, 188–192
Turkic people 175
Turkish Islamic identity 33
Turko-Russian war of 1877 164
Turks 62, 138, 177, 180, 192
Tweed, Thomas 63

*ʿulama*ʾ 29
ʾUmar al-ʿAntābī 204
ʿUmar ibn ʿAbd al-ʿAzīz 33
umma (global Islamic community) 10, 22–24, 138, 157
Umm Hanī bint Abī Ṭālib 20
United Arab Emirates 19, 24–25, 100, 138, 145–147
United Nations High Commissioner for Refugees 2, 18, 48, 57, 67, 181

United States of America 10, 18–19, 112, 121, 174, 183, 186, 188–189, 224
universal humanism 28–29, 41–42
universal human sanctity 36
UNRWA 48, 57
uprootedness 80, 84–85
Urfa 58
'Urf 7, 28–29, 38, 41–42, 44–45
'urfī marriage 85
Urumqi riot (2009) 179, 184
uṣūl al-fiqh 38
Uyghur American Association 184
Uyghur Americans 183
Uyghur culture 174, 179
Uyghur diaspora 180–183, 192
Uyghur empire 177
Uyghur history 177
Uyghur Human Rights Project 184
Uyghur identity 174, 182, 189
Uyghur identity-construction spaces 189
Uyghur independence movement 186
Uyghur language 179
Uyghur nationalists 178
Uyghurness 189–190
Uyghur refugees 11, 180–181, 184–185, 191
Uyghurs 10–11, 174–175, 177–192
Uyghur separatist activists 184
Uyghur social institutions 190
Uzbek 175

victimhood 68–69, 81, 84, 88
victimizing 68
violence against migrants 121
visa requirements 49
vulnerability 81, 83, 88

wāfid (newcomer) 103
wājib al-ḍiyāfa (duty of hospitality) 15
wājib al-hijra (duty of migration) 15
al-walā' wa-albarā' 41
waliy al-amr (person in charge of the affairs of Muslims) 92, 97, 100, 104–105
Washington 10, 174, 183–184
Waṭaniyya (nationalism) 138. *See also* nationalism
Weber, Max 112–113
West Asia 143
Western hegemony 68
Western white man 24
West Turkestan 180
white colonizers 24
white Europeans 23–24
White Mountain Khoja 177
white Western world 23
widows 8, 67, 70–72, 80
Wild-Dādā, 'Abd al-Qādir Muḥammad 121
World Uyghur Congress 184
World Vision 34
World War I 22
World War II 3, 18, 67

Xinjiang 10–11, 174–188, 191–192, 215
Xinjiang Uyghur Autonomous Region (XUAR) 174, 178
XUAR *see* Xinjiang

Yakub Beg 177
Yasīn, Abū 56–57
Yathrib 3, 154–155
Yemen 19, 25, 143, 155, 178, 200
Yūsuf al-Yakhsāwī 161

Zakariyya al-Anṣārī (Shaykh) 206
Zambia 18
Zamorin 199–200, 202–205, 207–209
Zamorin (non-Muslim) 205
Zamorins of Calicut 202
ẓannī (speculative, open to interpretation) 39-40
zawāj al-sutra (protection or shelter marriage) 67, 70
Zaynab 20
Zayn al-Dīn al-Makhdūm al-Ma'barī 202, 207
Shaykh Zayn al-Dīn al-Makhdūm al-Ṣaghīr 204
Zuo Zong-tang 177–178